P9-BYU-319

What others are saying about
Straight A's Are Not Enough

While this survey of best practices in learning is targeted to college students, its recommendations are useful for learners of all ages.

Howard Gardner
Hobbs Professor of Cognition and Education
Harvard Graduate School of Education

In STRAIGHT A's ARE NOT ENOUGH, Judy Fishel covers everything a young person needs to know in order to gain a first-class education. Her emphasis on authentic learning is a breath of fresh air, and will inspire young people to form lifelong learning habit. This is a great book for the student in your life, whether they need to polish their study skills or are ready to tackle more advanced strategies for learning.

Daniel H. Pink
author of DRIVE and A WHOLE NEW MIND

I must say, as a higher education professional, I found this book to be very refreshing. The book challenges the reader to go beyond the culturally acceptable forms of educational attainment through extrinsic recognition i.e. grades, and instead to strive to learn for the sake of learning.

Mirtha Novalien Bailey
Assistant Program Development and Recruitment
Nova Southeastern University, Orlando, FL

Using succinct and engaging language, this book provides clear steps to becoming an intentional and lifelong learner. I plan to implement many of Ms. Fishel's principles of time management, willpower, and concentration. As a graduate student, future school counselor, and older sister to two teenage boys, I would highly recommend this book.

Ms. Esther Noel
Graduate Student: University of Central Florida, Orlando, FL

One major focus of the book is to learn how to learn. The book overflows with strategies that dissect the learning process, identify inefficiencies, and debunk long-standing assumptions about study skills. Well-researched and exquisitely organized, Straight A's Are Not Enough is the answer to a motivated student's prayer: achieve improved results with less effort.

Learning to learn is only part of the benefit this book provides; it offers many strategies for increasing organization, presentation and communication sills – all of which are integral to success, not only in school, but in the world after graduation.

This book dazzled me with its depth and practicality. After reading it, I realized how horribly inefficient my approach to learning was. It includes a smorgasbord of approaches from which students can select the strategies that best suit their learning styles. It offers ideas for everyone.

Gayle H. Swift
Co-founder GIFT Family Services; Author: ABC, Adoption & Me

Straight A's
Are Not Enough

Breakthroughs in Learning for College Students

Judy Fishel

Flying Heron Books
2015

Published in 2015 by
Flying Heron Books
516 SW River Point Drive North
Stuart, FL 34994

For permissions
check www.flyingheronbooks.com

For bulk purchases,
contact Pathway Book Service 800-345-6665 or www.pathwaybook.com.

Copyright © 2015 Judy Fishel
All rights reserved. Copyrights promote free speech, creativity, and the sharing of in-formation and ideas. Thank you for complying with copyright law by not reproducing, scanning, or distributing the book or any part of it in any form without permission except for brief excerpts used in published reviews and as permitted by Sections 107 or 108 of the 1976 United States Copyright Act.

ISBN 978-0-9906112-0-2

Three Zits comic strips
Used with permission ©
Zits © 2013 Zits Partnership, Dist. By King Features
Zits © 2010 Zits Partnership, Dist. By King Features
Zits © 2013 Zits Partnership, Dist. By King Features

Cover and book design by Jim Bisakowski
All illustrations created by Judy Fishel
Edited by Mark Woodworth

Library of Congress Control Number: 2014918139

Publisher's Cataloging-in-Publication
(Provided by Quality Books, Inc.)

Fishel, Judy.
    Straight A's are not enough : breakthroughs in
learning for college students / Judy Fishel.
        pages cm
        Includes bibliographical references and index.
        LCCN 2014918139
        ISBN 978-0-9906112-0-2

    1. Study skills.   I. Title.

LB2395.F57 2015   378.1'70281
                            QBI14-600185

WHO IS THIS BOOK WRITTEN FOR?

- This book has been written for college students who wonder if there is more to getting a good college education than just making good grades.

- This book is based on recent research about how we learn. It should be helpful to all college students who want to develop or improve their learning skills and who wish to get a really great education.

- This book is also appropriate for high school students taking advanced classes or preparing for college.

- Teachers who work with either high school or college students should find much of this material helpful.

- Adult learners should also find much of this book helpful.

CONTENTS

THE LIST OF STRATEGIES

ACKNOWLEDGMENTS

When I was in fifth grade, my teacher, Hazel Orman, gave me a C in Citizenship. Used to getting A's, I asked what I'd done wrong. Her response was that I'd done nothing wrong but that, even with straight A's, I wasn't reaching my full potential. Her statement could have been rephrased: *Straight A's Are Not Enough.*

Here, I want to acknowledge and thank Mrs. Orman and others who helped me reach my potential.

When I was in junior high school, I had questions about evolution. My pastor, Rev. Goddard Sherman, encouraged me to question everything. I have always been grateful for this advice and have asked many serious questions, including those found in this book.

At about the same time, I heard someone say MIT was the best college in the world. I immediately announced that I would attend MIT and become a nuclear physicist— the most important job I could think of. I am grateful to my parents, Arthur and Virginia Ruhnke, and to my teachers, because none of them laughed at me. They all believed I could do absolutely anything. (But no, I didn't go to MIT.)

In college, my botany professor, Dr. Alan Conger, was the best teacher I ever had. I took notes on his teaching methods. He hired me to work in his lab and became my mentor.

I want to thank the 15 to 20 professors who let me sit in on their classes without being registered, sometimes because I couldn't fit in the lab; sometimes, as with calculus, to relearn a subject I'd forgotten; and sometimes because I was over my limit on credits. I'm especially grateful to the professor who allowed me to sit in on a graduate seminar when I was a freshman—–as long as I did all the assignments, including a class presentation. I worked harder for no credit and no grades than I did for my regular classes.

Thanks to two middle school principals, Jim Macedo and Michael Carbone, who encouraged and supported my creative teaching methods and my decision to focus more on my students than on the subjects I was teaching.

Thanks also go to the following:

- Edward Hughes who allowed me to retell his amazing story and who added new insights found in this book

- Barbara Reilly for her constant encouragement, leading to my decision to teach middle school

- Rachel McAnallen for her amazing workshops on Math Madness

- Susan Rabiner for extremely helpful advice

- Foster Heine for showing that I was right—that he really could do something great with his life

- Leona Bodie and all the Palm City Word Weavers for their continuing help and support

- Mark Woodworth, who added much that improved this book and made editing fun

- Jim Bisakowski, who made this book look so great

- And all the students who are telling their friends about this book.

Both of our children have inspired me with their determination and hard work. Our daughter, Thamora, began her education in neighborhood schools in India, Malaysia, the Philippines, and the Marshall Islands. In sixth grade, her first year in an American school, she started far behind the rest of her class. With determination and hard work, she soon caught up and kept on going, earning her Ph.D. from Cornell.

Our son, Tony, in spite of being severely dyslexic, was determined to reach his goals. Even when he failed classes, he refused to give up. Tony also visited my classes one day each year from the time he was in seventh grade until he finished graduate school. On those days, he taught my students what it means to be dyslexic, that having a learning difference doesn't mean you're stupid, and how he still planned to go to college. He told them they could also reach their goals if they worked hard enough. My students encouraged their friends to come listen to Tony and, for many of these students, Tony's message stuck with them. And yes, he got his degree in physics as well as an M.A. in education, and he reached his goal of becoming a physics teacher.

Most of all, I must thank my husband, Bob, who has supported and encouraged me in writing this book, as he has done all though our adventures together, from marching in Selma, to living and teaching in Asia for eight years, and now traveling and bird-watching around the world.

To Bob

Who has always encouraged me to reach my potential,

Who always believed in me and
in the potential of this book,

Who insists that I stop writing long enough to enjoy meals together,

Who understands and agrees that
Straight A's Are Not Enough.

WHY I HAD TO WRITE THIS BOOK, AND WHY YOU NEED TO READ IT

No one bothered to teach you the most important academic skill: how to learn.... Most students exhaust themselves with inefficient, laborious, and sometimes completely counterproductive study methods because they have misconceptions about what actually goes on in school. — Adam Robinson

I was in seventh grade when I began asking myself an important question: "I work really hard and make good grades but I still don't learn much in school. Isn't there a better way to learn?"

College students who were among the best in their high school classes are often baffled to discover that, after reading a chapter or listening to a lecture, they remember so little. They spend long hours cramming for tests, but even students who do make straight A's soon forget nearly everything they "learned." Sometimes they wonder if this isn't a terrible waste of their time and money. Certainly this cannot be what is meant by getting a good education. They may sometimes say to themselves, *there really must be a better way to learn.*

That is why I had to write this book.

This book deals with three Big Questions:

1. Why do so many students work hard, make good grades, but quickly forget what they "learned"?

2. How can you learn more, understand deeply, and remember longer?

3. How can you get a great education?

Other books on study skills don't have the answers. Many of them are actually part of the problem, reinforcing the idea that grades are the only things that matter.

This book takes a radically different approach, starting with the concept that *Learning is more important than grades*. Based on current research, *Straight A's Are Not Enough* explains some of the reasons why hard-working students often learn so little. It goes on to describe key learning breakthroughs as well as practical strategies for enabling students to get the great education they want and need.

Used with permission Zits ©2010 Zits Partnership, Dist. by King Features

Jeremy, the main character in these comic strips, has the right idea but, like many students, he isn't putting his theory into practice. Students who really believe learning is more important than grades spend their time learning, not procrastinating.

When students read only to find facts they might be tested on, when they take notes but can't identify the main ideas, and when they prepare for tests in the only way they know—by cramming—they soon forget everything they've learned, partly because they are using the least effective strategies.

Straight A's Are Not Enough challenges you to:

- set meaningful and specific personal, educational, and lifetime goals.

- plan your time intentionally—including more than just study-time.

- expand your interests to include many areas of learning.

- rediscover intrinsic motivation—a new love of learning.

- make connections between what you know, learn, and experience.

- try new approaches to learning—learning for deep understanding.

- use mental processing strategies—organization, thinking, and memory.

- develop the critical skills you need to be successful in and beyond school.
- reflect on your beliefs, values, experiences, goals, and learning.

I had to write this book because, as long as you and thousands of students like you don't understand these ideas, you will continue working hard, sometimes making excellent grades but still learning little.

And *you* need to read this book so you can get the education you want and need.

About the book

Although the chapters cover different topics, the main concepts are interwoven throughout the book, with earlier chapters sometimes referring to ideas found in later ones. If you choose to read the book a second time, you are likely to get an even better understanding of how the concepts fit together.

The main content of this book is found in parts 1, 2, and 3. Part 4 is supplementary, dealing with skills for your future including the skills employers want most. You will also find these skills helpful as you continue through your educational journey. But, if you are a freshman and just getting started, you might concentrate on the first three parts and the conclusion.

About the website

Check the website that goes with this book, **www.choose-learning. com,** where you can:

- find weekly study tips.
- share questions, insights, and experiences on the forum.
- enter one of the monthly contests (yes, there are prizes for most contests!)
- read a regular blog written by and for college students; if you'd like to write a blog, please let me know.

When you tell your friends about this book, suggest they check out this website. They can read the table of contents and a sample chapter, the one on Flexible Time Management (chapter 4).

About ASK JUDY

On the website, **www.choose-learning.com**, you can post questions that will be answered on the website for all to read, or you can ask Judy personal questions and she'll respond by email.

About the money-back guarantee

If you decide this book isn't helpful, I will happily refund your money. If you suspect that you might not find the book helpful, you need to do two things:

1. Save your receipt. You will need it.
2. Do not write in the book.

Go to the website, **www.choose-learning.com**, to find the instructions for mailing the book back to me and to tell me how to make out the refund check and where to send it.

> *There's an old truism…that says you can't shoot a deer from the lodge. The same goes for learning: You have to suit up, get out the door, and find what you're after. Mastery, especially of complex ideas, skills, and processes, is a quest. It is not a grade on a test, something bestowed by a coach, or a quality that simply seeps into your being with old age and gray hair.[1]*

Questions for Reflection

1. What do you want to learn from this book?

2. Think about the idea of shooting a deer from a lodge. How does this apply to students? What would it mean for you to suit up, get out the door, and find what you're after?

3. Malala Yousafzai, who was awarded the Nobel Prize for Peace in 2014, said:

   > *In some parts of the world, students are going to school every day. It's their normal life. But in other parts of the world, we are starving for education…. It's like a precious gift. It's like a diamond.*

   If Malala could speak to you, what do you think she would ask you? What advice might she offer?

CHAPTER 1

Eight Giant Steps: A Brief Introduction to Part 1

Unless you try to do something beyond what you have already mastered, you will never grow. — Ralph Waldo Emerson

You probably don't remember this game but, when I was young, we often played a simple game called "Mother, May I?" The child playing the mother stood alone. The children stood about 20 feet away and took turns asking Mother if they could take a number and kind of steps. "Mother, may I take 7 baby steps?" "Mother, may I take 3 giant steps?" "Mother, may I take 4 jumping steps?" The goal was to be first to reach the mother. The mother could say yes, say no, or give you permission to take a different number or different kind of steps.

From this game, the terms "giant steps" and "baby steps" have become part of our language. A giant step is defined as the longest step you can possibly reach. This book is *not* about taking baby steps. You'll be challenged to stretch as far as you can, to take giant steps forward in your learning skills and in making decisions to prepare for greater success in life and in your career.

In each chapter, you'll be asked to begin with a simple exercise, reflecting on a topic to be discussed in the chapter. Each exercise should take only a few minutes. If you want to get the most from this book, use a notebook or reflective journal for your answers. You will learn even more if you add further reflections after you finish each chapter. For each question you can always choose one or more suggested answers, or (better yet) write your own.

Exercise:
What Are Your Main Reasons for Getting an Education?

---

1. What is the real reason why you came to college (or plan to go)?
   A. My parents expected me to go
   B. All my friends were going
   C. To have a good time
   D. To get a great education
   E. To earn a diploma so I can get the kind of job I want
   F. Because students with a college education earn more money
   G. Because I really enjoy learning and want to learn as much as I can
   H. Because, even if learning isn't fun, it's important for my future

2. How important to you is it to make good grades?
   A. Extremely important
   B. Very important
   C. Somewhat important
   D. Not very important

3. Why do you care about making good grades? Choose as many answers as you'd like, and feel free to add others.
   A. I'm not really concerned about grades. I think learning is more important than grades.
   B. I don't care about my grades as long as I pass all my classes. I'm here to have fun.
   C. I want to make good grades to please my parents—and gain the respect of my teachers.
   D. I need top grades to get into graduate school, medical school, or law school.
   E. I need good grades to get the kind of job I want.
   F. I want to make good grades because I take pride in being the best student in the class.
   G. I want to graduate with honors—perhaps summa cum laude and Phi Beta Kappa.
   H. I just enjoy making good grades. I do it for myself. It's challenging. It's fun.

4. Why did you choose this book to read? What do you hope to learn from this book?

5. What are three giant steps you could take immediately that would help you learn far more effectively than most college students?

A true story: students often don't learn

It is always nice to start with a story. This is a story *about* a story. I was teaching a seventh grade science class about gravity. Because I believe we often learn more through stories than through lectures, I began by telling the story of Galileo dropping heavy and light objects from the leaning tower of Pisa. I explained that most people agreed with Aristotle that heavy objects fall faster, but that Galileo was an independent thinker. He wanted to test this idea for himself. I'm sure you know the story. The objects landed at the same time.

The next day I checked to see what my students had learned. I held a good-sized rock in one hand and a sheet of paper in the other and—to my students' horror—I climbed up and stood on top of my desk. The students warned me nervously that the principal might catch me! Personally, I thought he'd be impressed, seeing that every student was paying close attention. I held up the rock and the sheet of paper and asked, "If I drop them at the same time, which will hit the floor first?"

"The rock," they agreed. Why? "Because it's heavier," they said in unison. I dropped them and the rock hit the floor first. The students weren't surprised. They knew they were right.

I then suggested we do a little experiment. "Would it make any difference," I asked, "if I folded the paper?" The students shook their heads. "No, why should it?" I folded the paper repeatedly until I couldn't fold it any further. "Now," I asked, "I have the same rock and the same paper. Which will hit the ground first?"

"The rock!" Not one student questioned this apparently obvious conclusion. They all gasped when the rock and the paper hit the floor at the same time.

"Can anyone explain why this happened?" I asked, hoping someone remembered Galileo.

After a long pause, one boy raised his hand. "When you fold paper," he explained solemnly, "it gets heavier."

It was hard not to laugh. I looked around the room, hoping another student would suggest a better answer. "How many of you believe this?" I asked. Every hand was raised. Not one student could think of an alternative. "Does it make sense that folding paper would make it heavier?" I asked.

"No," said the boy. "I never would have believed it, Ms. Fishel, but you just proved it."

—•◦•—

I seriously hope you aren't agreeing with my students—either about rocks falling faster because they are heavier or about paper getting heavier when it's folded. There are, sad to say, many college students who memorize what seem to be important facts, make straight A's on tests, but never understand the basic concepts. There are students taking college physics who still don't understood the laws of motion, often taught in middle school. Some of these physics students even believe rocks fall faster than paper because they're heavier.

Learning involves far more than memorizing facts. Genuine learning requires reflecting on what you believe, considering the evidence, and being willing to change your ideas. While my seventh graders enjoyed the Galileo story, they didn't change their beliefs. As you read this book, I hope you will be prepared to examine and perhaps rethink and revise some of your opinions, beliefs, and even behaviors.

Beginning a journal—or maybe several

You might want to stock up on simple notebooks. In this book, you'll find many suggestions that you begin a new kind of journal. The first suggestion, earlier, was that you use a reflective journal for writing answers to the exercises and add further reflections at the end of each chapter.

As a college student, I kept four journals. The first was a daily diary, with occasional reflections on what I'd learned from my experiences. The second was my financial record; my family didn't have a lot of money so I recorded every penny I spent and planned ways to spend even less. The third journal, my "Boyfriend Journal," may sound silly, but it was the most helpful; as each relationship ended, I took time to reflect on the happiest times, on mistakes I made, and on what I learned from the experience. The fourth journal, my "Thinking Journal," included reflections on my

Big Questions. I spent nearly two years trying to answer a single question: "What is the purpose of life?" (To read my answer to this question, check the website.)

Here I am already suggesting that you start a second journal, a "Learning Journal." You may be surprised to find how this will affect how much and how well you learn.

STRATEGY *1.1*

KEEP A LEARNING JOURNAL

Step 1: Each night before you go to sleep, write about the most important things you learned that day in your classes.

Step 2: Add something you learned outside your classes. Often, what we learn outside of class is even more important than what we learn in class.

Step 3: Write one or more things you'd like to learn or to understand more completely. Sounds easy? It is easy but it really will help you learn.

The Eight Giant Steps

The first three giant steps are described in the next three sections of this chapter. The other five are dealt with in the next five chapters. They include examining your approach to learning, your goals, your time, your mindset, and your willpower. These chapters are far more than an introduction to the book.

Each chapter includes research-based information and suggestions that can help you take a giant step toward earning better grades, learning more, and getting the kind of education you want. Take each chapter seriously. But be warned: taking "Giant Steps" is never easy. Each step takes determination and courage. These chapters ask you to stretch as far as you can.

While all these steps are about familiar topics, you might be surprised that the first three are among the most important steps to learning. Most students don't understand this. They do the opposite of what they should be doing and, as a result, their learning suffers.

The First Giant Step: Get enough sleep

Some researchers believe that poor sleep habits are the most important reason why students make poor grades.

When the brain is tired or exhausted, it actually shuts down several of the mental processes that are needed for learning.... To be ready to pay attention, you must find a way to get enough sleep; otherwise, you are making new learning difficult.[1]

But what do most college students do? They stay up late to study, to join interesting discussions, or to party. Then they wonder why they read without understanding, find it difficult to concentrate during lectures, and can't remember the material on tests.

I speak from experience. For my first semester in college, I was tired all the time. Then I changed my habits. When you make a time schedule, be sure to allow eight hours of sleep every night of the week. When you are not tired, you will learn more in less time and enjoy it more.

Showing up to class without proper sleep and exercise and without eating or hydrating your brain will cause your brain to operate inefficiently and make learning much more difficult.[2]

The Second Giant Step: Get regular exercise

According to Dr. John Ratey, a clinical professor of psychiatry at Harvard, "Getting adequate exercise is the single most important thing a person can do to improve their learning."[3]

Most college students go from a more-active lifestyle in high school to spending long hours in college sitting in classes, crouched over a desk to study, or hanging out with friends for long discussions. So why is getting exercise important? Recent research on the brain offers several reasons.

"What is amazing is that exercise does at least three things. First, when you exercise, your brain releases important neurochemicals that improve human ability to take in, process, and remember new information and skills....

"Second, exercise leads to the development of new synapses in the brain. Synapses, the connections between neurons, are important for memory and for learning new information. In other words, exercise makes it easier for you to grow smarter."

And, as if that's not enough, the third thing exercise does is to increase "the development of new brain cells" in an area of the hippocampus that "controls learning and memory."[4]

How much exercise do you need? Dr. Ratey suggests at least 30 minutes of fairly strenuous exercise four or five times a week. For you, this means adding regular exercise to your weekly schedule—and taking it seriously.

Among other things, exercise appears to boost brainpower—specifically the ability to carry out tasks that require attention, organization and planning, reduce symptoms of depression and anxiety in some people, and enhance the immune system's ability to detect and fend off certain types of cancer.[5]

The Third Giant Step: Focus on learning

We learn best with focused attention. As we focus on what we are learning, the brain maps that information on what we already know, making new neural connections.[6]

More and more often, students who should be paying close attention in a class or lecture, or while they are studying alone, are texting, checking email and posting to Facebook, or playing a game—thinking they can do all this and pay attention at the same time. *They can't.* As a result, they make lower grades and learn far less. When I was a student, the main distraction was television and, along with many of my fellow students, I chose not to watch any television at all while in college.

Your focus is your reality. — Yoda

To focus on learning, you must make a firm decision about your digital devices. One good plan is to set aside blocks of 30 minutes each morning and 30 minutes each evening to read and answer emails, to check and comment on Facebook or other favorite social media sites, to listen to and respond to voicemails, and to make any important phone calls. At the very least, you must choose to turn off your cell phones, iPads, and other devices when you are in a classroom, when you are studying, and whenever you are face to face with other people.

According to Professor Dumbledore in the *Harry Potter* books, "It takes a great deal of courage to stand up to your enemies, but a great deal more to stand up to your friends." So true. Choosing when you will and when you will *not* use digital devices might upset your friends, But then, if you can explain your decision, you might even convince them to do something similar, to their eventual gain.

All three of these—sleep, exercise, and focusing on learning—require giant steps. They are not easy. It will take firm decisions and a great deal of willpower to stick to your decisions. But, if you can manage this, you will find you are better able to concentrate. You will learn more with less effort and will find it easier to remember what you have learned.

> *It takes enormous courage and dedication to take control of your own education.... Yet, it is probably the only approach that makes any sense of the college experience and certainly the one most likely to bring you self-satisfaction. — Ken Bain[7]*

Questions for Reflection

1. What are some of your Big Questions?
2. Have you made any choices about the first three "Giant Steps"?
3. Which will be most difficult for you to do?
4. What surprised you in this chapter? What was the most important thing you learned? How will you use what you learned?

CHAPTER 2

The Four Approaches to Learning

Students frequently get through basic math and science courses with no more than a superficial understanding of the concepts and relationships that are central to these subjects they have studied and without the ability to apply these concepts effectively to real-world problems. – Raymond Nickerson[1]

When you were 4 or 5 years old, you were incredibly excited about learning. Whether your special passion was learning about dinosaurs, superheroes, or sports, or whether you knew everything about Angelina Ballerina, Winnie the Pooh, or Curious George, learning was a grand adventure. You were eagerly anticipating first grade when you'd learn to read for yourself.

Then something unexpected—something truly terrible—happened to you and nearly all your classmates. You lost that marvelous delight in learning. To understand how this happened, you first must know about the monkeys.

Eight monkeys with puzzles

It is commonly believed that people work harder when they are rewarded for their efforts. This seems totally logical. Daniel Pink describes fascinating research showing that what seems so logical is totally false. He tells the story of Harry Harlow who, in 1949, did an interesting experiment with eight rhesus monkeys. Harlow wanted to see if monkeys could solve a fairly tricky puzzle. "Solving it required three steps: pulling out the vertical pin, undoing the hook, and lifting the hinged cover." Harlow put his puzzles in the cages so the monkeys would get used to seeing them before researchers began their tests.

What happened next surprised the researchers. "The monkeys began playing with the puzzles with focus, determination, and what looked like enjoyment." The researchers still expected the monkeys to work even harder when given rewards, but again they were surprised. When the monkeys were given raisins as rewards for solving the puzzles, they seemed to lose interest. They made more mistakes and spent less time working on the puzzles.

To explain this unexpected behavior, "Harlow offered a novel theory: 'The performance of the task provided intrinsic reward.' The monkeys solved the puzzles simply because they found it gratifying to solve puzzles. They enjoyed it. The joy of the task was its own reward."[2]

Twenty years later Edward Deci did a similar experiment using college students. Students *did* work harder when offered money for solving puzzles but later, when the rewards were stopped, they lost interest, while the students who had never been offered rewards continued to work harder each day.

According to Deci, human beings seem to have an "inherent tendency to seek out novelty and challenges, to extend and exercise their capacities to explore, and to learn."[3] He later added, "One who is interested in developing and enhancing intrinsic motivation in children, employees, students, etc., should not concentrate on external-control systems such as monetary rewards."[4] He could have added to this statement *"or grades."*

Perhaps you could see this coming. When you and all the other children started school, you were rewarded for learning. You got grades. Perhaps you even made the honor roll. You pleased your parents and teachers. All too soon, as with the eight curious monkeys, these rewards took the place of your original excitement about learning. Most of you no longer used your spare time to learn; it wasn't fun anymore. In place of your former intrinsic motivation, instead of learning for fun, you worked for grades. Your motivation was now extrinsic.

Your parents and teachers never intended to destroy your love of learning, but that's exactly what they did. One of the purposes of this book is to help you avoid the trap of extrinsic rewards like working for straight A's, and to allow you to rediscover the excitement and love of learning you had as a child.

What is intentional learning?

In this book, the term "intentional learning" is used to describe learning that takes place when students take charge of their own education and focus on studying subjects they find most interesting and most important. Intentional learning is therefore intrinsically motivated. To further explain intentional learning, we will consider two important questions in this chapter:

- What are the different approaches to learning and why do they matter?

- What does it mean to get a great education?

Exercise: How Do You Approach Learning?

Choose the answers that describe you most of the time. If your answer depends on the subject, the teacher, or something else, then describe when you use each approach.

1. Would you say your motivation to learn is mainly intrinsic or extrinsic? Would you keep studying if you didn't get grades?

2. When you read a chapter or article you will be tested on, do you usually:
   A. read without much thinking, concerned mainly with completing the assignment?
   B. search for facts and definitions you expect to be tested on and memorize these?
   C. focus on understanding the main ideas well enough to be able to explain them?

3. What is your main goal in college?
   A. Preparation for a job?
   B. Getting a good education?
   C. Making top grades?
   D. Or something else?

4. What do you mean by getting a "good education"?

The discovery at Göteborg

It all began in Göteborg University in Sweden. A group of researchers gave college students an article to read, explaining that they would be tested on the material. After students finished the test, the researchers asked each of them to describe how they had gone about reading the article. Their responses fell into two main categories.

Many students searched the article for important terms and facts they expected to be tested on, and then tried to memorize this information; they wanted to get a high score on the test. Other students read for understanding; they wanted to be able to explain the ideas. Both groups did well on tests but, when tested again weeks later, the first group remembered little. The second group remembered the information far longer.

The three approaches to learning and why they matter

These researchers labeled the first approach to learning "*Shallow*" and the second approach "*Deep*."[5] Some years later other researchers identified a third approach to learning: "*Strategic*."[6] Perhaps, partly because these terms use metaphor, they resonated with researchers and educators around the world. Teachers found it easy to identify the shallow, strategic, and deep learners in their classes. These terms, however, are not intended to describe particular students; rather, they describe approaches to learning. Students often use a combination of approaches

Shallow learners have little interest in understanding what they read. Some are concerned only with completing the assignment. Others look for isolated facts and try to remember them.

Strategic learners work mainly for top grades, often for straight A's. They may study for understanding when they expect essay tests. They believe grades are more important than learning. This shouldn't be a surprise. Isn't this what we have all been taught by teachers and parents? We were rarely praised for what we understood or learned on our own. Instead, we were praised and rewarded mainly for making top grades.

Strategic learning is actually an overlapping category. There can be shallow strategic learners, deep strategic learners, and others who are somewhere between the two.

Deep learners want to understand the basic concepts. They love learning and firmly believe learning is more important than grades. They may spend many hours a week reading and learning material not related to any classes. Some deep learners have a genuine need for top grades to get into medical school or graduate school. These students often combine the strategic and deep approaches.

What about *you?* Based on your first two answers in this exercise, are you motivated extrinsically or intrinsically? Would you consider yourself a shallow, strategic, or deep learner? Is there a connection between the two answers?

Who are the best students?

This is a tricky question. To many students (and even professors), the answer might seem easy; the best students would be the deep learners, the deeper the better. Some professors are trying to understand how to develop deep learners in their classes by focusing more on tests for deep understanding.

We might, however, ask "Best for what purpose?" Those early researchers may disagree with me, but I don't believe there is one best approach.

The Fourth Giant Step: Choose Intentional Learning

My response to this question is to suggest a fourth approach to learning: Intentional Learning. To become an intentional learner, a student must first understand that different approaches to learning exist. If you know only one approach, you don't have much of a choice.

Intentional learners choose their approaches to learning based on their personal goals. They decide what they want to learn and what grades they want to make. They may choose a shallow approach in one course, a strategic approach in another, and a deep approach in the courses that seem most important or most interesting. Like students using a deep approach, intentional learners enjoy learning because they are focusing on what and how they want to learn. Chart 2.1 was created to compare the four approaches to learning.

Chart 2:1 A Comparison of the Four Approaches to Learning

Approach	Shallow	Strategic	Deep	Intentional
Goals	Have fun – Party Graduate	Make top grades Get approval	Learning Understanding	Choose the approach Liberal education
Motives	Avoid work Extrinsic motivation	Earn respect Extrinsic motivation	Answer questions Intrinsic motivation	Reach personal goals Intrinsic motivation
Strategies	Take easy classes Scan book for information Recognize answers Short-term memory	What professor wants Know the kind of test Study for tests Memorize	Understand concepts Organize information Study arguments Memory understand	Take hard classes Multiple strategies Independent study Association memory
Questions	Why should I learn this? Why is it so boring? Why do they work so hard? What's the point?	How remember all this? What, when, and where? How make higher grades? How can I be successful?	How do they know? Why does it happen? How to explain? Do I under-stand?	Asks Big Questions What else is possible? What's my purpose? Can I make a difference?
Future	Worker Do what they're told Works for money	Routine expert Knows the answers Works for respect	Thinker Researcher Works to accomplish	Leader/Innovator Entrepreneur Works to reach goals

Notice that students using the shallow and strategic approaches are both extrinsically motivated. They work for rewards such as good grades, but they respond differently to failure. When shallow learners fail, they are likely to blame their problems on bad luck. They might say the test didn't include the information they'd expected. When strategic learners fail or don't do as well as they'd hoped, they often suffer a loss of self-esteem. They no longer feel confident that they are among the smartest and hard-est-working students in their classes. This can lead to anxiety, sometimes to deep depression.

Students using both the deep and intentional approaches to learning are intrinsically motivated. Their reward is learning itself, not the grades. They are less likely to judge their self-worth by their grades. Since they believe learning is more important than grades, they are able to use their mistakes and failures as learning experiences. They often reflect on ways they could have been more successful so they try again, using more effective strategies.

These differences carry over into students' careers. Shallow learners often take simple, routine jobs. They would rather have someone tell them what to do and how to do it. Strategic learners get better jobs because they work harder, but they seldom get promotions because they are so afraid of taking risks and making mistakes.

Deep and intentional learners, by contrast, are less dependent on what others think. They are willing to take greater risks, sometimes leading to failure, sometimes to success. They often end up in positions of leadership or start their own businesses. Entrepreneurs, for example, may fail repeatedly before being successful, sometimes hugely so.

Who chooses the goals for your education?

At each college and university, the faculty and administration decide what it means for students to get a great education and they develop a core curriculum to meet those goals. Students take required classes but rarely understand how these classes are expected to provide that "good education."

The professors decide what students should learn in their courses. Their goals may have little relationship with the school's image of the ideal education.

Many students make an effort to understand what their professors consider important and study that material for tests. In doing this, they allow the professors to determine what their education should include. Certainly it is easier to simply "go with the flow," but this may not lead to a great education.

Intentional learners decide for themselves what sort of education they need and want, based on their personal goals and interests. In required classes, they choose which topics are most interesting and important and spend more time studying these topics. They understand that no one will *give* them the kind of education they want; they need to get it for themselves.

How is your concept of a great education the same as what your school has planned on your behalf? How does it differ? What can you do to get the kind of education you want and need?

STRATEGY 2.1

BECOME A MORE INTENTIONAL LEARNER

Step 1: Describe the education you intend to get and how you plan to get that education.

Step 2: List at least five ways you plan to be more intentional in your learning.

Step 3: What will you do differently *today*?

In this chapter, you have learned about two main types of motivation and four approaches to learning. You have been asked what it means to get a great education. This is only the beginning. As you continue reading this book and, as you go through college, pause occasionally to consider your motivation, your approach to learning, and whether you are getting the kind of education you want and need.

> *Intentional learners...take the initiative to diagnose their learning needs, formulate learning goals, identify resources for learning, select and implement learning strategies and evaluate learning outcomes.*[7]

Questions for Reflection

1. What surprised you in this chapter? What was the most important thing you learned? How will you use what you learned?

2. What did you discover about yourself? Did you like what you learned?

3. In what ways are you a shallow or a strategic learner? In what ways are you already a deep or an intentional learner?

3

The Five Characteristics of Meaningful Goals

There may be no more important process in the world than goal setting. We know from the world of business that success-ful managers are ones who set reasonable, attainable goals for themselves and their employees.... When students do set goals for their own learning, they profit by improving their achievement levels, developing more of an internal locus of control, and becoming more aware of their own problem-solv-ing capabilities. — John Barrell[1]

There are many kinds of goals. This chapter will cover everything from helping you set lifetime goals to creating a goal and a plan for every course you take. You can even set goals for brief study sessions.

A. Lifetime Goals

These are long-term goals. What do you want to do with your life? What kind of person do you plan to be? What do you want to accomplish?

B. Educational Goals

These can include fairly long-term goals as well as semester goals and goals for tomorrow's test. What kind of education do you want? What do you need to reach your lifetime goals? Do you want to attend graduate school or simply improve your GPA? What skills do you want to improve this semester? What grades do you want to make on your midterms?

C. Personal Goals

What practical steps could you take that would make you happier? Do you want to lose weight or stop smoking? Do you want to make new friends or strengthen existing friendships? Do you want to be better organized, more confident, or a more careful listener? Do you want to improve your relationships with your family? Do you want to get married, buy a car, start a band, or build an app?

D. Compassionate Goals

What would you like to do to make a difference, either locally or globally? Those who have a purpose beyond self-centered wishes are likely to live a more rewarding and meaningful life.

> *Figure out for yourself what you want to be really good at, know that you'll never really satisfy yourself that you've made it, and accept that that's okay.* — Robert Reich

---
Exercise: List Your Goals

List at least three to five goals in each of these four categories:

1. Your Lifetime Goals
2. Your Educational Goals
3. Your Personal Goals
4. Your Compassionate Goals

Don't spend too much time on this, though; after you finish the chapter you should do a serious job of rewriting your goals.

Reflecting on goals with a true story

When I was a teenager I met a good-looking boy at the beach. After we got to know a little about each other, I asked him about his goals. His answer was memorable: "I want to go to a nice college, make good grades, and then get a good job. I want to meet a nice girl and get married and we'll find a really nice house in the suburbs."

My response was utter disgust. I made an ugly face, said a most emphatic "Yuuck," turned around, and left without looking back. The poor boy probably had no idea what he'd done wrong. He probably thought his goals made sense.

The truth is that these were completely generic goals. Even if he still hadn't chosen a college or thought seriously about a job and a wife, he could have described what he was looking for. Was he more interested in getting a good liberal education, or did he want to learn skills that might help him get the kind of job he wanted? What did he mean by "good" grades—C's, B's, or straight A's? Was he more interested in getting rich or in doing the kind of work he enjoyed? Did the girl need to be pretty and sweet? Would it be more important for her to be intelligent, strong, highly motivated, and perhaps independent?

Many college students have "goals" that are just as generic and meaningless as that unfortunate young man. Their goals all seem to include: making good grades (at least pretty good grades), having a good time in college, graduating, getting a good job...and maybe getting rich. The only specific goal on this list is graduating. We understand exactly what it means to graduate. What about the goals you wrote? Are they generic or are they meaningful?

Five characteristics of meaningful goals

1. **Meaningful goals are specific.**
   "Making good grades" is not specific. A better goal might be making a 3.5 GPA or, more specifically, getting an A in English Literature; at least B's in Ancient History, Calculus, and Sociology; and hopefully a C in Organic Chemistry. Being specific means these are *your* goals, not just the goals of the average student. Saying you want to be a doctor is certainly better than "getting a good job," but it would be more specific yet to say you want to become a cardiologist or a general practitioner working around the globe with Doctors Without Borders.

2. **Meaningful goals are connected to your other goals.**
   If you're planning to be a doctor, your educational goals should involve making the grades you need to get into medical school. If one of your life-time goals is writing great books, your educational goals might include taking classes in creative writing.

3. **Meaningful goals are challenging.**[2]
   If you are dyslexic, making passing grades might be a challenging goal. But, if you have the ability to make top grades, making only passing grades isn't much of a goal.

4.   Meaningful goals are realistic.

If you have a poor singing voice, being an opera singer or singing on Broadway are not realistic goals. But sometimes goals that appear unrealistic do come true. Some athletes have done well in spite of being smaller than the other players on the team. Some contestants on *American Idol* with little musical training go on to be finalists and then to be successful in the music field.

5.   Meaningful goals are taken seriously.

If you aren't planning to work hard in your classes, making straight A's isn't a meaningful goal. People laugh at New Year's resolutions because these resolutions tend to be no more than wishful thinking. If your goal is to improve your grades and you regularly skip class and don't do assignments, that wasn't a goal; it was merely wishful thinking. If your goal is to make a 3.5 GPA, you will create a time management chart plus a study plan for every subject. You will never skip a class. You will do all the assignments as well as you can. A true goal is something you act on.

> *The reason most people never reach their goals is that they can't define them, or ever seriously consider them as believable or achievable. Winners can tell you where they are going, what they plan to do along the way, and who will be sharing the adventure with them.* — Denis Watley

STRATEGY 3.1

SET MEANINGFUL GOALS

Step 1: Brainstorm. Start with your wildest dreams.

If you could do or be anything in the world, what would it be? The world is changing rapidly. Think about possibilities that don't exist today. What kind of person do you really want to be? What work would be most fulfilling?

Step 2: List your own strengths and weaknesses.

Write down your interests. Do you have a purpose in life or have passion to do something? If so, write it down.

Step 3: Reflect on the goals you wrote earlier.

Reflect on your wildest dreams. You might discover a few dreams you could turn into reality. Would you be willing to spend the time and effort required to work toward these goals?

Step 4: Rewrite your goals and evaluate them carefully. Ask yourself six questions:

1. Is this goal personal and specific? Will I know when I have reached this goal?

2. Is this goal connected to my other goals? Will it help me reach my lifetime goals?

3. Is this goal challenging? Is this the highest goal I can imagine or reach?

4. Is this goal realistic—not necessarily easy, but possible?

5. Will I take this goal seriously? Am I willing to take steps every day to reach this goal?

6. Am I willing to change my life to reach this goal?

Step 5: When you have a well-written set of goals, write or type them neatly.

Put one copy on your bulletin board, by your mirror, above your desk, or on the door where you'll see it every day. Put a small copy in your wallet, so you can occasionally take it out and read it.

People with clear, written goals accomplish far more in a short period of time than people without them could ever imagine. — Brian Tracy

The Fifth Giant Step: Working to reach your goals

The reason most people consider New Year's resolutions a joke isn't that there's a problem with these "goals"; the problem is that we don't take them seriously. We don't do what we need to do to reach these goals. We decide to lose weight, we eat too much one night, and we think it's the end of the diet. With real goals, we still slip up and make mistakes but we don't quit; we work harder.

If you're serious about a goal, you will create a plan and a schedule. If you want to lose weight, you'll decide how to change your eating and exercise habits and when you'll reach your first weight-loss goal. You might start a notebook to record what you eat each day, and also keep an exercise record. At the end of each day or each week, you will study the records and decide how well your plan is working and what you need to do differently.

We all have dreams. But, in order to make dreams come into reality, it takes an awful lot of determination, dedication, self-discipline and effort. — Jesse Owens

STRATEGY 3.2

PUT GOALS INTO PRACTICE

Step 1: Look at your list of goals every day.

Just a quick glance will help you remember them.

Step 2: Take time to read your goals at least once a week.

Think of steps you can take in the coming week to help you reach your goals.

Step 3: Share your goals with a close friend.

They might ask how you are doing on particular goals, especially on short-term educational goals. You can do the same for them.

Step 4: At least once a year, take time to review your goals.

Over time, we discover new interests and learn more about ourselves. Rewrite your goals as needed.

STRATEGY 3.3

CREATE AND USE A STUDY PLAN

For every class you take, you should set goals and develop a plan to reach them. Here is a plan that worked for me. You don't need to follow my plan. Go ahead and develop a plan that makes sense to you, but it's important to create some kind of plan. I used only one page for each course plan, and I always began with five basic types of information.

Step 1: Basic Info: The course, the date, the professor, the book, and the author.

Step 2: Goals: Decide what grade you plan to make and what you want to learn and remember.

Step 3: Plan: Describe what you will do to reach your goal.

Step 4: Strategies: List strategies that seem most effective for this course.

An example of a study plan I actually used

Basic Information: Invertebrate Zoology – Spring 1984 – Dr. Wall – *Invertebrate Zoology, 4th Ed.* by Robert D. Barnes. (The book is over 1,100 pages long. It covers 37 phyla, most subdivided into subphyla, classes, and orders, giving me 101 invertebrates to study.)

I anticipated test questions asking me to compare the respiratory systems of the sponges and the corals, or comparing the excretory systems of the five classes of echinoderms. This was enough to scare most students away; it made me even more determined. Clearly, I needed a good plan.

Goals:

1. I will make an A. I'd really like to get the top grade in this class. It's my most exciting course.

2. I want to know and remember basic information I can use to teach biology.

3. For invertebrates I can find in this area, I want much more information.

4. To hold student attention in classes I teach—and just because it's fun—I want to learn the most interesting ways invertebrates have sex, especially the stories that are really weird.

Plan: (This was the plan written before the first class. It changed later.)

1. Study the table of contents and decide if an outline or concept map is most useful.

2. Read introduction and chapter headings for the first 3 chapters.

3. Read chapter 1 before the first class. Compare chapters and lectures to see if they cover the same or different material. Decide if it's best to read chapters before or after lectures.

4. Make a list of questions about invertebrates for which I expect or hope to find answers.

Strategies: (Again, this was just my first plan.)

1. Draw a concept map or outline for each chapter, showing structure and including detailed information.

2. Copy diagrams showing different body systems.

3. Create "compare and contrast" charts to show how organisms are similar and different. Since I expect test questions comparing different organisms, this will be especially important.

4. Write potential test questions, especially essay questions, and practice writing answers.

What happened next?

By the time I had created my master plan, I knew I could read 50 pages a day, and could even read the book from cover to cover, but I wouldn't remember much. Remembering how Echinoidea and Holothuroidea were different would be impossible.

When I started to survey the third chapter, I discovered something important: Nearly every chapter covered the same nine systems: (1) External Anatomy, (2) Circulatory or Circulatory System, (3) Nutrition/ Digestive System, (4) Locomotion, (5) Gas Exchange or Respiratory System, (6) Excretion/Excretory System, (7) Nervous System, (8) Sense Organs, and (9) Reproductive System and Development.

After much thinking, I designed a page for note-taking with spaces for the chapter, phylum, subphylum, class, and order, as shown in Chart 3.1. The rest of the page was divided into spaces for the nine systems. This, alone, made studying easier. I completed one page for each of the 101 groups. The actual chart covered a whole page, leaving enough space for me to take detailed notes on each system.

Chart 3.1 My Chart for Taking Organized Notes

Chapter _____ Phylum _____ Subphylum _____ Class _____ Order_____
External Anatomy
Circulatory
Digestive
Locomotion
Respiratory
Excretory
Nervous
Senses
Reproduction

I then developed a far more exciting plan. I created a huge matrix chart. I divided the chart into 11 sections horizontally: one for the name, one for the taxonomic classification, and the rest for the nine systems. These were listed down the left side, as shown in Chart 3.2.

Chart 3.2 The Giant Matrix Chart (Showing Only a Small Section of the Blank Chart)

	Sponges	Anemones	Jellyfish	Comb Jellies	Flatworms	Ribbon Worms
Taxonomy						
Ext. Anat.						
Circulatory						
Digestive						
Locomotion						
Respiratory						
Nervous						
Excretory						
Senses						
Reproduction						

The 101 groups were listed along the top, each with spaces wide enough to write basic details. This chart was over 50 feet long. It covered one wall and part of the next. As I read about each type of invertebrate, I first filled in the details for each system on my note-taking pages. Then I copied the highlights on the matrix. Each time I started a new column (a new invertebrate), I compared the organisms in the current chapter to those I had studied earlier. If 10 or 15 groups used the same sort of digestive system, I circled them all with a highlighter. Systems that were unique were circled in red.

The secret of using this method is that I first studied all the material vertically, one chapter at a time, but I rehearsed the material horizontally. I could now describe the changes in the nervous system, for example, as the animals became more complex. I prepared for essay questions like "Compare the digestive systems of the jellyfish, octopus, and insects."

I not only made my A+, I really *did* get the highest grade in the class! It wasn't because I was the smartest student in the class. *It was because I had a good study plan and an amazing strategy.* The matrix won't work for all courses, of course. You'll need to find the best strategies for each particular course and textbook.

Do I really need to write a study plan?

Writing a study plan pushes you to think carefully about what you need to do to reach your goals. The more effort you put into creating the plan, the more likely the plan is to work well. You could grab the notebook you plan to use for a class and quickly write out some goals and a plan on the inside cover, but a carelessly made plan will not get you very far. The more carefully you plan, the better your chances are of success.

Linda Nilson puts it this way.

> *Deep, lasting, independent learning requires a range of activities...that go far beyond reading and listening. It entails, first, setting learning goals for a class period, assignment, or study session. Then the learner must plan how to go about the task effectively—perhaps actively listening, taking notes, outlining, visually representing the material, occasionally self-quizzing, reviewing or writing a summary.*[3]

I was thrilled to read Nilson's book. It not only reaffirmed a large part of what is included in this book, it's the only book I've seen that suggests having an actual plan for each class period, assignment, or study session. She would certainly agree that, for every course, it's wise to begin with a goal *and* a plan. How exciting it would be if you had classes with professors who use these strategies.

And then, who would expect a statement like the next one to be made by an artist?

> *Our goals can only be reached through a vehicle of a plan in which we must fervently believe and upon which we must vigorously act. There is no other route to success. — Picasso*

Questions for Reflection

1. Which of your goals is actually the most important?
2. Are you just dreaming or are you really serious about this goal?
3. If you're truly serious about this goal, what should you be doing now to make it possible?
4. What surprised you in this chapter? What was the most important thing you learned? How will you use what you learned?

CHAPTER 4

Flexible Time Management

If you want to make good use of your time, you've got to know what's most important and then give it all you've got. — Lee Iacocca

College juniors and seniors often say the one thing they wish they had known as freshmen is the importance of time management. While a few study-skills books recommend using a "To Do" list instead of a weekly study schedule, that's like putting a Band-Aid on a big cut; it might help a little, but most of the time it's useless. As you will discover in this chapter, time management not only helps you get your work done with less anxiety, it also helps you get a great education.

Exercise: How Do You Manage Your Time?

Rate yourself from 0 (never true) to 5 (usually true):

1. I have a regular study schedule and get my work done on time.
2. I study when I have time, but I never have a plan.
3. No matter how hard I work, I get further and further behind.
4. I always have a lot of work to do but I never know what to do first.
5. I tried using time management but it was too much work.
6. I'm a procrastinator. I put things off until the last minute and it hurts my grades.

Which of the above sentences above describes you best?

What does research say?

According to research, "freshmen are particularly prone to underestimate the amount of time an assignment will take and put off starting it. Time mismanagement and procrastination explains 30% of the variance in first-year college grades, more than the factors of SAT scores and high school grades combined."[1]

Richard Light discusses a study in which researchers "interviewed sophomores about their freshman year. One group of students did well academically and socially. The others had a difficult year. 'They quickly discovered that one difference, indeed a single word, was a key factor.... The critical word is time.' Those who did well discussed time management— scheduling their time."[2]

Edwin Locke describes the need for time management this way:

> *The two main ways that students mismanage their time are by wasting it and by trying to do too much work. Wasted time is often due to lack of purpose which results in numerous types of unproductive activities.... Time overload is typically due to too heavy a course load; time-consuming and/or fatiguing outside jobs; and excessive extracurricular activities such as dating, sports, club work and hobbies.*[3]

Flexible time management doesn't take time; it MAKES time

Students who don't use time management may spend many hours each day studying but somehow, they still get further and further behind. They could save time and worry less if they'd make a plan and follow it.

Some students shy away from time management because it sounds complicated. In fact, time management is *not* hard; studying without good time management is far more difficult. Without time management, students often find that it takes longer to get work done and this leads to increasing levels of anxiety.

STRATEGY *4.1*

BASIC TIME MANAGEMENT

Step 1: Begin by reading your goals carefully.

Ask yourself what you should do each week or each day to reach your goals.

Step 2: Use a calendar for long-term planning.

Mark on your calendar all tests, due dates for papers and projects, doctor appointments, interviews, and even parties and social engagements. Check your calendar regularly. Creating a well-marked calendar is a total waste of time if you don't use it.

Step 3: Make a weekly study schedule.

Some people prefer a vertical format; I find it easier to write on a horizontal chart. If you don't have a chart, you can use Tables to create a chart with 8 columns and 15 or 16 rows. You can also go to the website **www. choose-learning.com** and print the blank schedule found there.

Step 4: Fill in the schedule with your courses.

If you have a job, meetings, or other regular obligations add these. Make extra copies; you'll want to revise your schedule several times. I usually highlight classes in bright colors so they stand out clearly. If you miss a study period, you can make it up later, but you can't make up a missed class.

Step 5: Add study time.

Many schools suggest at least 2 to 3 hours of study for each hour of class. Some colleges and universities take this very seriously. For a three-hour class, you might need 6 to 9 hours of study each week. At other schools, you might manage with a little less study time.

If you have any doubts, start with a ratio of at least 3:1 for classes you think will be difficult, 2:1 for classes you think will be about average, and 1:1 if you're sure the class will be easy. After the first several weeks, you'll probably find you can manage well with less time, at least in some courses. Other courses might take far more time than you'd expected.

Step 6: Add time for everything else.

Schedule time for three meals a day; at least eight hours' sleep a night; showering and dressing; doing laundry and running other errands; time to spend with friends and/or family; and time to call home, call friends, check email, Facebook, and similar activities. When these things are scheduled, you will be less tempted to do them during study time.

Many shorter periods of time won't show up on your schedule. While eating, you can also spend time with your friends or practice your flash cards. You can study while waiting for clothes to wash or dry. You might even practice your Spanish while in the shower or redraw a diagram while your professor checks attendance or returns papers.

A time management schedule for Jane

Jane planned to take five classes her first semester. Chart 4.1 shows her schedule with just the classes.

Chart 4.1 Jane's Study Schedule with Classes

	Monday	Tuesday	Wednesday	Thursday	Friday	Saturday	Sunday
6 AM							
7							
8	Math	Math	Math	Math	Math		
9	Spanish	Sp. Lab	Spanish	Sp. Lab	Spanish		
10	Biology		Biology	Bio Lab	Biology		
11				Bio Lab			
Noon				Bio Lab			
1 PM							
2	Writing		Writing		Writing		
3		History		History			
4		History		History			
5							
6							
7							
8							
9							
10							
11							

Many students create a rough chart like this before registering for classes. They want to avoid having two classes at the same time. They also consider the distance between classrooms. They want to avoid racing all the way across campus for one class and then racing back for the next. If you have a class far from your other classes, schedule that class on a different day or when you have a break between classes.

With the first chart, Jane seems to have an amazing amount of free time. Don't be misled by this. There is much more to be included. When Jane adds an hour each for breakfast, lunch, and dinner, the schedule is no long quite as empty. Next, Jane will add three hours of study time for each hour of class, plus extra for Spanish practice. She also adds time for regular exercise. A schedule like hers, shown in Chart 4.2, can help students decide if they have taken too many courses.

Chart 4.2 Jane's Schedule with Study Time, Meals, and Exercise

	Monday	Tuesday	Wednesday	Thursday	Friday	Saturday	Sunday
6 AM							
7	Breakfast	Breakfast	Breakfast	Breakfast	Breakfast		
8	**Math**	**Math**	**Math**	**Math**	**Math**	Breakfast	Breakfast
9	**Spanish**	**Sp. Lab**	**Spanish**	**Sp. Lab**	**Spanish**	Bio HW	Hist HW
10	**Biology**	Math HW	**Biology**	**Bio Lab**	**Biology**	Span HW	Span HW
11	Math HW	Span HW	Bio HW	**Bio Lab**	Bio HW	Write HW	Span HW
Noon	Lunch	Lunch	Lunch	**Bio Lab**	Lunch	Lunch	Lunch
1 PM	Span HW	Hist HW	Write HW	Lunch	Span HW	Hist HW	Write HW
2	**Writing**	**History**	**Writing**	**History**	**Writing**	Span HW	Span HW
3		History	Math HW	**History**	Math HW	Span HW	Laundry
4	exercise	exercise	exercise	exercise	exercise	exercise	exercise
5						Span HW	Write HW
6	Dinner	Dinner	Dinner	Dinner	Dinner	Dinner	Dinner
7	Write HW	Laundry	Bio HW				
9	Hist HW	Hist HW	Write HW	Write HW			
10	Span HW	Bio HW	Span HW	Math HW			
11							

As you might imagine, Jane is horrified. She wouldn't have time to do anything but study! Even her weekends are full. The only good part of the schedule was that she fit in exercise and she had a free hour every day. She also managed to keep Friday, Saturday, and Sunday nights free for dating and social events.

Most descriptions of time management charts stop at this point, and such a chart is certainly better than nothing. If, however, you intend to be an intentional student, you should take five more steps. Two require extra time; three steps suggest ways to use your time more effectively. Notice that HW (homework) is written instead of "study" only because it's shorter. Use the term you prefer.

What is flextime and why is it important?

There is nothing flexible about Jane's schedule. To make a schedule flexible, we add what I call *flextime*: time that is available for finishing work not completed during your scheduled study hours. It's especially helpful when working on major projects, such as research papers. When you don't need to do extra work, flextime is free time, scheduled free time. With flextime, you'll get more work done and worry less. In fact, many students work harder in their regular study time so they'll have this time free.

STRATEGY 4.2

FLEXIBLE TIME MANAGEMENT

Step 1: Add 8–10 hours a week of flextime.

If this seems like a lot, imagine needing to write a 20- to 30-page paper. How many hours a week would you want available? You should never plan to do your research and write your papers in time meant for studying. Remember that, when you don't need flextime to get your work done, it counts as free time.

Step 2: It's a good idea to include at least one hour of flextime each day.

If you didn't finish an assignment because you spent that time talking to your professor or chatting with friends, it's helpful to have a scheduled time to get the work done that day.

Step 3: To show flextime on your schedule, you might just highlight the spaces in yellow. You'll know what it means but your schedule won't look quite so full.

What is independent study time and why is it important?

Autonomy—the freedom to make your own decisions—is important to intentional students. Daniel Pink, in his book, *Drive*, writes: "A sense of autonomy has a powerful effect on individual performance and attitude. According to a cluster of recent behavioral science studies, autonomous motivation promotes

- greater conceptual understanding,
- better grades,
- enhanced persistence at school and in sporting activities,
- higher productivity,
- less burnout, and
- greater levels of psychological well-being."[4]

Research shows that, with even a short period of autonomy, people reap these benefits. Begin by scheduling five hours of independent study a week. You might use only three hours a week when you're busy and ten hours a week when you have more time.

You can choose one topic per semester or change topics every day. You could use this time to learn more about a topic in one of your courses, or you could enjoy exploring a topic simply because it's interesting. You can read. You can talk to a professor—even one whose courses you aren't taking. You could create a business plan that you might use after graduation, or outline a book you'd like to write. You might even invent something. Use your time productively.

Sure, it takes time; anything important does. But it will increase your motivation and eagerness to learn in many areas. You might even find yourself wanting more time for independent study. You could use flextime when you don't need it for special projects.

Some of what you learn might lead to a research paper or a future thesis. Some of what you learn might help you get the job you want or even start your own business. It might also lead to a lifelong passion or hobby. For some students, independent study is the most exciting part of the day, possibly the most significant part of their entire education.

STRATEGY *4.3*

ADD INDEPENDENT STUDY

Step 1: Schedule five hours a week to begin with.

Step 2: Set independent study goals.

Create a list of at least 10 topics you'd like to study.

Step 3: Brainstorm ways to learn.

Will you read? You're already doing a lot of reading. Will you talk to professors other than your own? Are there other people in the area you might talk to? Will you discuss a topic with an expert by exchanging email? Will you use the Internet to do research? Will you create or write something yourself?

Step 4: Evaluate your progress.

For the first several weeks of a semester, keep a record of how you spend your time. What changes should you make for more effective independent study?

Chart 4.3 leaves little free time. While some students would be willing to put in this much study time, Jane was not. Her first schedule had looked so simple. She has scheduled only one hour of homework/study for each hour of class for math, but she is still worried about Spanish. Instead of nine hours of study time for Spanish, she increased it to 12 hours, a wise move. Taking five classes without the two labs wouldn't have been quite as bad. But now, just looking at this schedule makes Jane feel very anxious. She decided to drop Spanish.

Chart 4.3 Jane's Completed Study Schedule – A Very Full Schedule

	Monday	Tuesday	Wednesday	Thursday	Friday	Saturday	Sunday
6 AM							
7	Breakfast	Breakfast	Breakfast	Breakfast	Breakfast	Breakfast	Breakfast
8	**Math**	**Math**	**Math**	**Math**	**Math**	Bio HW	Hist HW
9	**Spanish**	**Sp. Lab**	**Spanish**	**Sp. Lab**	**Spanish**	Bio HW	Hist HW
10	**Biology**	Math HW	**Biology**	Bio Lab	**Biology**	Span HW	Span HW
11	Math HW	Span HW	Bio HW	**Bio Lab**	Bio HW	Write HW	Span HW
Noon	Lunch	Lunch	Lunch	**Bio Lab**	Lunch	Lunch	Lunch
1 PM	Span HW	IS-Time	IS-Time	Lunch	IS-Time	Hist HW	Write HW
2	**Writing**	**History**	**Writing**	**History**	**Writing**	Span HW	Span HW
3	IS-Time	**History**	Math HW	**History**	Math HW	Span HW	Laundry
4	exercise	exercise	exercise	exercise	exercise	exercise	exercise
5	FLEX	FLEX	FLEX	FLEX	FLEX	Span HW	Write HW
6	Dinner	Dinner	Dinner	Dinner	Dinner	Dinner	Dinner
7	Write HW	FLEX	FLEX	FLEX			
8	Bio HW	Math HW	Hist HW	Span HW			
9	Hist HW	Hist HW	Write HW	Write HW			
10	Span HW	Bio HW	Span HW	Math HW			
11							

Chart 4.4 Jane's Schedule After Dropping Spanish – Her Weekends Are Free Again

	Monday	Tuesday	Wednesday	Thursday	Friday	Saturday	Sunday
6 AM							
7	Breakfast	Breakfast	Breakfast	Breakfast	Breakfast		
8	**Math**	**Math**	**Math**	**Math**	**Math**	Breakfast	Breakfast
9	Math HW	Math HW	Math HW	Math HW	Math HW		
10	**Biology**	Volunteer	**Biology**	Bio Lab	**Biology**		
11	Bio HW	Volunteer	Bio HW	Bio Lab	Bio HW		
Noon	Lunch	Lunch	Lunch	**Bio Lab**	Lunch	Lunch	Lunch
1 PM		IS-Time	IS-Time	Lunch	IS-Time		
2	**Writing**	**History**	**Writing**	**History**	**Writing**		
3	IS-Time	**History**	Write HW	**History**	Write HW		
4	exercise	exercise	exercise	exercise	exercise	exercise	exercise
5	FLEX	FLEX	FLEX	FLEX	FLEX		
6	Dinner	Dinner	Dinner	Dinner	Dinner	Dinner	Dinner
7	Write HW	FLEX	FLEX	FLEX			
8	Bio HW	Math HW	Hist HW	Hist HW			
9	Hist HW	Hist HW	Write HW	Write HW			
10	Write HW	Bio HW	Laundry	Hist HW			
11							

As chart 4.4 shows, dropping Spanish was a great decision. Jane also cut back study time from six hours to five hours a week for history and biology. Now she can do her math HW right after class. Her weekends are totally free and she is breathing a sigh of relief.

She was even able to add two hours to volunteer in a Special Education classroom, which she really wanted to do because she's thinking about majoring in Special Ed. Since she'll be learning a lot by doing this, she could even count it as part of her independent study time. She also got back two hours of free time each day if she doesn't need it for flextime. Her revised schedule, Chart 4.4, still looks like a full schedule, but Jane is pleased with it.

Study means more than reading

In math classes, study time is used for solving problems. In language classes, there may be some reading and perhaps some translation, but most of the time is spent memorizing the vocabulary and grammar.

In most other classes, students often use study time to read their assignments and then think they're finished. This is part of the reason they learn so little and forget it so quickly. While reading can be one small part of what it means to study, genuine study goes much further. Part 3 of this book, "Mental Processing," describes what it means to study.

"Mental Processing" includes organizing information in a variety of ways, thinking deeply about the information, and using several of the pathways to memory. While mental processing is the key to learning, it's not found on the schedule. This is about to change.

STRATEGY *4.4*

INCLUDE MENTAL PROCESSING

Mental processing applies mainly to classes based on information from lectures and textbooks. For math classes, keep "Math HW" on the schedule. For writing classes, most of the homework is writing, so the schedule includes "Write HW." For language classes, you'd have to decide what to include, based on your first several weeks' experience.

Step 1: Indicate what specific activities will be done, such as previewing a chapter, mastering vocabulary, writing questions, and more. For each activity, there is a suggested abbreviation. If you don't like these, create your own.

1. Preview the chapter	Prev
2. Master the Vocabulary	Voc
3. Write Questions	Ask
4. Read and take notes	Read or Re/No
5. Organize the information	Org
6. Think	Think
7. Memory	Mem
8. Self-Testing	ST
9. Condense notes for regular review	Cond
10. Regular Review.	Rev

If your schedule is large enough, use the whole words. Otherwise, you might use these shorter terms. You will see examples done both ways in chart 4.

Step 2: Consider dividing each one-hour study period into two parts, such as preview/vocabulary or reading/organization. For many students, it's difficult to concentrate on what they're reading longer than 20 or 30 minutes at a time.

Step 3: Be aware that you'll need to adjust your schedule. You might have a lot of vocabulary to learn in one chapter and very little in another.

Chart 4.5 Jane's Partial Schedule, Using Mental Processing Activities for Homework

Monday	Tuesday	Wednesday	Thursday	Friday
Breakfast	*Breakfast*	*Breakfast*	*Breakfast*	*Breakfast*
Math	**Math**	**Math**	**Math**	**Math**
Math HW	Math HW	Math HW	Math HW	Math HW
Biology	Volunteer	**Biology**	**Bio Lab**	**Biology**
Bio Prev/Voc	Volunteer	**Bio Condense**	**Bio Lab**	**Bio Review**
Lunch	*Lunch*	*Lunch*	**Bio Lab**	*Lunch*
	IS-Time	IS-Time	*Lunch*	IS-Time
Writing	**History**	**Writing**	**History**	**Writing**
IS-Time	**History**	Write HW	**History**	Write HW
exercise	exercise	*exercise*	exercise	*exercise*
FLEX	FLEX	FLEX	FLEX	FLEX
Dinner	*Dinner*	*Dinner*	*Dinner*	*Dinner*
Write HW	FLEX	FLEX	FLEX	
Bio Read/Org	**Math Review**	**Hist Org/ST**	**Hist Condense**	
Hist Prev/Voc	**Hist Read/Org**	Write HW	Write HW	
Write HW	**Bio Org/ST**	*Laundry*	**Hist Review**	

Notice on Chart 4.5 that the time and the weekends have been removed to provide extra space. The classes and all other information that stayed the same were shown in smaller type. You don't need to be able to read these. The parts that were revised were enlarged.

With biology and history, the first study session is labeled Prev/Voc. This means preview the chapter and learn the new vocabulary. The second study session is labeled Read/Org, meaning read the chapter, which might take most of the time, and do the first organization. Next is Org/ST, meaning use one or more new ways of organizing information and also use self-testing.

Then you'll find Condense, which means to boil down the notes, including reading notes, lecture notes, and the organization charts. (This will be covered in chapter 13 on Test Preparation.)

Finally, you have one study session each for Review in biology, history, and math. These hour-long reviews should include self-testing and will cover everything you have learned in this course so far. At first, you'll spend most of your review time on the current week. Later, you'll be spending more time reviewing earlier material. This kind of test preparation means you'll never need to cram for an exam. As you read further in the book, this will become easier to understand.

Jane has also decided to read and respond to email, text messages, voicemail, and Facebook after breakfast, which won't take a full hour, and again after exercise, since she plans to exercise only 30 minutes a day.

Jane wants to join one or two campus organizations. Other students want time to watch or participate in sports. Jane will move some of her study time to the weekend to have time for her new activities.

STRATEGY *4.5*

USE LEARNING SPRINTS

One way to get more done in less time is to do some of your work in short, intensive periods of time. Instead of reading a chapter in one hour, prepare yourself to work extremely hard and see how much you can learn in 20 or 30 minutes. You can do a sprint for any of the learning activities.

Step 1: For each kind of study sprint, begin by setting goals for the next 20 or 30 minutes.

Step 2: Don't work at the same speed, doing only half the work. You should, instead, try to cover very nearly everything, but do it rapidly.

Step 3: When you finish doing a study sprint, take time to evaluate how much you learned or accomplished. Compare this to what you would have accomplished in an hour.

For a Preview Sprint, your main goals are to discover how the chapter is organized, learn the main ideas, and spot unfamiliar vocabulary. You should aim to complete a thorough preview of a chapter in half the time you usually use.

For a Study Sprint to organize information, don't worry about the beauty of your visual organizers or even the spelling.

When you Sprint to memorize, do not work with a small list of vocabulary words or other flash cards. Your goal is to do just as much work in less time. This means concentrating harder.

Reading Sprints are like a rapid version of SQ3R (survey, question, read, recite, and review). You still do a quick preview. You skim instead of reading sections, but you still take some notes and you still test yourself at the end of each section. If you can't remember what you're reading, stop sprinting and read in the usual way.

In a marathon, runners must pace themselves so they can keep going for 26.2 miles. But at the end, most runners take every ounce of energy they have left and sprint to the finish. This is exactly what you want to do in a Study Sprint. Some people enjoy this so much that they schedule several Learning Sprints throughout the day. I often find that I learn more in an intense 20-minute sprint than I do when reading the usual way for an hour. Give it a try.

If sprinting doesn't work for you, there is no need to keep trying. Different strategies work best for different learners. Even in a marathon, there are runners who aren't sprinters. They continue their steady pace to the finish line.

The Sixth Giant Step:
Use flexible time management

To make a schedule and not use it is like creating a budget yet not changing your spending habits. You were able to follow a regular schedule in high school. This isn't much different except that now, with a flexible time management chart, *you* make the schedule and you have built-in flexibility. Ask yourself if you get more work done this way.

*In truth, people can generally make time for what they choose
to do; it is not really the time but the will that is lacking. — Sir
John Lubbock*

STRATEGY *4.6*

USE YOUR SCHEDULE

Step 1: When you finish your study schedule, make several copies. Put one
on your bulletin board or desk. Keep a smaller copy in your wallet. I taped
copies on the inside covers of all my notebooks. You may want to refer to
your schedule several times a day.

Step 2: Over the first several weeks, make adjustments for classes where you
need more time or less time. You might also find better times of the day to
study certain subjects.

Step 3: Take time weekly to evaluate how well your schedule is working. What
problems make it hard for you to get your work done? What can you do to
prevent these problems or handle them differently?

Nine ways flexible time management helps you learn

1. Simply creating the study schedule helps you make informed decisions
    about the number of courses to take and whether there's time for a
    part-time job. Some students are comfortable with a heavy schedule
    and little free time. Most prefer having a reasonable am ount of free
    time to spend with friends or to participate in other activities.

2. When you know you have exactly one hour to read a chapter, you're
    likely to use your time more efficiently. You can accomplish more work
    in less time.

3. Picture yourself working on that research paper. With flextime, you
    have the time to do a great job on the research. You might finish writ-
    ing, reorganizing, or revising it several times, and then have it ready
    several days early. None of your other classes has been affected. You
    feel more relaxed. You might even enjoy working on the paper.

4. Before exams, you will be able to relax. Use your flextime for final
    reviews.

5. You will never feel guilty when you use flextime to spend time with
    friends or do something special. You'll have finished the work you
    needed to do. When you have available flextime, go ahead and enjoy
    yourself.

6. Knowing what and when to study, and knowing you'll have time set aside to finish research papers or finish work you weren't able to complete in the expected time, will greatly reduce anxiety. With less anxiety, you will understand more of what you read and do more work in less time.

7. Adding mental processing strategies to your schedule will help you use a variety of strategies. You will learn more effectively and remember longer. It will also prepare you for tests.

8. Spending time on independent study makes it clear that you are taking charge of your education. You may discover that learning can be exciting again. If you're lucky, this excitement might even extend to your regular subjects.

9. Flextime helps you fit in extracurricular activities—an important part of your education. Jane's schedule with flextime leaves two hours a day free for extracurricular activities, so she can easily shift her schedule if she needs more, to be with friends or do volunteer work. She could also move some of her flextime to the weekends.

Your time is valuable

If someone gave you $10,000 and told you it had to last a full year, you would probably put this precious gift in a safe place and plan carefully how you'd spend it. Each of us is also given another gift: the gift of time. For the next year, you've been given 8,760 hours to spend. Don't waste them.

Flexible time management will help you choose the best ways to spend that time.

You wouldn't let someone else tell you how to spend that money. You would decide for yourself. The same should be true about spending your time. Some students, once they create a time management chart, let the chart tell them what to do.

A time schedule is not something you absolutely must follow. Rather, it's a guide to help you make the best use of your time. At any point, you can change your schedule. On any day, if you make a choice to do something else instead of studying, that's your right. It is your time to spend. Spend it wisely.

> *The key is in not spending time but investing it. — Stephen Covey*

Questions for Reflection

1. How would you feel about having flextime for special projects?
2. How would you feel about having time for independent study? Some find it exciting but others feel overwhelmed. Are you willing to give it a try?
3. How might time management be helpful after graduation? How will time management on the job be different from time management in college?
4. What surprised you in this chapter? What was the most important thing you learned? How will you use what you learned?

CHAPTER 5

Mindsets and Stereotype Threats, and What You Can Do About Them

The goal is to work toward a world where expectations are not set by the stereotypes that hold us back, but by our personal passion, talents and interests. — Sheryl Sandberg

Consider this sentence: "Although her parents want her to go to law school, Melissa has her mind set on studying art." Having one's mind set on something is related to a passion rather than a rational decision. It will be hard for anyone to get Melissa to change her mind.

A "mindset" is not quite the same. It is a set of ideas, beliefs, and stereotypes that permeate every part of your life. It is also very difficult for you to change your mindset, even if you wish you could. But, while we know very well what we have our minds set on, we are generally not aware of our own mindsets.

Some examples include the ideas that fat people are lazy, that children learn a lesson when they are punished, or that wealthy people are happier. Some mindsets are simply mistaken ideas; some are biased thinking; some are statements of opinion. Several of the most important mindsets affect both our behavior and our performance on tests. It is these mindsets that will be discussed in this chapter.

Exercise: Examine Your Mindsets

With some of these questions, you may not know the answer. Write down what you believe is true. If you can't answer with a yes or a no, describe what you *do* believe.

1. Is intelligence set or changeable? Is there anything you can do to become more intelligent?

2. Is it possible to change or improve someone's brain? Can you improve your own brain?

3. Imagine you are taking a fairly difficult course. On the first test your grade is 37 (out of 100). Would you conclude that you aren't good at that subject and drop the course? If not, what would you do?

4. You made an A in a difficult course. Would you believe you got the A because you were smarter than the other students or because you worked harder?

5. Is math really difficult for most people to understand? Is it especially difficult for women?

6. Are people of one racial or ethnic group generally smarter than others? If you think so, which ethnic group do you think is the most intelligent?

7. Would you prefer to take a challenging course or an easier class in the same subject where you'd be sure of an A but would learn less?

The responses of children to difficult puzzles

Carol Dweck, author of the book *Mindset*, used a simple experiment that brought attention to the idea of mindsets. She invited some 10-year-old children, one at a time, into her office and asked them to try doing some puzzles. Each child began with easy puzzles and all were successful. Later, the child was given more difficult puzzles—ones that were actually impossible to solve.

Some children gave up quickly, saying they weren't smart enough, and asked to do more of the easy puzzles. Other children were excited. They worked harder and harder, hating to give up.[1]

Why is this important? Dweck had first divided the children into two groups. Children in one group believed they could learn well because they were smart but thought there was nothing they could do to get smarter.

Children in the second group believed they learned more and got smarter if they worked hard.

The first group, when faced with failure, blamed it on the puzzles' being too hard or on their own lack of ability. "I can't do it. I'm not smart enough." The children who thought they could get smarter if they worked harder were excited. They enjoyed the challenge. Many felt confident they would eventually solve the puzzles.

Dweck describes the first group, those who thought they weren't smart enough, as having a "Fixed Mindset." They believed their intelligence was fixed and couldn't be changed. Those in the second group were described as having a "Growth Mindset."[2]

Reflecting on the Exercise

Can Intelligence Be Improved?

Did you recognize a relationship between this story and the questions you were asked earlier? The first question asked whether intelligence is set or changeable and whether there is anything you can do to become more intelligent. When I was growing up, we were taught that intelligence was not changeable, that no one could change their IQ. We were certain that brains could not be improved. Let's consider the evidence to the contrary.

- Alfred Binet, who created early IQ tests, wrote, "With practice, training, and above all, method, we manage to increase our attention, our memory, our judgment, and literally to become more intelligent than we were before."[3]

- Reuven Feuerstein, an Israeli psychologist, worked with immigrant children who had been diagnosed as severely mentally retarded. Many of these children later tested at the normal level of intelligence or above. Some went on to graduate from college. Feuerstein taught that "Intelligence is not fixed but modifiable."[4]

- The SAT tests your mental abilities rather than what you have learned. It is often described as another test of intelligence. We know that students taking SAT Prep classes raise their test scores significantly. Have they improved their intelligence? If they learned new skills for the test and soon forgot them, the answer would be no. If this training improved their reasoning abilities and the change was permanent, we really *could* say these students increased their own intelligence.

Can brains be changed?
Can we change our own brains?

Over recent years, the response to these questions has also gone from "No, that's ridiculous," to "Yes, of course!"

- Marion Diamond and others did research on rats showing that those in enriched environments (larger cages, more toys, and with other rats) had larger brains.[5]

- Norman Doidge wrote that "The idea that the brain can change its own structures and function through thought and activity is, I believe, the most important alteration in our view of the brain since we first sketched out its basic anatomy and the working of its basic component, the neuron."[6]

- Barbara Arrowsmith-Young, whose story is told in Doidge's book, went on to write her own book. Born with multiple physical and mental disabilities, she developed strategies while in graduate school and used them to change her own brain. She now runs a school using these strategies with learning-disabled children.[7]

- The National Research Council found that "1) learning changes the physical structure of the brain, 2) learning organizes and re-organizes the brain, and 3) different parts of the brain may be ready to learn at different stages of development."[8]

Identify your own mindset

The third question asked what you'd do if, on the first test, your grade was 37. Would you conclude that you aren't good at that subject and drop the course, or would you decide that you'd need to work much harder, perhaps using better strategies and actually welcome the challenge?

First, we must consider the circumstances. If you've taken a very heavy course load, it might be wise to drop this course. But students who give up whenever a course or anything else is too hard—students who give up because they believe they aren't smart enough—could be described as having a "Fixed Mindset."

Students who refuse to give up, who understand that this course is going to be harder than they'd expected but look forward to the challenge, who are certain they can do better if they only work harder, can be described as having a "Growth Mindset."

In the fourth question, you've made an A in a difficult course—perhaps the top grade in the class. Those who believe it's because they are smarter than the other students have a "Fixed Mindset." Those who believe it was because they worked harder have a "Growth Mindset."

Students with "Growth Mindsets," are more successful in school, at work, and even in social relationships.

The problem with math

The fifth question asked whether math was hard for most people, especially for women. This is a common belief. Girls get this idea, sometimes from their parents, often from elementary teachers, many of whom suffer from math-anxiety. "The more anxious teachers were about math, the more likely girls (but not boys) were to endorse the commonly held stereotype that 'boys are good at math and girls are good at reading' and thus lower the girls' math achievement."[9] The only real problem with math is that so many people believe this stereotype.

Why 5,000 girls didn't get credit for AP calculus

An important experiment showed that, when students took the usual AP Calculus exam, the boys made much higher scores than the girls. But, when students filled out personal information (including the check box asking if they are male or female) *after* the test, girls made higher scores than boys. This apparently happens because, when students are reminded of their gender, they (usually unconsciously) are reminded of the stereotype that boys are better in math. This decreases the confidence of the girls and increases the confidence of the boys.

We might assume that responding to this question after the test means that none of the students are affected by the stereotype. If this is true, girls are actually better in math than boys; at least they are better at taking math tests. In spite of these studies, the AP Calculus test continues to ask this and similar questions before the test and girls continue to make lower scores.

One study estimated that the average scores of the girls who answered the questions before taking the test were 33% lower and that, based on the number of girls taking the test each year, moving these questions to the end of the test "could increase women receiving AP Calculus credit by more than 4700 every year."[10] Since that estimate was made in 2008, the number is likely to be over 5,000 per year now.

If you didn't think mindsets were important, this should change your mind. It is painful to think about these 5000 talented girls who don't get credit on an AP exam – every year, simply because of their mindset, because of a lie, even if they didn't believe it was true.

Are people of one racial or ethnic group generally smarter than others?

Are Asian students smarter than non-Asian students? Are they better at math? Are white students smarter than African-American and Latino students? Judging from average test scores, the answers would appear to be yes. But, as you might suspect, it is stereotype threat again raising its ugly head.

When students, about to take a difficult test, are told they are simply doing a "problem-solving exercise," African-American and white students do equally well. When they are told this test is a "good indicator of their underlying abilities," African-American students make much lower scores.[11]

On tests like the SAT or ACT, all students realize that these are tests of their intellectual ability. It should be no surprise, then, that the white students, aware of the stereotype that they're smarter, do better than minority students who are aware of the stereotype that they aren't as smart.

It's also true, much like on the math tests, that when students are required to indicate their racial or ethnic background before taking a test, African-Americans and Latino students make lower scores. White men are at a disadvantage when tested along with Asian students in math, science, and computer studies, because of the stereotype that Asians are superior in these areas.

It is often suggested that students are affected by the stereotype because they lose confidence, but research shows that it involves far more than this. Students, whether or not they believe the stereotypes, often experience anxiety in test situations. Anxiety causes their blood pressure to go up, and higher blood pressure leads to difficulty in thinking clearly. Anxiety also changes the parts of the brain that are most active, and this leads to problems accessing memory.[12] When students experience problems in both thinking and memory in a high-stakes exam, it is easy to understand why so many students make lower grades.

In addition to causing lower grades, it has also been found that these same stereotypes make it harder for minority students to learn in the first place. It also appears that all students are affected by one stereotype or another. Even some Asian students, aware of the stereotype that they are superior in math and computer science, are anxious about not doing as well as everyone expects them to do in these areas.

STRATEGY 5.1

PREVENT STEREOTYPE THREAT

Step1: Warn other students about stereotype threat.

Students who are aware of stereotype threat, and who realize these stereotypes are not true, are affected less. If you have read the last several pages, you should realize that *none of these stereotypes is true*.

Step 2: Write about your goals.

Experiments have shown that stereotype threat is reduced when students review their goals and write for 20 to 30 minutes about their own values. It should also help them to remember having done well on similar tests.

Step 3: Get enough sleep.

When preparing to take a test, it's a good idea to get a good night's sleep and eat a meal with plenty of protein and few carbohydrates (carbohydrates can make you sleepy).

Step 4: Relax.

If you still experience anxiety on a test, whether from stereotype threat or something else, it is often beneficial to put down your pen, lean back a little, and take several long, slow, deep breaths.

Step 5: Try positive self-talk.

"I know I can do these problems. They're just like the problems in my homework." "I have no reason to be anxious; I am well-prepared for this test." Or "This really is a tough test but all I need to do is relax and do my best."

The Seventh Giant Step: Develop a Growth Mindset

Would you prefer to take a challenging course where you'd need to work hard, or a much easier class in the same subject where you'd be sure of an A but would learn less? This question is about far more that choosing a class. Would you prefer a job where you'd need to work very hard and might not succeed, or would you rather take a job where you'd have no problems?

Students who choose the more difficult course, who care more about how much they learn than about the grade they'd make, get the best education. People who apply for the more challenging jobs might fail now and then but, if they learn from their failures, they may go on to success and enjoy their work even more. This is another way to understand what it means to have a "Growth Mindset."

Stereotypes lose their power when the world is found to be more complex than the stereotype would suggest. — Ed Koch

Questions for Reflection:

1. What stereotypes are you aware of that might affect your ability to learn?

2. What information in this chapter was most surprising? What was the most important thing you learned? How will you use what you learned? Who should you tell about what you learned?

3. Would you have believed this information if the chapter hadn't included supporting research?

CHAPTER 6

Develop Willpower, Resilience, and Concentration

Of all the virtues we can learn, no trait is more useful, more essential for survival, and more likely to improve the quality of life than the ability to transform adversity into an enjoyable challenge. — Mihaly Csikszentmihalyi

Self-control is generally understood as taking charge of emotions, desires, and choices. Self-discipline involves doing work you decide to do, completing tasks, and finishing what you start. A person without self-discipline might be described as disorganized, as lazy, or as a procrastinator.

When you were younger, your teachers and parents enforced discipline. They set goals for you and made sure you did the necessary work to reach them. In college, you must set your own goals and be self-disciplined.

Willpower, resilience, and concentration are all related to self-discipline. Some authors refer to this area as "self-regulation." All these areas are important for effective learning; all were once seen as nearly impossible to change; and in each of these areas, researchers have now found ways you can improve.

Exercise 1: Reflect on Your Willpower

1. Have you ever used the excuse "I can't do that because I just don't have the willpower" or perhaps "I'm just not motivated"?

2. Would you describe yourself as a hard worker? Do you generally try to do your best?

3. Do you often procrastinate, choosing to put work off until the last minute?

4. Do you ever set goals but do nothing to reach them? Do you create a study schedule or budget but not follow through?

5. Would you rather have $50 today or $60 in one week?

6. Imagine you just started a diet but friends want to go out for pizza. Would you join them and have some pizza, figuring you can start your diet the next day? Would you go along and order a salad?

Understanding willpower

Research shows that "self-discipline outdoes IQ in predicting academic achievement."[1] A person with willpower is self-disciplined. With willpower, the focus is on the determination to succeed and the ability to keep working. A person with willpower hates the idea of giving up. A person without willpower gives up easily, makes impulsive choices, and doesn't carry through with decisions.

While doing the exercise you were probably clear about which behaviors involved willpower. If you answered yes to numbers 1, 3, or 4, and no to 2, your willpower is weak.

On question 5, the person with willpower is likely to choose $60 next week rather than $50 now. They might consider anyone taking the money now to be foolish and short-sighted. They have learned to "delay gratification," to wait for the greater benefit. On question 6, they'd happily join their friends going for pizza but they'd order a salad for themselves. They wouldn't worry about temptation and would never moan about how much they'd love to have some pizza and how hard it was to stick to their diet.

Students with willpower are not so rigid that they must study history only in the time period on their schedule for studying that subject. Instead, they make choices based on their goals. They know that not studying history now means doing it later during flextime.

Children with marshmallows

The classic study of willpower by Walter Mischel involved research with 4-year-old children who were offered one marshmallow now or two marshmallows later. All the children chose two marshmallows later but, when left alone with that single marshmallow sitting in front of them on the table, some children just couldn't wait.

Some children ate the marshmallow just as soon as the researcher left the room. Some resisted temptation for a time but finally gave up and ate their marshmallow. Other children found ways to distract themselves, looking the other way, singing, or thinking about something else. They waited the whole 15 minutes and earned that extra marshmallow.[2]

Picture a younger brother, a sister, or another child you know who is about 4 or 5. What would they do in that situation? What do you think you'd have done as a 4-year-old?

"So what?" you might ask. "It isn't surprising that some children can wait more patiently than others."

But this isn't the end of the story. Years later, Mischel managed to find hundreds of these children and asked follow-up questions. These results were stunning.

The children who had shown the most willpower at age four went on to get better grades and test scores. The children who managed to hold out the entire fifteen minutes went on to score an average of 210 points higher on the SAT than the ones who had caved after the first half minute.[3]

Students with the most willpower were also more popular in later life, held jobs with higher salaries, were less likely to be overweight, and experienced fewer problems with drugs. This might lead us to believe that willpower is either a genetic trait or a result of early training. Nothing seems to change after age four.

One reason there is so little change was that the children were still in the same families. Their parents had not changed their behaviors. In some families children were still rewarded for working hard, avoiding impulsive choices, and not giving up easily. Their willpower was strengthened. In other families, children's willpower was further weakened.

Just as I finished writing this book, I learned that Walter Mischel had just published a book with new information on willpower. Some of the children who were tested years earlier were tested again "at midlife" with an MRI. The students who couldn't wait for their marshmallows as children showed higher brain activity in an area of the brain tied to addiction. The students who were able to wait long enough to get that second marshmallow (or other treat) as children showed more activity "in the prefrontal cortex area, which is used for effective problem solving, creative thinking, and control of impulsive behavior."[4] Still, there is good news. Strategies have recently been developed to help people strengthen their willpower.

Exercise 2: Reflecting on Resilience

---

1. You want to study physics but failed both physics and calculus in your freshman year. Would you give up and change your major? Or would you refuse to give up and take both classes again?

2. Imagine that you had a good job but the company downsized and you were left unemployed. How many times would you apply for new jobs before giving up? 10? 100? 1,000? Would you refuse to give up?

3. You are on the cross-country team and tried your best, but you came in last in every race. Would you decide you don't have what it takes and try a different activity? Would you practice harder and give it one more try? Would you keep practicing and keep doing your best?

Understanding resilience

While self-discipline generally describes the decision to work hard and willpower describes the determination to keep on working, resilience describes the ability to keep going after encountering a problem or failing to reach a goal. It's often described as the ability to "bounce back."

On question 1, you were asked what you'd do if you failed calculus and physics. Many students would simply give up, saying they weren't smart enough or they weren't willing to work that hard.

My son (who is severely dyslexic) is the best example I know of will-power and resilience. Tony planned to major in physics so he could teach high school physics but, in college, he failed both calculus and physics—not just once but three times. He still refused to give up. He tried again and again and finally, he got his degree in physics and a master's degree in education. It wasn't easy but he reached his goal.

On question 2, you were asked if you lost a job, how many times you'd apply for a new job. Those who keep trying are the most resilient. On question 3, you were asked about coming in last on every race. While there is no shame in trying a new activity, resilient people are more likely to relish the challenge. They might double their practice time, get extra coaching, and strengthen their muscles at the gym or with a trainer in their effort to improve their skills.

A person who is *not* resilient sees mistakes and poor results as an indication that they are failures. We might call it defeatism: giving up hope, or a loss of confidence. Roger Crawford describes this beautifully:

> *We can't control which difficulties we'll encounter, but we can control how we'll respond to them. We can choose to be victims or victors, winners or whiners, optimistic or pessimistic.*[5]

In physics, resilience describes materials that, when pushed or pulled, return to their original size and shape. Elastic is resilient. Balls that bounce when dropped are resilient. My parents used to say "when you fall off a horse, you should get right back on again," but the adage was never really about horses; it was about not letting failures get in the way of success.

> *Too often, when people suffer a major loss, they also lose their sense of identify and purpose in life. But with a resilient core, you keep a clear inner vision of your strength and flexibility in the face of challenges.*[6]

I often think of students who are failing all their courses and are tempted to run away, or even commit suicide, rather than return home as a failure. What would *you* do if you were failing your classes? How long would it take you to tell your parents? Would you stay in your dorm and cry—or do something else?

I especially think of the student who was spied on by his roommate doing no more than kissing another man. Tyler Clementi, an 18-year-old freshman at Rutgers, was a talented violinist. When he learned that his roommate and others had watched him several times through a webcam, Tyler made complaints to the school, but the humiliation was obviously more than he could take. He committed suicide.

Tyler apparently couldn't see that he had alternatives. He could have dropped out and started over at a different college. He might even have been strong enough to stand up to the bullies. He could have found others to support him, pointing out the unacceptable behavior of the roommate and of others who thought it was so funny. They might have opened up a discussion about respecting all students regardless of sexual orientation. He could have accomplished a great deal if he had been resilient. Instead, he felt he had no other choice but to take his own life. What a tragic loss.

Resilient students feel the same shame and pain as other students who flunk out or who are bullied, and they experience the same dread of discussing problems with their parents. Resilient students, though, are faster to analyze the problems and set new goals. Those who flunk out might get a job and work for a year or two while taking classes at a community college and, when they're ready, return to college prepared to work harder. Others might admit honestly that they never wanted to go to college in the first place. Instead, they might get vocational training to help them reach their goals.

It's often said that when one door closes, a new door opens. When you lose one job, it's an opportunity to find a better one. When you break up with someone you cared about, it's an opportunity to find someone even better suited to you. When you flunk out of one college, you have the opportunity to learn from your mistakes and start over again somewhere else. When you're being bullied, you can always make it clear that you did nothing wrong and force the bullies to recognize that their behavior is not acceptable.

But not everyone sees the new doors open. Some are too busy feeling sorry for themselves. Because resilient people expect to find those new directions and possibilities, they find them more easily.

Exercise 3: Reflecting on Concentration

1. Do you daydream or find your mind wandering during classes or while studying?

2. During classes or while studying do you answer your cell phone or call or text a friend? Do you talk to or write notes to another student? Do you surf the net, check Facebook, or play games? Do you ever do homework for one class while in another class?

3. Do you ever read a chapter in the book or listen to a lecture and later realize that you have no idea what it was about?

4. How often, during class or while studying, do you find yourself so focused on the subject that you ignore all distractions and can't believe how quickly time has passed?

Understanding concentration

Concentration is the ability to focus deeply on a single topic for a reasonable period of time. If you answered the first three questions with "yes," you need to develop your powers of concentration. If you answered the fourth question with a "yes," you probably have excellent powers of concentration. Your experience is sometimes called "flow."

People who aren't able to concentrate have not disciplined their minds. They allow distractions to interfere with their concentration and let their minds wander at will.

The problem has become far more serious and widespread in recent years with the increasing number of electronic devices that distract students when they should be learning. Several studies have reached the obvious conclusion that students who attempt to multitask during classes or while "studying" learn less and make significantly lower grades.

In one study of 774 college students ranging in ages from 18 to 55, students were asked which activities they had participated in during class in the past 30 days. The results are shown in Chart 6.1.[7] While the researchers didn't include playing games on cell phones, tablets, or laptops, I'm sure many students would also have checked those.

Chart 6.1 Student Activities Done During Class

	Number	Percent of students
No multitasking	44	5.9%
Text messaging	392	50.6%
Facebook	191	24.7%
Work on other classes	136	17.6%
Email	116	15%
Instant messaging	102	13.2%
Listen to music	51	6.5%
Talk on cell phone	25	3.2%

What was most interesting in this study was the discovery that students who multitasked more frequently not only made lower grades, they were also most likely to drink more alcohol, smoke more, use more marijuana and other drugs, binge drink, drive or ride with a driver who'd been drinking, and have multiple sex partners—all in the past 30 days.[8]

It is important to realize that this is *not* proof of cause and effect. Rather, it is a correlation. The study doesn't prove that risky habits cause students to be distracted when they should be studying, and it doesn't prove the reverse—that the distractions cause students to smoke and drink more and have multiple sex partners. It may simply be that students who are not strongly goal-oriented, students who are not intentional learners, are more likely to allow themselves to be distracted and also more likely to be involved in risky behaviors.

Many students appear to be addicted to their electronic devices. Some seem to suffer genuine withdrawal symptoms when they must go even an hour without texting or checking their email and Facebook pages. It would require a great deal of willpower to break these habits.

According to Daniel Goleman

> There are two main varieties of distractions: sensory and emotional.... The biggest challenge for even the most focused, though, comes from the emotional turmoil of our lives, like a recent blowup in a close relationship that keeps intruding into your thoughts.... The more our focus gets disrupted, the worse we do.... The power to disengage our attention from one thing and move it to another is essential for our well-being. The stronger our selective attention, the more powerfully we can stay absorbed in what we've chosen to do.[9]

You should not be surprised to learn that students who can concentrate on the lecture or on what they're reading will understand it better, remember it longer, and make better grades. Students frequently complain about or excuse their poor grades on the grounds that they "just can't concentrate." Instead of complaining, they should develop their skills in this area.

It might help to understand exactly what happens when we concentrate. According to Dr. Daniel Siegel, "when we focus intently, we do three things in the brain." His description is somewhat technical, but easy enough to understand if you concentrate on the information rather than skimming it.

First, one part of the brain secretes acetylcholine, which is spread all over the brain.

Second, "Paying close attention intensely activates specific circuits."

Third and perhaps most important:

When we pay close attention to one thing, the acetylcholine bathing those activating circuits works with the localized release of another neurochemical...to optimize how genes become expressed to produce the proteins necessary to strengthen the connections among those firing neurons. In short, when you pay close attention, you optimize neuroplastic changes that are the basis for learning.[10]

In other words, when we concentrate on or pay close attention to what we're learning, this causes actual changes in our brains, making it possible for us to understand more deeply and remember much longer. When we are distracted, multitasking, or paying only partial attention to what we're learning, our brains are not changed. The information will not become part of our long-term memory, so we forget most of this information quickly. We have learned nothing.

As Siegel remarks, "Without the lasting structural changes in the brain, no long-term learning can occur. The exam comes and the exam goes just like the divided attention that prevented any synapse growth from occurring."[11]

The most striking part of this new understanding of learning is that it's not about learning a little more or a little less. It is absolute. If you concentrate, your brain is changed. You understand and you learn. If you don't concentrate, there is no change in your brain. You might remember information long enough to pass a test but, in the long term, you have learned absolutely nothing.

Concentration leads to the ability to form accurate and penetrating knowledge, which allows more effective learning and provides access to our power of discrimination and intuitive knowledge. — Phil Nuernberger

The Eighth Giant Step: Strengthen willpower, resilience and concentration

Two Australian researchers looked for a way to build or strengthen willpower. They recruited volunteers who wanted to improve in one of three areas: physical fitness, money management, or study habits. Half the people in each area were asked to wait (the control group).

The physical fitness group got a free gym membership and a personal trainer, the money management group had someone to help them create and use a budget, and the study skills group got help setting goals and using study schedules. The three groups were treated the same in three ways:

1. In each group, participants had an expert who taught them how to improve.

2. In each group, participants kept a log of their time, their spending, their study habits, or whatever was appropriate.

3. In each group, participants wrote in journals daily, describing their problems, successes, and feelings.

The surprising results

As you might expect, all the participants improved in their particular areas. The surprise was that participants also showed improved willpower in other areas. Those working on physical fitness, for example, became more careful about saving money and developed better study skills. They also "smoked fewer cigarettes and drank less alcohol. They washed dishes instead of leaving them stacked in the sinks, and did their laundry more often. They procrastinated less. They did their work and chores instead of watching television or hanging out with friends first. They ate less junk food, replacing their bad eating habits with healthier ones." Those in the control groups showed no change.[12]

STRATEGY *6.1*

IMPROVE YOUR WILLPOWER

Step 1: Select one area to work on.

It might be physical fitness, weight loss, living within your budget, improving study skills, or stopping a habit like smoking.

Step 2: Find someone to help you.

There might be someone at your college fitness center who will advise you. Someone in your school's study center or tutoring center might assist with study habits. A doctor in the school infirmary or someone who recently quit smoking could help in that area. But you can always ask a friend to help. If they can advise you, that's good—but their main task is to hold you accountable. They should ask each day, or at least several times a week, to see your log, to ask how things are going, and to encourage you to keep working. Discussing your efforts and problems with someone else makes it easier for you to keep working.

Step 3: Keep a detailed log of your efforts.

For weight loss, keep a list of what you ate at each meal or between meals, and perhaps also the calories, and your weight (checked every week). For study skills, keep a list of time spent studying each subject, the time of day and location, the strategy you used, and how much you think you learned. For smoking, keep track of the number of cigarettes smoked, time of day, and reason for smoking.

Step 4: Write in a journal every evening.

Reflect on what you did well that day, what problems you faced, and what you might do differently next time.

Step 5: Continue this effort for at least two or three months.

You might feel it helpful to continue keeping the log and writing in your journal even longer.

STRATEGY 6.2

IMPROVE YOUR RESILIENCE

Resilience is quite different from willpower. You cannot practice facing problems unless you have problems to face. But, when that moment comes, return to this strategy.

Step 1: Accept what has happened.

You cannot undo the past. Do NOT waste your time saying or thinking "If only I had…" or "I know I should have…." Face the truth. You didn't do those things. Thinking about the "If only" ideas will just make you more miserable.

Step 2: Don't blame someone else for your problems.

That won't change anything and it won't help you develop resilience.

Step 3: Focus on the future, not the past.

When you face a difficult situation, look for a way to do something positive. Set new goals. Make new and better plans.

Step 4: Be brave.

It never helps to deny or try to run away from your problems. Face reality. Set new goals. Tell your parents the unfortunate news sooner rather than later. Certainly they will be upset. They may even be mad at first, but that will pass. When they understand how terribly upset you are, most parents will want to comfort you. Let them know how much you appreciate their understanding. Share your plans for the future. They might add some helpful suggestions. Be sure to thank them for their help even if you don't like the ideas.

Step 5: Use positive self-talk.

If you find yourself blaming others for your problems or thinking you couldn't help it, or that you just aren't smart enough, you need to talk some sense into your head. Here are five examples of positive self-talk:

1. When you make a low grade on an essay, don't complain that the professor expects too much or grades too hard. Tell yourself, *I have a lot to learn. This will be a great opportunity to improve my writing skills!*

2. If someone bumps into you, causing you to spill your drink, don't think or say she did it on purpose, or she should have looked where she was going. Tell yourself, *Relax. I know she didn't do it on purpose. I'm sure she's embarrassed. I could easily have bumped into someone else like that.* Accept her apology with a smile and say, "Don't worry about it; it will all wash out."

3. When you have difficulties solving a math problem, don't give up and think *Math is too hard. I'm not good at math.* Tell yourself, *These problems are challenging but, with a little help, I know I can learn this. I certainly will not give up.*

4. When you break up with your boyfriend or girlfriend, don't keep thinking about how much you hate them. Instead, remind yourself: *I'm sad that it's over, but I will always have happy memories of the good times we had together. I'm sure I will eventually find someone else I will love even more.*

5. When someone makes a rude or hateful remark that upsets you, do not reply in kind. Do not tell yourself or your friends what a terrible person he or she is. Instead, try to understand their problems. Were they raised to be prejudiced? Be glad you weren't taught hateful ideas. Perhaps they were having a really bad day; maybe they just failed a test, or got a poor grade on a paper. Either say nothing or reply, "I'm sorry you feel that way. Maybe, when you're in a better mood, we could get to know each other better."

STRATEGY 6.3

IMPROVE YOUR CONCENTRATION

Step 1. Recognize that you are in charge of your own brain.

You decide whether or not to pay attention.

Step 2: Identify all the distractions that prevent you from concentrating.

If you are texting, checking email, going on Facebook, or doing anything other than paying attention in class or while studying, make a firm decision to avoid this in the future. Follow the procedures for improving willpower. Keep a record of the number of times you are distracted or not paying attention in each class and in each study period. Was the problem something you could avoid in the future? Do you need to sit somewhere away from your friends?

You might also turn off your cell phone as soon as you walk into class—a good habit to use at movies and concerts, too. Even better, you might have two 30-minute times in your schedule, one in the morning and one at night, for communications. In these scheduled times, you'll make all your phone calls, do all your texting, and check Facebook.

Step 3: Keep a separate journal strictly for improving concentration.

Write in it each evening describing your successes and failures and listing strategies you'll use in the future to prevent these problems.

Step 4: Many people have found it helpful to meditate or practice mindfulness.

From what I can tell, they use these exercises to relax and clear the mind of all the desires and distractions. Some people simply practice concentrating. They concentrate on a spot on the wall for 5, 10, or even 15 minutes. They practice concentrating on their breath, on slowly breathing in and breathing out. You might also concentrate on a single goal or an inspirational quote. Whatever you concentrate on should allow you to avoid thinking about your emotions and desires.

Step 5: Choose something short and interesting to read.

Practice concentrating for 5 minutes the first day and gradually increase the time each day.

Step 6: Improve concentration while reading or listening to a lecture.

Begin by being well-prepared. In particular, describe what you already know on the topic and make a list of questions for which you'd really like answers. As you read or listen, be alert for three things:

1. Is this information you already knew?

2. Does this answer any of your questions?

3. Is this new information that you really need to know or that you find especially interesting?

Step 7: Learn more about the subject.

The more you learn, the easier it will be to concentrate.

Step 8: When you reach the point that you are so focused on your subject that you hate to stop, you will have succeeded in learning to focus your attention. You are really learning!

———

No one expects to learn the rules to a sport and become a star without a great deal of practice. No one expects to pick up a saxophone or other musical instrument and become a skilled musician without many years of instruction and practice.

Why is it, then, that we believe we can learn new study skills and expect to be instant experts? Don't despair when you try some of these strategies and don't succeed immediately. Keep practicing. And, as with most skills, if you stop practicing, those skills become rusty. Choose the habits, skills, abilities, and strategies you want to do well—then practice them regularly.

Optimistic people tend to interpret their troubles as transient, controllable, and specific to one situation. Pessimistic people, in contrast, believe that their troubles last forever, undermine everything they do, and are uncontrollable. — Martin Seligman

Questions for Reflection:

1. Try to remember when you practiced very hard to develop a particular skill or ability. How did you manage to keep working? Why didn't you give up?

2. Which of the mental strengths in this chapter seems most important to you?

3. What surprised you in this chapter? What was the most important thing you learned? How will you use what you learned?

CHAPTER 7

High School Skills Are Not Enough: A Brief Introduction to Part 2

No one would expect to be able to succeed as a neurosurgeon or as a pro football quarterback without training, but countless thousands of students assume they can succeed in college even if they are not skilled in reading, writing, listening and other basic skill activities.[1]

I f you are in college, we can assume you had some of the best learning skills in your high school. But that doesn't mean that your skills are adequate for college. Part of your college experience should include developing stronger basic skills.

Exercise: Evaluate Your Learning Skills

1. In each of these skills, compare yourself to others you know. Rate yourself from 1 to 10; 1 means your skills are among the weakest and 10 means your skills are among the very best. Try to be realistic. People nearly always rate themselves far too favorably.

Some 93% of people interviewed say they are better than average drivers. And a little closer to home, 94% of college professors think their teaching is above average.

a. Reading	g. Writing
b. Understanding what you read.	h. Vocabulary
c. Note-taking	i. Public speaking
d. Using the notes you take	j. Test preparation
e. Research	k. Study skills
f. Computer skills	l. Test-taking skills

2. In which of these areas are you most interested in improving your skills?

3. Many students work extremely hard, make good grades in their classes but, within days or weeks after the last exams, forget nearly everything they'd "learned." How much do you remember of what you learned last year?

4. Explain why students forget so much of what they "learned." Certainly this could not be considered getting an education.

Why do students work so hard, make top grades, and still forget most of what they learned?

This is the first of the Big Questions asked at the beginning of the book. We have described many parts of the puzzle in earlier chapters. The reasons why students forget most of what they learn involve the student's approaches to learning, their goals, use of time, mindsets, willpower, resilience, and concentration. This section of the book covers the importance of strengthening basic learning skills.

These skills are also an important part of what employers want most. They are frustrated when new employees cannot understand or write acceptable reports, when they can't do effective research, or when their computer skills are inadequate for the job.

Chart 7.1 The Empty Head

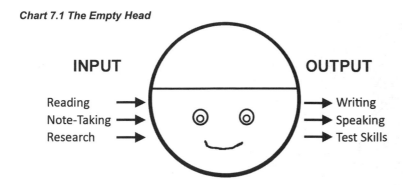

In Chart 7.1 The Empty Head, you will see the six basic skills covered in this part of the book, with three main input skills on the left and three main output skills on the right. We could also include computer skills both as part of the input and of the output skills.

The Empty Head shows information entering the head and going back out again *without* being processed by the brain. This is one of many reasons we forget so quickly. The next section of the book explains ways to avoid leaving your head empty. I call this a visual metaphor.

Zits, a favorite comic strip of mine, provides another visual metaphor related to this section of the book. We often hear people say "It just went in one ear and out the other." We might say those people are listening with their brains turned off. Here, Jeremy is reading with his brain turned off.

Used with permission Zits © 2013 Zits Partnership, Dist. by King Features

Before covering mental processing skills, it is important to have information to process. For this you must begin by strengthening your basic learning skills.

Merely accumulating information is of little value to students. Facts are soon forgotten, and the sheer volume of information has grown to the point that it is impossible to cover all important material or even to agree on what is most essential. Concepts and theories have little value unless one can apply them to new situations.[2]

STRATEGY 7.1

LEARN WITH YOUR BRAIN TURNED ON

Step 1: When reading, stop at the end of the first section.

Remember as much as you can. Could you explain what this section was about? Could you have understood the information more deeply? You might go back and read it again, this time increasing your concentration, reading with your brain turned on. Continue this several times until you begin to read each section with your brain turned on.

Step 2: During lectures, stop very briefly from time to time.

Reflect on how well you've listened and taken notes. Were you listening and taking notes with your brain turned on? Learn to concentrate as you take notes.

Step 3: When you're studying, pause occasionally.

Ask yourself if you are studying with your brain turned on. It does take more energy to work or study with your brain turned on, but you'll learn more in less time.

There's a wonderful analogy told at many times and in many places. We know Abraham Lincoln, for one, related this story. More recently it's found in Stephen Covey's book *The 7 Habits of Highly Effective People.*[3]

A man walking through the woods stops to watch a woodcutter struggling to cut down a tree. The woodcutter complains that his saw isn't sharp enough. But when the observer suggests that he stop and sharpen his saw, the woodcutter says he doesn't have time. We can only shake our heads at such a foolish response. We understand that if the woodcutter would only spend a few minutes sharpening his saw, he would complete his work far more quickly.

When students are asked why they don't take some time to sharpen their basic skills, they respond the same way: "We don't have time." Sharpening your basic skills will both save time and help you learn more.

Learning is not just knowing the answers. It is not just acquiring the bits and pieces of general knowledge.... Learning is a lifetime adventure. It's a never-ending voyage of exploration to create your own personal understanding. — Colin Rose and Malcolm Nicholl

Questions for Reflection:

1. Do you ever read like Jeremy, with the words going in one eye and out the other?

2. How much time are you prepared to spend to sharpen your learning tools?

3. Which of your learning tools do you want to work on first?

4. What surprised you in this chapter? What was the most important thing you learned? How will you use what you learned?

CHAPTER 8

Rediscover the Excitement of Reading

A book is a device to ignite the imagination.
— *Alan Bennett*

You do remember when reading was exciting, don't you? When your mother called you to dinner you might have begged, "Please, can I just finish this chapter?" You might have hidden a book under the covers at night and read with a flashlight long past your bedtime. In school, you might have hidden the book you *wanted* to read inside the book you were supposed to read.

And yet, of all the tasks done by college students, one of the most disliked tasks is reading. Many students understand less of what they read in college than they did in high school. Certainly, textbooks are not as thrilling as adventures, mysteries, or romances, but reading can still be exciting. Most students who hate reading assignments never learned how to read a textbook.

Oprah Winfrey said, "The door to freedom is education." We should all reflect on and learn from her attitude toward reading. She also said:

> *Books showed me there were possibilities in life, that there were actually people like me living in a world I could not only aspire to but attain. Reading gave me hope. For me, it was the open door.*

Exercise: What are the most effective reading strategies?

John Dunlosky and four other researchers studied hundreds of previous studies on the effectiveness of 10 common learning strategies considered most effective. They are listed below.

Of the strategies on this list, which do you think are the two most effective? Which do you think are the four least effective?

1. Explaining why something is true
2. Relating new information with what is known
3. Summarizing information
4. Highlighting and underlining main ideas
5. Comparing information with sounds
6. Using mental images
7. Rereading the book
8. Testing yourself
9. Distributed practice (reviewing at regular intervals, such as daily or weekly)
10. Interleaved practice (studying two or more subjects in rotation)

My system for becoming a better reader

When I was in fifth grade, I decided to read every book in the elementary library (a rather grand goal). One of my classmates decided he would read the encyclopedia. At a recent class reunion, I asked him how far he had gotten. He never finished that first volume and doesn't remember anything he learned. It made me feel a little sad. Both of us had high ambitions, but neither of us set goals that made much sense. Reading six or seven Nancy Drew books in a single day might have increased my reading speed, but I didn't learn much.

According to Mortimer Adler, "In the case of good books, the point is not to see how many of them you can get through but, rather, how many of them can get through to you." None of those Nancy Drew books got through to me. Later, I was lucky. I found many books that *did* get through to me; some of them even changed my life.

When I was in junior high school, I decided there were three ways to improve my reading skills. I applied these rules with great seriousness. They still seem a good way to begin:

1. Improve your vocabulary. It's easier to read when you understand the words.

2. Read as much as you can. Read many different kinds of books.

3. Sometimes, read really hard books. Read adult books, not kids' books.

When I was young, there were no YA books for teenaged readers. My small public library had two small rooms: one for children's books and one for adults. By the time I was in fifth grade, I began reading books for adults. One summer I read *A Handbook of Psychiatry*. It was pretty heavy reading for a 14-year-old. I'm sure it added many words to my vocabulary and, believe it or not, it really was fascinating.

I still recommend my three rules. In addition to reading assigned books, college students should continue to read widely. Read novels, magazines, newspapers, a little poetry, and some good nonfiction. Don't skip over words you don't know; learn what they mean. Sometimes, when you're feeling brave, read more-challenging books—ones that are far more difficult than your textbooks. They may also be more interesting.

Evaluating your Responses on the Exercise

The two strategies rated by the researchers as most effective were numbers 8 and 9: self-testing and distributed practice.

The five strategies rated least effective included numbers 3, 4, 5, 6, and 7: *summarizing, highlighting and underlining*, relating information and sounds, using visual imagery, and *rereading*. The three most commonly used study methods are emphasized. Notice that all three commonly used strategies are among the least effective.[1]

How well did you guess the answers? How often do you use the least effective strategies?

Why college students can't read

Many college textbooks are poorly written. They focus on information and pack far too many facts into each page. A better approach, in my view, would be for textbooks to focus on relevant issues and explore Big Questions in the field.

Many college textbooks also introduce a large number of new terms in each chapter, making it harder to read. Readers have three choices: They can study the vocabulary before they begin reading, they can look up each new terms as they come to them, or they can skip words they don't know and try to understand the chapter without them. Most students simply skip words they don't understand.

We cannot blame textbooks, however, for most of the reading problems. Most textbooks do a great job of organizing information, making it easier for students to find the main ideas. They often include summaries and practice questions. Take advantage of what the authors have done to make your job easier.

A more serious problem is that reading should involve thinking but many students don't seem to realize this and almost never question what they read. One writer believes that this eventually changes. He explains that many students "come in believing textbooks are authoritative but eventually they figure out that textbooks and professors don't know everything and then they start to think on their own."[2]

The biggest reading problem, however, might be caused by underlining and highlighting. In high school, you weren't supposed to write in your books. As you read an assignment, you needed to either take notes or remember the important information without notes.

Now that students own their books, they like the idea of writing in them. Some are taught to use this strategy but students rarely use these strategies effectively. They are now so intent on using their beautiful multi-hued highlighters that they no longer concentrate on understanding what they're reading. We might refer to this activity as *"reading with their brains turned off."*

"No problem," students say, "I'll go back later and read everything that is highlighted. Then I *will* understand." This might work if students correctly highlighted the topic sentences and main ideas but most of the time they highlight a large number of randomly selected facts that might (or might not) be important. You might compare what you highlighted in one chapter to what other students marked. In many cases, the apparently "important" information is quite different.

Students also make several common mistakes in highlighting: They highlight too much, too little, or the wrong information. Sometimes they highlight scattered words that make absolutely no sense at all when they reread what they highlighted.

The strategies in this book are suggestions for reading *"with your brain turned on,"* reading for understanding, reading to learn and remember. Nine strategies are listed: five for preparing to read, three for skimming, and one strategy with several variations for serious reading.

Five strategies for preparing to read

You may have used some of these strategies in high school and found them boring and not very helpful. The harder the material is, the more important these strategies will be. The better you prepare for reading, the easier it will be to understand what you read.

Many students think they can skip these strategies, especially when they're in a hurry to finish. What a shame. When they skip these simple strategies, they'll find the material harder to read and harder to understand and remember.

With many lists of strategies, students can choose one to use. With these strategies, though, it's important to use the first four every time you read. We might describe them as four parts of a single, extremely important strategy. The fifth strategy is only needed when taking a course covering unfamiliar and difficult material.

STRATEGY 8.1

READ WITH K-W-L

The letters represent three simple steps: what you **K**now, what you **W**ant to know, and what you **L**earned.

Step 1: What do you *know* about the topic?

In your notebook, write what you are *sure you know*, what you *think you know*, and what *you "kind of" know*. You can list the information, write an outline, or create a concept map.

Why is this important? Recalling this information reactivates the part of your brain where these memories are stored. When you recall what you already know, the new information will seem more familiar, making it easier to understand. Best of all, the new information connects with what you already knew, making both old and new memories stronger. The neurons in your brain physically connect the old information with the new, and the new information moves quickly into long-term memory.

Step 2: What do you *want* to know?

> *Question making has a huge payoff in learning. Question making is the tool that allows you to get inside your brain and know what you know and what you don't know. — Ruby Payne*

List your questions, starting with what you need to know for class. Add questions about topics that you find interesting. Leave space for answers. Mark questions that are most important.

You learn more when you're interested, when you really want to know something. But you knew that already, didn't you? Writing down what you want to know focuses your attention on these topics and questions. When you find the answers, you experience satisfaction.

Step 3: What have you *learned*?

When you finish reading, write a list or brief summary of what you learned. This step is so helpful that you should do this after each lecture or class, as well as after each chapter you read. *If you cannot describe what you learned, you didn't learn anything.* Writing the main ideas helps you retain this information longer and in greater detail.

You might have noticed that I am reminding you to write reflections at the end of each chapter. You might add further questions like "What else do I want or need to learn about this topic?"

> *Informal evaluations indicate that the K-W-L Strategy increases the retention of read material and improves students' ability to make connections among different categories of information as well as their enthusiasm for reading nonfiction.*[3]

STRATEGY 8.2

SURVEY THE BOOK AND CHAPTER

Surveying a *book* usually takes from 30 minutes to 2 hours and sometimes longer. Surveying a *chapter* is likely to take only 20–30 minutes. You think you can't afford to spend this much time? *You can't afford not to.* At the end of the survey, most students understand the main ideas in a book or chapter better than students who didn't do a survey but who did read every word. Sometimes, after a good survey, you'll decide you know the material well enough. At other times, the survey provides a strong framework upon which you can add important details as you actually read the material.

Step 1: Always take notes as you do the survey. You will need them for the last step. You will also want to refer to your survey notes on the book before reading each chapter. Be sure your notes are neat and well-organized. You will read them many times.

Step 2: Read the title. Write it in your notes. What do you expect to learn in this book?

Step 3: Write the names of the author(s) and the date the book was published.

Step 4: Check the back matter and add notes. Skim the Index. Which topics are found on many pages throughout the book? Is there a Glossary? Is it short or long? Are most of the words unfamiliar, long, and hard to pronounce? Does the Glossary show you how to pronounce them? Does the Bibliography include mainly books, or are there a lot of research articles from journals? If the books and journal articles were all published in the past year or two, you know the author is covering the most recent research. Check Appendices to see what's included and whether any of it seems important.

Step 4: Read the Table of Contents carefully. Is the Table of Contents divided into larger parts as well as chapters? If so, the author is providing clues to the structure of the book.

Step 5: Organize the main ideas. (This is the most important part of the survey.) If chapter titles are informative, you can begin organizing information immediately. If the chapter titles aren't informative, skim each chapter, looking for the main ideas. Read introductions, summaries, and main headings. This is usually enough to describe the main points of the chapter. You might use an outline, a concept map, or a structural chart (shown in chapter 16). You have now finished surveying the book. Stop and reflect. Have you learned enough?

With some materials, especially supplementary readings, you might be finished. You know the main ideas. If you need or want to learn more, you could select several chapters or sections that are closely related to what you're learning and read these in detail. With textbooks or other important reading, you will usually need to read further or at least skim for important details. The survey of the book will be a framework upon which you can build. If you decide to read further, the next step is to survey the first chapter or section you plan to read.

A most informative story

Dr. William G. Perry, a professor at Harvard University, did a simple study. He gave 1,500 Harvard freshmen just 20 minutes to read a 30-page chapter from a history textbook. Students were told that, after 20 minutes, they'd be asked to remember main ideas and write an essay on what they learned. Could you read 30 pages in 20 minutes? What would *you* do?

The students did well on a multiple choice test but not on the essay. Only 15 students could write a paragraph about the chapter. What did these students do differently? They went to the end of the chapter and read the summary.[4]

It's hard to believe that 1,485 Harvard students started to read, beginning with the first word, hoping they could read enough in the allotted time. Even knowing that they'd need to write an essay didn't make them wonder if there was a summary. Had there been no summary, they would have done better to read and organize the headings and subheadings before hunting for important information. They probably thought they didn't have enough time.

STRATEGY 8.3

SET READING GOALS

Step 1: What do you want to learn from this chapter or reading assignment? Set clear and specific goals.

Step 2: What grade do you plan to make in this class?

Step 3: How important will this material be for making that grade? How important is it for what you want to learn? Will it be more important to learn vocabulary, facts, main ideas, or concepts?

Step 4: How much time will you need for this assignment? Will you be doing the assignment all at once or dividing it into several shorter sections?

Step 5: What strategies will you use?

If you're in a hurry, just copy and fill in the blanks.

"My goal in the next ___ minutes is to read (or study) pages ___ to ___ in order to learn _____ I will use the _____ strategies."

Step 6: After you finish reading, evaluate yourself. Did you reach your goals? If not, when will you continue working?

Notice that when you have specific goals, you are more likely to accomplish them—plus you'll get more out of your reading. What matters most is not what your goals are, but that you *have* goals; not what strategy you use, but that you *use* a strategy.

STRATEGY 8.4

MASTER THE VOCABULARY

Start with K-W-L, a survey of book and chapter and goal setting.

Step 1: When you survey the chapter, look for unfamiliar vocabulary. Most words should be learned before you begin reading.

Step 2: You can set aside a page of your weekly notes for vocabulary or write them directly on flash cards.

Step 3: List the unfamiliar words, and write most definitions in your own words. If you don't understand a definition, try a dictionary or check the Internet. *Never memorize definitions you don't understand.* You might also include examples. If you still don't understand the term, talk to your professor or TA. Some terms are more difficult than others.

Step 4: To learn these words you might:

A. Read the definition several times. Can you relate it to other words that you already understand?

B. When possible, learn a group of related words at the same time. When you look up "monograph," you might also learn the words "monotone" and "monogamous." Understanding one word beginning with mono makes it easier to understand and remember all other words starting with mono.

C. Create your own flash cards. I prefer 3x5" cards cut in half. They fit comfortably in a pocket. Write the word on one side. Write the definition and maybe an example on the other side. Wrap the cards with a rubber band and keep them in your pocket or in a section of your backpack. When you have a few free minutes, review your flash cards.

D. Review the words just before going to sleep and first thing in the morning when your brain is fresh.

E. If you're a commuter student, make a recording of the words, leaving 5–10 seconds for a response, and then give the definition. Listen as you drive or take the subway or bus, saying the definition before the recorded answer pops up.

F. *Never* throw away your cards. Before the next test, go through all your cards for that class or subject. Before midterms and final exams, go through all your cards again.

Each time, you'll remember more of them but will have forgotten others. Each time you relearn the words, you will remember more of the words. This is more than just memorizing; this is an example of both self-testing and distributed practice.

Just before starting a related course, review your vocabulary cards again. It's surprising how much easier it will be to learn the new material.

STRATEGY 8.5

READ EASY BOOKS FIRST

As you start to survey a textbook, you may find the subject unusually difficult. This is most likely to be true if you didn't take related classes in high school. According to studies done by J. A. Langer and many others, "Irrespective of students' reading abilities, high prior knowledge of a subject area or key vocabulary for a text often means high scores on reading comprehensions measures."[5]

Students with high prior knowledge also tend to make the highest grades.

Step 1: Check to see if the college offers an easier introductory class. For a class like physics, be sure you have adequate math skills.

Step 2: In many subjects, it's helpful to first read *easy* books.

    A. Go to a public library and start with the children's books. Let's say you plan to take astronomy. The librarian will help you find children's books on astronomy. Take notes on what you learn.

    B. Then look through adult books on the topic and select several books that look "readable." They might bear titles like *Astronomy for Amateurs*, *Astronomy for Beginners,* or *Astronomy for Dummies*. Check out several of these.

    C. If one book is especially helpful, you might buy a copy. You could read a chapter in the easy book just before reading the related material in your textbook. This will build your confidence, develop your vocabulary, and make the concepts easier to understand.

Step 3: If you're struggling with a literature class, perhaps on Shakespeare, you can find children's books on the subject. You can also use CliffsNotes or something similar. Do not use these instead of reading the actual books. Read these first to get a clear idea of the plot so you understand what's happening. Read them to get acquainted with the main characters and the setting, or to understand what your professor means by "themes."

Three strategies for skimming the content

STRATEGY 8.6

SKIM FOR FACTS

This strategy is useful to prepare for multiple-choice, true-false, or short-answer test questions. It will *not* help you understand the material.

Step 1: Start with K-W-L, a depth survey of book and chapter, and goal setting.

Step 2: Skim each small subsection for one or several facts. Choose a few that seem most important and write them in your notes. Writing helps you remember.

Step3: Repeat until the end of the chapter.

Step 4: Go back through your list of facts and mark them according to importance. Spend your study time appropriately.

Step 5: Finish with the last part of K-W-L. Write what you've learned.

STRATEGY 8.7

SKIM FOR MAIN IDEAS

This strategy will help you learn the material fairly well. It will prepare you for both objective and essay questions.

Step 1: Start with K-W-L, a depth survey of book and chapter, and goal setting.

Step 2: Skim each paragraph for the main idea. Write the main ideas in your notes.

Step 3: Stop when you reach a new heading. Look through your notes and write a brief summary or explanation of the main ideas in the section in your notebook. Repeat for each section.

Step 4: When you finish the entire chapter, look over your section summaries and write a summary of the whole chapter.

Step 5: Finish with the last part of K-W-L: Write what you learned. You can substitute outlines or concept maps for summaries. If you have outlined subsections, you may want to summarize sections and do a concept map for the chapter.

Using different ways of organizing information makes you think in different ways, which leads to both deeper understanding and lasting memory.

STRATEGY 8.8

QUESTION – SKIM – ANSWER – EXPLAIN

This takes more time than the other skimming strategies, but it will give you the best understanding of the material. If you use it to prepare for a test, write the kind of questions you expect to find on the test. If you're reading for understanding, write questions that test your understanding of the material and write about topics you find most interesting. Obviously, you can ask different kinds of questions.

Step 1: Start with K-W-L, a depth survey of book and chapter, and goal setting.

Step 2: Based on your survey of the material, write questions, leaving spaces for answers. As you read, you will answer some questions and continually write further questions. You might want to mark your questions according to importance.

Step 3: Skim one section at a time, looking for answers to your questions. If you find answers, write them in your own words. Repeat until the end of the chapter.

Step 4: If you have unanswered questions, check the book's index. The answers might be elsewhere in the book. You might also look for answers on the Internet or check the library.

Step 5: Evaluate your understanding of the material. Are there parts of the chapter you don't understand? If so, go back and read the sections quickly and then write questions and answers that describe what you learned.

Step 6: Do the last part of K-W-L: Write what you learned.

The strategy for serious reading: SQ3R

While this is described as a single strategy, it is actually a flexible strategy that can be modified in many ways, depending on the difficulty of the content and what works best for you.

STRATEGY 8.9

SQ3R WITH VARIATIONS

SQ3R means: Survey – Question – Read – Recite – Review

Some books call this strategy SQ4R, Survey, Question, Read, Recite, Record, and Review. Notice that they Record or write notes *after* they recite.

Step 1: Start with K-W-L, and set goals.

You will find it helpful to *read once*. Do not think you'll understand more when you reread. When you choose *not* to reread the material, you focus more carefully on getting the main ideas and understanding deeply the first time.

Step 2: Survey the book (if not already done) and the chapter you plan to read.

Step 3: Write a list of questions.

Leave space to write answers when you find them. Include questions on topics you expect to be tested on as well as ones you find interesting.

Step 4: Read a short section carefully.

In most books you can choose sections separated by subheadings or by main headings. If there are no headings, try several paragraphs.

Step 5: Recite mentally.

Summarize what you read and then check yourself. Did you remember the main ideas and all the important information? If not, check back and refresh your memory. *Repeat steps 4 and 5* (Read and Recite, plus taking notes and answering questions) until you finish the chapter or as much of it as you have time for.

You might also review by writing an outline or summary, or by creating a concept map from memory. Did you still remember the important information? If not, go back over your notes—not the chapter itself.

Step 6: Review. Some students prefer to do the first review mentally (rather than using written notes).

Step 7: Write down the last step of KWL: Write what you learned.

Step 8: Continue to review regularly—sometimes mentally, sometimes in writing, sometimes by creating or redrawing concept maps or other verbal and visual organizers.

Review later that day—again, before sleeping—and then (depending on the difficulty of the material) review daily for a few days, and gradually less often. Remember that review does not mean rereading. This involves both *Self-Testing and Distributed Review,* the two most effective strategies.

According to Terry Doyle and Todd Zakrajsek, who quote Payne et al. (2012):

> *"Sleep soon after learning can benefit both episodic memory (memory for events) and semantic memory (memory for facts about the world)."* This means that it would be a good thing to rehearse any information you need to remember immediately before you go to bed.[6]

IMPORTANT! If you don't review what you learned, you'll forget. That means you will have learned nothing. You were wasting your time.

SQ3R With Variations

A. Writing reading notes (Recording) is extremely helpful. After reciting, write the important information from that section in your own words. Never take notes until you are sure what information is most important. I would never read anything important without taking notes that then go into a reading notebook.

B. Write answers to any questions that have been answered, and write new questions.

C. You can use your highlighters.

I don't recommend it but, if you're determined to use your high-lighters, this is the time. When you're very clear on the main ideas in each section, go ahead and underline or highlight the material. There will still be two problems: You learn more when writing the main ideas than you do by highlighting or underlining. You'll also waste time later going through the whole chapter to find your highlighted material. It will be far more efficient to simply read your notes.

D. One last and very important suggestion: When you read slowly, the task seems tedious and you learn less. Try using a *Study Sprint,* a short period of high-intensity reading (described in chapter 4). You might discover that, in half the time, you can learn more, remember longer, and you might even enjoy yourself.

Six secrets for rediscovering the excitement of reading

> *You are the same today as you'll be in five years except for the people you meet and the books you read. — Charlie Jones*

1. When you prepare for reading by setting goals, you're making it possible to recover the excitement. Working to reach your own goals is always more interesting than reading just because you're supposed to.

2. While previewing the material, find new topics you'd like to explore.

3. Writing your own questions is critical. Searching for and finding answers to your own questions is far more exciting than merely finding answers to questions that might be on a test.

4. Doing further study on your favorite topics makes learning even more interesting.

5. Tell someone about the chapter in such a way that it sounds exciting.

6. Remember that you rarely need to read every word. Instead, read the important parts. Read the exciting parts—yes, even in textbooks! If some sections are really boring, chances are you wouldn't remember them anyway. Focus on what you think is important and the parts that are most interesting. According to William Armstrong:

Reading is thinking, it is a search, it is a challenge; and when done successfully, it is an adventure which involves two persons—the reader and the author. The reader must carry on a silent conversation with the author.... Reading is never passive acceptance. It is an energy-absorbing activity, requiring movement of mind and sometimes heart, out to meet the mind of the author and to grasp the meaning of another's thoughts.[7]

Questions for Reflection:

1. Which of these strategies comes closest to the way you usually read?

2. Which of these strategies would you like to try first?

3. When have you read a book and felt as if you were having a conversation with the author?

4. Do you remember any books that changed your life?

5. What surprised you in this chapter? What was the most important thing you learned? How will you use what you learned?

CHAPTER 9

Take Notes You'll Want to Study

If you aren't taking notes, you aren't learning. — Ben Casnocha

en Casnocha describes attending an important lecture when he "noticed something peculiar: almost no one was taking notes." He was taking notes, of course, but it appeared to him that only the experts were taking notes, that "novices didn't see the point."[1]

I read many of the comments at the end of Casnocha's blog and was surprised to see how many people disagreed with him, some saying that if they take notes they can't listen.

Exercise: Reflecting on Your Note-Taking
---

1. If you chose to attend a lecture by an expert in your field, would you take notes?
2. Do you have problems listening and taking notes at the same time?
3. How often do you take notes in lectures: never – sometimes – most of the time – always?
4. How often do you rewrite your notes after the lecture?
5. How often do you go back over your notes before the next class or to review for a test?
6. How would you describe your notes: terrible – not very good – OK – fairly good – excellent?
7. What could you do to take better notes?

When taking notes is a problem

Recent literature indicates that the activity of taking notes can potentially aid or hinder memory for classroom lecture information. — Gary S. Thomas[2]

Read the above statement again, carefully: Have you ever heard someone suggest that taking notes can cause problems for students – that they might actually learn less when taking notes? Most study skills books don't mention this possibility.

Obviously, note-taking helps most students learn. Even if they never read their notes, it helps students focus on main ideas—or at least keeps them awake during the lecture. While some students might not learn much from the lecture, I needed to think about how note-taking might actually interfere with their learning.

Then it was obvious; this was true for our son. Tony started college with a third grade reading level but with two advantages: He is extremely intelligent and he has an amazing memory. He tried taking notes but, with his terrible handwriting and even worse spelling, no one could have made sense of them. And, while focusing on writing notes, he missed hearing much of the lecture. Tony chose, instead, to never miss a class, to concentrate his listening with the intention of remembering what he considered important, and to mentally review the lecture afterward.

Few students who have problems taking notes are dyslexic, and even fewer can compensate with a fantastic memory. The main problem is that many students find it difficult to listen, understand, and write at the same time.

If this doesn't describe you, you might want to skip down to the section *Five strategies for taking great notes*.

Three problems can make it hard to listen and take good notes

The most common problem is trying to write too much. Writing everything the professor says is nearly impossible. You may be finishing the second or third sentence while the professor is moving on to the sixth. Before long you're lost. You might skip to what the professor is saying now but you'll rarely get past the first words of a sentence. Nothing you write makes much sense. And, while you're fighting the losing battle of taking dictation, you miss the main ideas.

The solution is simple to understand but not easy to do: *Stop trying to take dictation. Write only the most important information.* Write key words and phrases instead of full sentences.

You might practice with a taped lecture. First, listen to the tape without writing. Do not sit back and relax; concentrate on the lecture. Listen for the professor's main ideas. Try to identify the introduction – point one – an explanation – an example – another example – point two…and finally, the conclusion.

Write a simple outline of the lecture by memory. Include the title; the introduction; each of the main points with details like definitions, explanations, examples, and finally the conclusion. Now write a summary of the lecture in your own words.

How well did you remember the material? This is another way of taking notes, but most students have trouble remembering all the important information.

Now try taking notes while listening to the same lecture. As you listen, write the main ideas and important details. Use short phrases rather than sentences. Compare your notes done by memory and those written while listening. Which is most complete? Which will help you understand the material better? Which would be most helpful if you needed to study for a test?

You might find a combination method most helpful. First, take notes during the lecture, writing an outline with the main points and a couple key words and phrases during the lecture. Immediately after the lecture, fill in additional important details you remember.

Don't expect to have perfect notes right away but, if you choose a method that seems helpful and continue to practice this skill, you will gradually improve.

The second problem with note-taking is writing too little. Some students sit with pen in hand but only write an occasional note, often something interesting or a fact they think they should memorize, but they are seldom aware of the main ideas. Good students often take 2 to 4 pages of notes in a 1-hour lecture. Their main problem might be the one described next.

The third problem is not recognizing the main points and other important information. This problem is not caused by note-taking. These students would have even more trouble if they *didn't* take notes. If you have trouble identifying main ideas, compare your notes with a few other students. Look at what they considered important. Ask how they could tell what was important. You should also find the following strategies helpful.

Five strategies for taking great notes

You might be all too familiar with this statistic: Apparently, within 24 hours after hearing a lecture, most students remember only about 5% of the information. Since some students remember considerably more, it's likely that many remember nothing at all. This familiar quotation describes the same problem.

> *A lecture is a process by which the notes of the professor become the notes of the students without passing through the minds of either. — R. K. Rathbone*

While Rathbone makes both giving the lectures and taking the notes seem to be pointless exercises, he provides a clue for making them meaningful. The information needs to pass through the minds of the speaker *and* the listeners. As I would describe it, *you need to take notes with your brain turned on.*

STRATEGY *9.1*

PREPARE TO TAKE NOTES

Step 1: Create a list of abbreviations to use.

Those listed here may help you develop your own list. Your actual list should be based on the subjects you are studying. Abbreviations used by a math major, a history major, and a chemistry major will obviously be quite different.

The math symbols used for words in the second section of the chart might mean: equal or the same, different, roughly or about, close to (plus or minus), temperature in Fahrenheit, increasing, decreasing, leads to, goes both ways, therefore, more than, less than (it's helpful, of course, if you can remember the usual symbols).

Chart 9.1 Common Abbreviations

Time	sec. min. hr. day. mon, yr. ASAP
Calendar	Mon, Tue, Wed, Thurs, Fri, Sat, Sun, Jan, Feb, Mar, 7/15
Measurement	in" ft' yd mi mm cm m km lb oz ton tsp T g cg mg kg L cl ml
Classes	Bio Chem Geo Astro Lit Hist Calc Bus Hum Psych Soc Anthro
Others	intro thru demo max min info def rep dem ind @ # $ & % ©
	(Those who do texting have many more abbreviations: lol)
Math symbols for words	$=$ $\neq$ $\sim$ $\pm$ °F $\uparrow$ $\downarrow$ $\rightarrow$ $\leftrightarrow$ $\therefore$ $+$ $-$
Other symbols	*important ***very important ? or ??? don't understand ! Wow
In Literature	Use initials or shorter names for characters
In History	Use initials or shorter names for people: Abe, Ike, JFK, LBJ
In Chemistry	Use chemical symbols like H_2O or $NaCl$
In Math	∞ $\sum$ $\leq$ $\geq$ π μ Δ

With the last two, you might describe a pig weighing a little more than 50 pounds as wt 50+ lb. or a pig weighing a little less than 50 pounds as wt 50- lb.

You might also include a large T in a circle for information that will be on a test, and NIB circled for lecture information that is Not In Book or is different from that in the book (and perhaps more up to date).

Step 2: Start with KWL. Writing what you already know on the topic and what you want to know will help you take better notes. Check your syllabus for the lecture topic or assume the lecture is about the chapter that was assigned.

Step 3: List vocabulary words and write definitions in your own words. Learn as many new words as possible. Look for commonly used terms that are long and create your own abbreviations. List your new abbreviations, with meanings, on top of your note-taking page.

Step 4: Read the chapter or do a good preview. Knowing the material before the lecture makes it easier to understand. You'll also need to write less this way.

Step 5: Review your notes from the previous lecture. Notice how the lecture was organized.

STRATEGY 9.2

DEMONSTRATE YOUR INTENTIONS TO LEARN

Step 1: *If you have a cell phone, turn it off and put it away.* Avoid distractions.

Step 2: *Stay awake, alert, and focused.* It helps to sit near the front where you can see and hear the professor better and where he or she will see you. Don't sit by friends who will whisper to you, write notes, or otherwise distract you.

Step 3: *Sit up straight.* You'll look more awake and you'll actually feel more alert.

Step 4: *Look at the professor.* The professor's facial expressions, gestures, and changes in tone or volume are important clues to let you know what's important. Some professors lean forward, step away from the podium, or raise an arm when delivering their most important information. They might also pause briefly, speak louder, or sometimes more quietly. When professors slow down and pause between words, they're saying it is important and should be in your notes.

Step 5: *If the professor writes something on the board, copy it.* It is important. If it wasn't important, the professor wouldn't have written it.

STRATEGY 9.3

RECOGNIZE LECTURE CLUES

Step 1: *Listen carefully to the introduction.* Some professors actually list all their main points in their introduction. At other times they tell you the number of points or at least the categories. If they suggest there will be five main points, be sure to number them and get all five points.

Step 2: *Look for clues that the professor is moving to a new main idea.* Some make it easy by saying, "*The second point* is...." Other professors may say something like "*The next cause* of the war was..." or "*After prophase comes....*" Some professors don't provide such clues; they expect you to recognize that they've finished one topic and moved to the next.

Step 3: When they say, "*Finally,...*" they expect you to understand that this is the last point of the lecture.

Step 4: After that final point there will usually be a conclusion or summary. The main points might be repeated. Make sure you have all of them in your notes. Listen for the anything important that you missed

STRATEGY 9.4

TRY DIFFERENT NOTE-TAKING FORMATS

Step 1: Try what's called a rough outline.

It's like an outline without Roman numerals, letters, or numbers. Write the main points far to the left. You might want to underline these. It still helps to number the main points.

Step 2: Indent major sub-points a little and minor sub-points further. Leave spaces between main points.

Step 3: Use one of the split-page formats. The Cornell Note-Taking System is the best-known and frequently described as the most effective.

We begin with the classic method, but many versions of this method can be found.

Chart 9.2 The Rough Outline

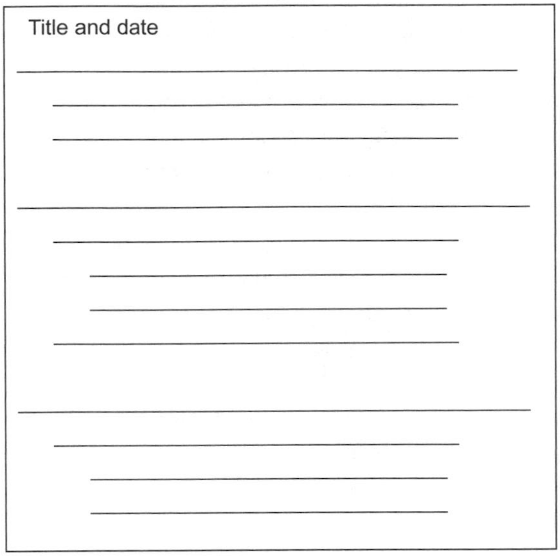

Title and date

_____

    _____

    _____

  _____

     _____

     _____

    _____

  _____

    _____

     _____

    _____

Chart 9.3 Cornell Note-Taking

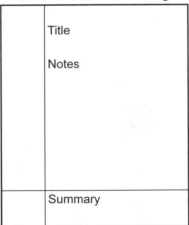

Title

Notes

Summary

1. Draw a horizontal line across the bottom of each page, 3–5 inches from the bottom. Draw a vertical line 2–3 inches in from the left side of the paper.
2. Write the title of the lecture at the top of the right section.
3. Take notes in the large section on the right, preferably using either a simple outline or a rough outline.
4. During or after the lecture add notes in the left column, usually stating the main ideas in the lecture.

5. After the lecture, fill in any details you remember and then write a summary at the bottom of each page. Your notes will cover at least three or four such pages.

6. The standard method is to write a summary of each page in the bottom section. You might prefer one longer summary at the end of the lecture. Try it both ways and see which is most helpful.

7. To use these notes for study, cover the right side where you took notes. Look at each main idea in the left margin, then explain or describe related information. Check to see what you missed and refresh your memory.

Step 4: Try a variation on the split-page systems.

1. Write questions in the left column that are answered on the right. Review by answering questions.

2. Compare reading and lecture notes. Draw the vertical line dividing the page in half. On one side, write reading notes. When the professor covers the same topics, underline what's stressed and only add new details that are not in the reading notes. (This only works when the lectures follow the book closely.)

3. In problem-based classes, show the problem on one side and the solution on the other side. If possible, number the steps to the solution.

4. You might also use the left column for reflection and comments. You might add notes like "compare to diagram in book." "Finally, this makes sense!" "I still don't understand."

5. You might also write questions to look up in the book or on the computer or to ask the professor later.

6. You can always add a list of topics or questions for review.

STRATEGY 9.5

USE YOUR NOTES WELL

Step 1: Review your notes soon after class, again that evening before going to bed, and then early the next morning.

Step 2: Remember that review is not rereading. It means self-testing and checking to see if you missed anything important.

Step 3: Review them several times that week. Just before the next lecture, review them once more.

Step 4: If you use the method of preparing for tests without cramming, you'll add these notes to your review folder and review them every week. Each time you review these notes, the material will be easier to remember—and you'll be glad that you learned to take such good notes.

Your goal is not to have the most detailed notes or to use the Cornell method properly. The goal, like the title of this chapter is to "Take Notes You'll Want to Study."

To copy your notes or not to copy— that is the question

While many teachers will tell you that copying notes is a waste of time, it always helps a little to write a new, clean version after the class. But, unless your handwriting is so bad that you won't be able to interpret it yourself, it's probably not worth your time.

A far better alternative is to *rewrite* your notes. It may sound like the same thing as copying, but it is totally different. Rewriting requires thinking and organization. Start with your lecture topic or title. It is critical that you know what the lecture is about. What does your professor want you to know on this topic? In other words, you can now write the notes you'd actually want to read.

STRATEGY 9.6

REWRITE NOTES TO LEARN

Step 1: State the main points clearly.

Step 2: Be sure each main point includes enough detail. Are examples and explanations clear?

Step 3: Organize your notes to reflect the structure of the lecture. Most students use an outline.

Step 4: If you study this information, will it help you make the grade you want? Will it help you learn what you want to learn? If not, find another way to organize the information that will be more helpful.

Step 5: Include a well-written, detailed summary.

Students often need to reorganize and rewrite their notes during the first several weeks. At the end of that period, you should find yourself doing it just as well the first time.

Once you learn to write great lecture notes, apply many of the same ideas to taking *great reading notes*. Try reorganizing and rewriting your reading notes several times so you understand how to take better notes.

Listening to a lecture is much like reading a chapter. Learning from either one requires keen mental focus, persistence, and reflective, inquiring interaction with the material. In addition, having a purpose—such as points to look for or questions to answer—helps listeners and readers concentrate.[3]

Questions for Reflection:

1. What surprised you in this chapter? What was the single most helpful suggestion for your note-taking in this chapter? How will you use what you learned?

2. Do you have any friends who are not paying close attention during lectures? What could you suggest to them that would be most helpful?

10

College Level Research Can Be Exciting

Imagine that your boss says, "I need you to learn everything you can about—another company—a new product or process—the possible causes of a problem you're experiencing, and get back to me ASAP. I need the information for the meeting tomorrow morning.[1]

Research is not only a key skill for writing papers in college; it's also one of the skills that employers want most. An article in the *Library Journal* makes this clear.

Employers expect college graduates to use effectively online databases (yes, they do subscribe to some of the same ones we offer) and Internet search engines for information retrieval. But they also want them to be equally skilled at using old-fashioned tools like phones and printed resources to gather information.... Overall, employers found students lacking in their ability to generate comprehensive reports, in a timely fashion, that demonstrated multiple approaches to research.[2]

As well as being a practical skill you need to learn, doing serious research can be exciting. Imagine you've been given a few clues and you are setting out on a grand treasure hunt. This chapter provides a number of clues. Your professor and your reference librarians will provide others. Then you're on your own. The treasures you seek are hiding in the library, on the Internet, and in the minds of other people. And, when you find the information you're searching for, you'll feel like you've found precious gems, one here and a few more there. Enjoy your adventures.

Exercise: Examine your Research Skills

1. List 10 or more ways you might do research without using your computer.

2. On your last (or best) research paper, roughly how many of your sources came from each of these?
   A. Encyclopedias
   B. Dictionaries
   C. Books
   D. Newspapers or magazines
   E. Wikipedia
   F. Scholarly journal articles
   G. Websites of respected organizations
   H. Other websites
   I. Interviews in person, by email, or by snail mail
   J. Blogs
   K. Other (describe)

3. Have you ever gotten an interlibrary loan?

4. Have you ever used online databases? Do you know what they are?

5. Can you explain how to use Boolean operators? Have you heard of Boolean operators?

6. If you wanted to search the Web for information comparing cats and mice, what search terms would you use?

My first research paper: "Thank you, Mr. Clark!"

My American History teacher, Mr. Clark, realized that students in our high school were graduating without ever writing a research paper, so he decided to do something. He taught us the basics of writing a research paper and added this to his course requirements. What was most surprising was that we were allowed to choose our own topics. They didn't need to be related to history or to any other academic subject.

I had recently read a short article in a newsletter, called "Science News." The article described a simple form of algae called Euchema that was being studied as a possible source of food that could be grown and eaten on long voyages in space. If my memory is right, a tablespoon of dried Euchema provided the same nutrition as one ounce of beefsteak.

I decided I'd write my research paper on this. Any sensible teacher or librarian would have discouraged me because there seemed to be no possible way I could find any information on this obscure topic. Perhaps they assumed I'd figure that out soon enough. Keep in mind that all this was done decades before the existence of personal computers.

I sent a letter to the Botany Department at the university where the research was done and asked how I could get some information for my paper, and whether there was some way I could buy some Euchema and try to grow it myself. Some kind person in that department sent me an order form for the algae, which I think cost about a dollar a tube. I bought three tubes then, and more later. They also sent copies of several journal articles on the subject. Each article included a bibliography.

With my precious articles in hand, I went to the school librarian to ask if there might be a library in a nearby city that would have these books. She knew none of the public libraries would have such technical books, so she wrote a letter to the library at the University of Florida. Two weeks later, a large box arrived at my high school and the librarian sent me a note. In that box there were seven very thick books for me to use. I had no idea that another library would do this.

The reading wasn't easy, of course, but in each book I only needed to read the short number of pages on my topic. With these books and my journal articles, I had enough information for my paper.

We weren't required to do anything beyond this, but I had ordered the algae, so I attempted over and over again to provide the proper nutrients. They always grew well—until I fed them. I killed every batch of algae I ordered.

When I got to college and was required to write research papers, I felt confident that I could do it, and do it well, thanks to Mr. Clark.

You don't write because you want to say something. You write because you have something to say.
                                                            F. Scott Fitzgerald

---

Reflecting on the Exercise

---

1. List 10 or more ways you might do research without using your computer.

My list includes newspapers, magazines, books, asking the librarian for other sources of information, calling a friend, writing an expert, consulting with a teacher or professor, doing a survey, checking the Yellow Pages, calling someone on the phone, checking a bookstore, and visiting a museum or historical society

2. On your last (or best) research paper, roughly how many of your sources came from each of the following?

While encyclopedias may have been acceptable sources in high school, your professors expect you to use academic books, scholarly journal articles, personal interviews, and research on the Web using articles found on websites of highly respected organizations. While you should almost never use Wikipedia as an authoritative source, it is an excellent starting point that provides both an easy-to-understand introduction to a topic and helpful sources you could find and read next.

3. If you aren't familiar with interlibrary loans, this is how I got my books from the University of Florida. Your library probably uses the Internet to find libraries with the book you need. In most cases, the book is loaned only if it's over one year old.

Exercise questions 4, 5, and 6 will be answered later in this chapter.

STRATEGY 10.1

BEGIN RESEARCH EARLY

Step 1: Never wait until the last minute. It's best to start on the day the paper is assigned. What do you want to learn as you write this paper? Do you want to learn about the content? about how to write a better paper? or both?

Step 2: Create a schedule and write it on a large calendar. Leave plenty of time. Each step will take much longer than you think it will.

Step 3: Generate a list of possible topics. You might look through lecture notes, reading notes, and the index in your textbook. List 10 to 20 possible topics. If you're assigned a particular topic, look for an interesting or creative perspective on the topic. My daughter, for example, wrote a paper on the Industrial Revolution as described by folk songs of that time.

Step 4: Take your list to the library and see what books you can find on the subjects. Skim these for related topics. Check the Internet for further ideas.

Step 5: Go through your list and choose the 3 to 5 topics that seem most intriguing. If you have questions, talk to your professor.

Step 6: Narrow your topic if it's still too broad. Some students need to narrow their topic 5 or 6 times. If there is a book on your topic, your topic is too broad.

STRATEGY 10.2

TAKING RESEARCH NOTES

Step 1: As you do your research, use index cards for each relevant chunk of information. The major advantage of index cards is that you can arrange them in various ways to plan the individual sections of your paper.

Step 2: You might use colored index cards for bibliography cards. Write the bibliography information in the citation style you should use for the paper. If in doubt, ask your professor. There are different styles for different subjects.

Step 3: Develop a system to identify the author and title on your other index cards. You might use the author's last name or, if this author wrote several books, add a date or first words of the title. This should be listed first on every card with information from this book or other source. Add quotes marked within clear quotation marks. For both quotes and paraphrased information, include the page numbers.

Step 4: When using information from Internet sources, you can copy the information onto your index card, or you can print the document, complete with bibliography information. Important information can be cut and taped to index cards.

Step 5: As you do your research, keep a list of interesting questions.

Step 6: Choose the single important question you want to answer in your paper. Your goal isn't merely to write a summary of what you read, but to come up with an original answer or thesis on the topic and to develop a logical argument to support your thesis.

STRATEGY 10.3

ORGANIZE YOUR NOTES

Step 1: Develop a simple outline. Try to organize your information in three or four main sections. It's always smart to create three or four simple outlines and choose the one that seems most interesting or that best fits your data.

Step 2: One way to create an outline is to sort your index cards into groups of related topics. These groups of cards can help you choose the main topics for your outline.

Step 3: Expand the outline with three or four sub-points under each main point.

Step 4: Arrange the index cards to fit your outline.

STRATEGY *10.4*

WRITE YOUR RESEARCH PAPER

Step 1: Begin writing your first draft. It doesn't need to be perfect—yet.

Step 2: Let your first draft sit a day or two.

Step 3: Read your first draft carefully, marking sections to delete, sections where you need more information, and ideas about how you might restructure the paper. You might need a new outline.

Step 4: Do additional research if needed and write the second draft.

Step 5: Again, let it sit for a few days.

Step 6: Print the paper and read it again. It should be in fairly good shape. Make changes that will strengthen your argument. Check your grammar and spelling. Have you used the best possible words?

Step 7: When you think you're done, read it aloud in a quiet place. Do the sentences flow naturally? Do you have a mix of longer and shorter sentences with varied sentence structure? Are all your sources written in the proper format?

Step 8: If you have time, let it sit once more. Read it aloud yet again. Print a clean copy and place it in a folder. Turn it in on time, and smile as you do.

While other students frantically tried to write their papers at the last minute and are turning in their first draft, you will be confident that you have done a good job.

Step 9: Evaluate what you learned from this experience. What were the most important things you learned? What will you do differently when you write your next paper?

Using Boolean operators to narrow your search

You may discover that you knew a little about Boolean operators but just didn't recognize the name. Boolean operators use "Command words such as AND, OR, and...NOT that narrow, expand, or restrict a search based on Boolean logic."[3] When you do a search on most search engines (or browsers), you can use these words. In a few cases, you'd write + instead of AND, and – instead of NOT. So far it's not hard, is it?

When you use the words listed below to search on Google or other search engines, you'll get very different results, depending on the Boolean operators.

When you type	You get
cats AND mice	websites that mention both cats and mice.
cats mice	the same thing. They assume you mean AND.
cats OR mice	all websites mentioning cats and all mentioning mice. (This is usually far too much information, with millions of hits.)
"cats and mice"	only the sites that mention this exact phrase.
cats NOT mice	all websites that mention cats but don't mention mice. This is particularly helpful when you type a word like *jaguar* and get a lot of websites on cars. Simply type *jaguar NOT cars* or type *jaguar –cars*.

The word "OR" is particularly useful when you want information on a term with several synonyms. You might search for *obese OR fat OR over-weight* to get all related information.

When you want many forms of the same word such as *dance, dancers, dancing,* and related terms, you simply need to type *danc** and you'll get all the words starting with these 4 letters. Notice that if you write *dance** you won't get *dancing*.

Using these simple tools will make it easier to get the information you want. You can also enter a search word and a date to get information on that particular year or month or day. You can search for an object with a price range such as *camera $100..$200;* Notice this uses only two dots. If you go to Google.com, click *Settings* at the lower right corner, and then click *Help*, you'll learn about several other useful search tools. Experiment with them on topics you find interesting.

Using research databases

Research databases can be defined as "organized collections of computerized information or data such as periodical articles, books, graphics, and multimedia that can be searched to retrieve information."[4] While many databases have been compiled covering general subjects such as car repair or popular magazine articles, databases are especially important to students and other researchers who want to read articles from the academic, peer-reviewed journals. Some of these databases include only an abstract and bibliography citation. Others include the entire articles.

Check out Wikipedia's "List of Academic Databases."[5] It gives the names of the databases, the subjects covered in each, whether it's free or you need a subscription, and the providers.

Ask at your school library for a list of the databases they have available and how to access them. Sometimes you must use a library computer but generally you can access them on your own computer by entering your library card number, Student ID number, or some other code. Once you get into one of these databases, check its instructions for searching in it. They're usually similar to those on Google.

According to one library's website, "Research databases provide information that has been reviewed and edited by experts and comes from reliable, authoritative, up-to-date published sources."[6] These articles are among the best sources of information for your paper. Ask your professor whether you should simply use the regular citation or if you should also include information about the database, such as where you located it and the date you retrieved information.

Doing research on Google

When doing research with Google or other regular search engines, you must make certain that your sources are reliable, that the article was written by an expert in the field, and preferably that it was published on the website of a highly respected organization, like the American Psychological Association (to give only one example).

I discovered a useful strategy that you might not need—though you never know. Since I lack access to research databases these days, I use Google Scholar.com, which is similar; but well over half the articles I search for are subscription only. So I read and take notes on the abstract. Then, back on Google, I search for authors and date published. Fairly often, I'll find the complete article on the website of either the author's university or the author's personal site, and sometimes also on an organization site.

A near disaster: learn from my experience

While searching for research on the importance of setting goals, I found this article as well as dozens of websites describing the same study:

> *"In the book 'What They Don't Teach You in the Harvard Business School,' Mark McCormack tells of a study conducted*

on students in the 1979 Harvard MBA program. In that year, the students were asked, "Have you set clear, written goals for your future and made plans to accomplish them?" Only three percent of the graduates had written goals and plans; 13 percent had goals, but they were not in writing; and a whopping 84 percent had no specific goals at all.

*"Ten years later, the members of the class were interviewed again, and the findings, while somewhat predictable, were nonetheless astonishing. **The 13 percent of the class who had goals were earning, on average, twice as much as the 84 percent who had no goals at all. And what about the 3 percent who had clear, written goals?** They were earning, on average, **ten times as much as the other 97 percent put together.**"[7]*

The title of the article is "Harvard Business School Goal Story: Study about the goals at Harvard MBA program 1979." Looks official, right? The URL is www.lifemastering.com/en/Harvard.html. The research was exactly what I was looking for. With the information provided, would you use this research in a paper? Why, or why not?

I had three problems with the story. First, I knew nothing of lifemastering.com and it didn't sound like one of the more trustworthy websites. But then, they had quoted from a book that looked legitimate, and many other websites shared the same information.

My second problem was that, although they quoted the book and provided the date of the original research, none of these websites had a reference to the original research. I wanted to find the original research before including the information in this book. (Is that being too picky?)

My third problem was that something about the numbers just didn't feel right. As much as I believe that setting goals helps you succeed, these numbers seemed greatly exaggerated. It made no sense that the 3% with written goals could make 10 times as much money as the other 97% together. Maybe the numbers got copied wrong from the original research? I wondered about that.

So I continued my search, finding the same study over and over. Finally I had the answer. A blogger, Sid Savara, had also been searching for the original research. He actually found over a thousand pages on the Internet describing this so-called "Harvard Study." But strangely enough, there were also reports of a very similar study at Yale in 1953, also with no citation. Finally, he found a page in the Yale Law Library that described earlier searches for this information. Researchers interviewed students from those classes both at Harvard and at Yale. The students all agreed that they had never heard of such a study. *The stories were...false.*[8]

A vaguely similar study was done at Dominican University in California with results that were not nearly as spectacular. Students with written goals did a little better than those who thought about goals but didn't write them. Yet in this study, students who gave a weekly progress report to a friend showed the greatest success.

I was very glad that, unlike the well-intentioned author, Mark McCormack, I did not use this information in my book.

The moral of the story? *Never trust what you find on the Internet*—even if it comes from a book (unless the author of that book is a respected expert in the field). You can also trust the story if it's found in a peer-reviewed journal that you located through one of the research databases. Even then, if the numbers don't seem right, you might express doubts about the research.

> *Even the most experienced writers can find writing a research paper to be a challenge. After all, unlike taking notes, answering test questions, participating in a discussion, or even writing an essay, writing a paper can take weeks and even months. If the other components that make up your semester grade can be considered sprints, writing a research paper is the marathon. But if you take a hint from the long distance runner by working systematically and pacing yourself throughout, when you finally reach the finish, you'll have something that you can be proud of.*[9]

Questions for Reflection:

1. What were the most important ideas you learned about research?

2. What surprised you in this chapter? What was the most important thing you learned? How will you use what you learned?

11

Effective Writing Begins with a Purpose and a Plan

Of all the skills students say they want to strengthen, writing is mentioned three times more than any other.[1]

Richard Light says of students, "I would have guessed that they value good writing but I didn't realize how deeply many of them felt about it or how strongly they hunger for specific suggestions about how to improve it."[2] He goes on to discuss a survey of alumni in their 40s who were asked how important different skills were on their job. "More than 90% of the alumni ranked 'need to write more effectively' as a skill they consider 'of great importance in their current work.'"[3]

Just as students often read without much thought, too many students look at an essay question and start writing before thinking about what to say. Even with longer essays, many students make the claim "I never know what I'm going to say until I've written it." Nonsense. While preliminary "free-writing" *can* help you start thinking about your essay, it should never be your final essay.

Writing a research paper was covered in chapter 10, on research. In this chapter, while the focus is on writing essay questions in tests, the same strategies apply to writing longer papers.

Exercise: Thinking about How You Write

---

1. As a high school student, what were the most important things you learned about good writing?

2. What writing skills do you still need to improve, now that you're in college?

3. If you were asked to write a 3- to 5-page essay, how much time would you need for research? To organize your ideas? To write the paper? To revise and proofread your paper?

Take your writing from acceptable to outstanding

Think about what it takes to become a good swimmer, perhaps even an Olympic medalist. There's no possible way for athletes to improve their swimming skills without getting in the water. But merely swimming for hours every day isn't enough. Swimmers need a coach to critique their techniques. They must practice those new techniques over and over again, often for years. To improve your writing, you need to write regularly, you need a coach to critique your work, and you need to practice the new skills you learn.

STRATEGY 11.1

IMPROVE WRITING SKILLS

Step 1: *Read.* Read many books, read all kinds of books, read better books. You might even reread books you read before and really liked.

Step 2: Study the writing in these books.

When you find an especially well-written book, take notes on what you like about the writing. Do you like the words the writer uses? Do you enjoy the descriptions, the characters, the action scenes? Do you like information that is well organized? The better you can identify what you like about someone's writing, the easier it will be for you to apply some of these ideas to your own work.

Step 3: Write regularly.

You might write in a journal, dream up stories and type them into your laptop, write a blog for friends and family, or compose short essays. What matters is that you keep writing.

Step 4: Find someone to critique your writing.

Just as swimmers need a coach, you need someone to correct your mistakes and suggest ways you can improve your writing. It might be a friend. You might have a writing center on your campus. You can even ask a professor to critique your writing.

Step 5: Consider taking one or more courses on writing.

In addition to having the teacher correct your mistakes and make suggestions, you will learn from lectures and class discussion. The discipline of writing a regular paper will also reinforce your decision to write regularly

Step 6: Work on your grammar.

Unless your grammar is close to perfect, you'll need to spend time working on it. The writing class will cover the subject.

You might read a book like the classic by Strunk and White.[4] You might find helpful information on the Internet.

One helpful website is smashingmagazine.com. Here you'll find links to 50 writing resources on subjects such as grammar, punctuation, style, and English as a second language, as well as many sites discussing common mistakes.[5]

Step 7: Improve your handwriting.

While professors rarely intend to grade your work based on your handwriting, spelling, or grammar, this is exactly what they do. Grading essays is not like grading a multiple choice test. Professors read your response and form an opinion. Whether they're aware of it or not, an essay that is sloppy or hard to read or that uses poor grammar does not make a good impression or a good grade.

Step 8: Keep your writing short and simple.

This and many of the following suggestions come from Strunk and White.

A. Use simple words. Never use a long, complex word when a short word will do. Don't say "utilize" if "use" will work.

B. Keep many of your sentences short. While it's important to vary the lengths of your sentences, you want them easy to understand.

C. Use shorter paragraphs. We understand material better when it's divided into many short paragraphs rather than in paragraphs that go on and on and on. Start a new paragraph for each main point.

Step 9: Say precisely what you mean.

Find the best words to express your thinking. Instead of writing "The woman walked down the street," make it clear whether she hurried, ambled, stumbled, or wandered.

Step 10: Recognize and use different styles of writing for different purposes.

These might include writing to describe, to persuade, to express opinions, to entertain, to summarize main ideas, or to state and support an argument.

The essay test: start by understanding the question

The short essays you write on tests, the essays you write when the entire test is a single essay, and the longer essays you write for a class—all have many things in common. First, you must read the questions carefully and understand what you are expected to write. *You must write with your brain turned on.*

The following story should make this point more clearly than anything I can tell you.

The little pine tree that didn't grow and why the whole class failed the test

I was taking an ecology course and, during the first week, we visited an area with many pine trees. I still remember the only young tree. It was about 6 inches tall—a sapling—and I'd have estimated it to be less than a year old. The professor explained that this tree was over 20 years old, but she didn't explain why it had grown so little. She kept asking us what else we noticed. We didn't observe anything significant. She finally asked, "What is missing? What would you expect to see here that isn't here?" Finally, we realized there were no pine cones on the trees or on the ground.

The first test in our course consisted of a single question: "On the basis of what you know about banking, explain why the little tree has grown so little, why there were no other small trees, and why there were no pine cones."

None of us knew the answers but it was a test, so we began writing. We described every reason we could think of to explain why there were no other young trees, why this one had failed to grow, and why there were no pines cones. Perhaps there was no longer enough rain, or maybe there was too much. Perhaps the weather had been too hot or too cold.

Every person in the class failed the test. The professor didn't discuss the answers; she simply said we'd take exactly the same test again in the next class. I spent hours wandering through the pine grove but could see no evidence of problems. I spent further hours in the library trying to discover what might cause this kind of problem. We all failed the test again.

The third time we took the test, one graduate student made a C. While that gave us a little hope, the rest of us failed again. Can you guess why we failed?

While I thought I knew the question well by this time, before taking the test for the fourth time, I reread the question very carefully. That beginning phrase stood out. "On the basis of what you know about banking…." This hadn't made much sense to any of us, so we had all ignored it. Actually, we didn't even remember that this phrase was part of the question.

What did I know about banking that was in any way related to pine trees? Nothing. What did I know about banking? You need to put money in the bank before you can take money out.

This time, I started with that simple statement about banking. My thesis was that for the pine trees to grow, they needed some environmental factors going in before the tiny tree could take it out in order to grow. This time, I got an A on the test.

While this painful experience didn't help me understand why the pine tree wasn't growing, it certainly taught me to read questions extremely carefully. And no, I didn't tell other students the answer, but I did suggest to a few that they read the question again—carefully. After the class took the same test several times more, the rest of the students finally passed. Someone had probably passed the secret along.

STRATEGY *11.1*

WRITE AN ESSAY

A well-reasoned paper will get you a B, maybe even a B+. But a well-reasoned paper backed up by facts and good writing will get you the A. To get an A+, you must be original. — Adam Robinson

Step 1: Always begin by studying the question. Good students never begin writing immediately. They pause to think about how they should approach the topic. They ask themselves what information the professor is looking for. How should they organize their ideas?

Step 2: Write a short outline or use a concept map, a compare and contrast chart, or another method of organizing information. Your outline might be only a few words, a list of your main ideas.

Step 3: Write an essay that answers the question and shows your knowledge, your reasoning, and your writing skills.

Step 4: If you have a very small space to write your essay, one paragraph may be enough if it has a topic sentence, three or so points, and a concluding sentence. Think of it as a basic five-paragraph essay reduced to five short sentences.

Step 5: For longer essays, follow the model of the five-paragraph essay.

You might use short paragraphs or longer ones, depending on the space and the time you have left. It's important that the professor can judge your knowledge, thinking, and writing skills when reading only the first and last paragraphs since they often read the first and last paragraphs and merely skim the others.

Step 6: The first paragraph is your introduction and should include your main idea or thesis. The following paragraphs will each state a main idea in the first sentence and then elaborate, using evidence and examples.

Step 7: The final paragraph is your conclusion. Restate your main idea or thesis, summarize your main points, and explain how these prove or support your thesis. Since this paragraph may be all your professor reads, it must show your thesis, structure, main ideas and your reasoning.

Five kinds of academic writing

Students are familiar with personal or informal essays. You wrote these when you were younger. They were based on your experiences and your opinions. You might remember "What I did last summer." You might also recall simple book reports that included what you liked and what you didn't like in the books. You rarely, or never, use this kind of writing in college.

Academic writing is more formal, it is based on facts often discovered through research, and it generally avoids personal words like *I, my,* and *me.* You should already have noticed that this book includes informal writing when I share an experience or express personal opinions. At other times, my writing is more formal and is based on the latest important research.

You will also discover that professors have an interesting habit of stating questions in a variety of ways. Do you know the differences between summarize, enumerate, explain, discuss, list, demonstrate, and justify? And these are only the beginning of a long list of terms used to express what professors want you to do in your essay.

Questions asking for the main ideas

Many students see the topic and write everything they know on that topic. Later, they wonder why they didn't get more credit. When professors want facts, they generally use objective tests with multiple-choice, true/false, or short-answer questions. These are easier to grade; grading essay tests requires significant time and effort.

Questions that ask you *to summarize, outline, describe, state, list, enumerate, or organize* all ask you to write about the main ideas. For example, you might be asked to summarize or describe mitosis. You should first define the term and then name each of its five stages, describing what takes place in each. Note that this is not the place to compare mitosis and meiosis.

If asked *to outline, list, or describe* the causes of the Civil War, you might begin by mentioning that there were many causes, then go on to list the main causes given in your book or lectures, explaining a little about each of them. If asked to enumerate the causes, do the same thing but either number your points or use the pointer words "first," "second"... and "finally." In either case, you might add that many other factors were involved in the run-up to the war, showing that you're aware there may be other causes than those listed in the textbook or given in the lectures.

A similar kind of question might ask you to *trace* something, as in "Trace the development of the computer." Again, you're writing the main ideas but this time you organize them in chronological order. It's especially helpful to explain how each event made the following events possible.

Another type of question where you show that you know something might ask you to *diagram* something. As you would expect, this means drawing the object and labeling all the parts correctly. If you're diagramming a typical plant cell and you learned about parts not shown on the diagram in the book, be sure to include those parts, too. Often you're asked to diagram and explain the function of each part. So draw a single diagram, then explain the functions of the parts, one at a time.

Questions that ask you to discuss, reflect, comment, or illustrate

Assume that you're asked to *discuss, reflect on, or comment on* the causes of the Civil War. You might start with the main ideas you learned: "According to our textbook, the three main causes of the Civil War were...." But this time, in order to discuss, reflect on, or comment, you must go one step further; you must add your own thoughts and conclusions. You might suggest several other causes of the war. You might discuss the fact that in spite of these causes, the people of the North and the South could have come to a compromise and avoided the war. You might suggest that, if Americans had known how much suffering this war would cause, they might have solved their problems another way. Start with the facts and then add your reflections.

Another kind of question asks you *to give an example or to illustrate* an idea. For instance, "Sometimes scientific discoveries are made because of a mistake or by accident. Give an example of how this might have happened." This instruction is quite clear.

On the other hand, if the question asks "Illustrate the ideas that scientific discoveries are sometimes made because of a mistake or accident," some students might think they should draw a picture of something. You "illustrate" an idea not by drawings but with one or several written examples. Begin by restating the main idea: "Sometimes a mistake or accident can lead to scientific discoveries." Follow this with your examples and end with a conclusion. You might point out in the conclusion that it requires a prepared or creative mind to understand the value of what scientists observed following the mistake.

Questions that require active thinking

The first type of question that requires active thinking involves comparisons. If you're asked to *compare* mitosis and meiosis, you should first list all the significant ways in which they are the same. Then, using categories, you should list ways in which they're different. If you're asked to *contrast* or *differentiate* two things, only include the significant ways in which they're different. Again, you begin with categories.

When contrasting elephants and giraffes, as an example, you might mention that while the elephant skin is thick, has little hair, and is solid gray, the giraffe's skin is not as thick, is covered with hair, and has a distinctive pattern of tan or yellow with brown patches. If this example isn't clear, there is more about *compare* and *contrast* in the sections on mental processing in chapters 15 and 16. Here, the categories are thickness of skin, color, and amount of hair.

A similar kind of question may ask you to *relate* two things. You might relate mitosis to growth. You might relate the industrial revolution to growth in large cities. There are many ways of relating things, events, or people. You might consider *cause and effect*. You might suggest that one event led to another or tell how the discovery of one thing led to yet another discovery. While some relationships show cause and effect, others might both have been caused by or affected by the same circumstances or events. Or they may simply have happened at the same time, by chance. They might have involved some of the same people. You might also include the most significant comparisons. If showing the relationships between elephants and giraffes, you could include similarities or differences in their natural environment, stating that both are often found in zoos, and pointing out that both are endangered in the wild.

Learning to explain

Questions asking students to explain something are often difficult to answer properly. "*Explain* Newton's three laws of motion" is a good example. It's not enough to list Newton's three laws, writing them as they are given in the book. Instead, you might begin by stating the laws and add "This means…," putting them in your own words, and then giving relevant examples not mentioned in the book or lectures.

Explaining how you solved a math problem involves how you pictured the problem, how you chose a particular formula or strategy, and how you worked out each step in detail.

Explaining a term means defining it in your own words and giving an example. When professors ask you to explain something, they want to know if you memorized an answer or if you truly understand. You might start with a textbook answer and go on to say, "In other words…."

Writing a critique or an evaluation

A *critique* is actually an *evaluation*. A movie critic watches and critiques new movies. A food critic visits restaurants and writes critiques of the food and service. There are art critics, music critics, poetry critics, and many more types. From these examples, it should be clear that a critique doesn't need to be negative. A movie critic sometimes describes the latest movie as one of the best movies of the year but doesn't stop there; he might point out which actors did a good job, what great work the animation team did on a particular scene, or who designed the original costumes and realistic settings.

Students generally are asked to *write a critique* of a scholarly article. You might respond, "Who am *I* to judge the work of a highly respected scientist, historian, or philosopher?" Your critique, however, is merely an assignment that allows your professor to evaluate (or critique) your understanding of the characteristics of the best scholarly articles. You are not being asked if you enjoyed reading it. Instead, you're expected to *evaluate* the work based on criteria such as clarity, use of evidence, fairness, and logical reasoning.

In your paper, you might first describe the author's question, thesis, or (in science) the hypothesis. Sometimes these are only implied. How did the experts approach the problem? Did they perform an actual experiment? If so, did it use a large enough sample and appropriate controls?

Sometimes the writer will use the method I use in this book. They will refer to research done by others. This is an accepted method, but you should still ask whether the research referred to was done by respected experts in their field and if the research was relevant, current, and properly done. You might look for possible problems in the methods or in the reasoning.

Do the results make sense? That's an important consideration. You'll remember the story I shared of research supposedly done at the Harvard Business School, comparing students who wrote their goals to those who didn't. In addition to the lack of any reference to the original research, the numbers simply didn't make sense.

In many reports of research, either the numbers or the conclusions don't make sense, or both. Perhaps the authors claimed to prove something was true when they showed only that it *might* be true. Actual proof is difficult. Perhaps they concluded that one behavior or event caused the other when, actually, it could have been the other way around or, more likely, there was a simple correlation, possibly because both might have been caused by or affected by some other factor.

You might also ask yourself whether the charts, graphs, and other displays of data are clearly labeled, making them easy to understand. Consider whether there's any sign of bias, whether the author has considered other points of view, and whether there are other possible interpretations of the evidence.

If you're being asked to critique art, music, literature, or other material, you'll do many of the same things, though you might need to begin by defining your criteria. The more often you critique work written by others, the more aware you will become of errors to avoid in your own writing or thinking.

Defend your thesis, support your argument, or prove your point

The final type of essay begins with verbs such as *prove, justify, argue, demonstrate, or support*. In some cases, you'll be given a thesis to support. At other times, you will be expected to first answer a question and then support that answer. You might, for example, be asked, "Do you think we are capable of reversing global warming? Explain and support your belief."

After you decide which alternative you want to support (possibly chosen because you know its evidence best), you need to plan your three to five types of evidence. You will not be judged on your opinion; you'll be judged instead on your ability to support that position through evidence and logical reasoning.

Good advice that helped improve this book

While beginning to organize this book, I read a book about writing nonfiction. One helpful statement was this: "Every book of nonfiction begins with a question the author has on the topic and ends with the answer the author wants to prove."[6]

I shouldn't have been surprised. This is what I've always done when writing an essay or research paper, but it suddenly struck me that this book wasn't based on a question. It didn't have a thesis. It had only a long series of good ideas. I needed to identify my main question—the one question I would attempt to answer.

Unlike with many study skills books, I was not asking, "How can students make better grades?" My question, as you might remember, is "*Why do students who work so hard, and make good grades, soon forget most of what they learned?*"

You may or may not be aware that, in many chapters in this book, parts of the answer are discussed. In the conclusion, chapter 23, the question will be considered again and the answers, at least the parts of the answers I have discovered, will be summarized.

When you need to write an essay or longer paper, think first about your question. As you find answers to the question, state your thesis—the answer you will try to prove in your paper.

Two final comments

The best way to prepare for an essay test is to write your own questions and to practice writing essays. You might have a friend or even your professor evaluate your efforts so you can understand the difference between an essay that is just OK and one that is outstanding.

Finally, as you read the various strategies for organizing information verbally and visually in chapters 15 and 16, and learn ways of thinking in chapter 17, you will notice something: Those strategies will sound eerily familiar. The words that professors use in essay questions are closely related to those strategies. So the more you use those strategies, the better you'll be prepared to deal with essay questions.

> *People learn to write well, not by studying grammar, sentence structure, and spelling but by reading good writing and trying to imitate it. — Grace Llewellyn and Amy Silver*

Questions for Reflection:

1. What information in this chapter was new to you?

2. What have you decided to do to improve your writing skills?

3. What surprised you in this chapter? What was the most important thing you learned? How will you use what you learned?

Develop Your Speaking Skills

The success of your presentation will be judged not by the knowledge you send but by what the listeners receive. — Lily Walters

O ne of the skills employers value and see as important for advancement is the ability to make effective presentations. If you have the opportunity, take a class in public speaking. In class, you and the other students are all beginners. You will all understand when members of the class get nervous, lose their place, or suffer from "stage fright." It is far better to make these mistakes now with sympathetic listeners rather than later when your boss asks you to make a presentation at an important meeting.

If your school doesn't offer a class, you might collect a group of your friends or classmates and start a Public Speaking Club. Take turns doing 3- to 5-minute talks and critiquing each other. You might even find a good book on public speaking, read a section or a chapter, and discuss it before doing your speeches. Another alternative is joining a local chapter of Toastmasters, an organization that helps people develop skills in public speaking.[1]

Exercise: How Do You Feel about Speaking in Public?

1. A professor asks you to describe your position on an issue and explain why you believe you are right. How well will you be able to speak logically and clearly? Would you feel nervous?

2. You are part of a team working on a class project. Your task is to do a 5- to 10-minute presentation of what your team learned. What would you do to prepare? How confident would you feel?

3. You are president of a campus organization and want to suggest a service project. You want your members to agree that this is a good idea, to believe it will work, and to be eager to participate. Can you do this effectively?

Stating your opinion in class can start with a quick plan

A three-point outline can prepare you to state your opinion and give a few reasons.

STRATEGY 12.1

SPEAK IN CLASS

Step 1: Decide what you want to say.

Step 2: Do a quick three-point outline listing points you want to make.

Step 3: With an outline, you no longer need to think and talk at the same time. Concentrate on stating and explaining your position clearly.

Step 4: Look and sound confident. Stand tall. Look at the people you're talking to. Speak loudly and clearly enough to be heard and understood by everyone in the class.

Step 5: If you are nervous about speaking in class, you might want to practice answering questions in private to build your confidence.

STRATEGY 12.2

MAKE A PRESENTATION

Making a presentation in class will take a great deal more planning.

Step 1: You and your team should work together to collect information on the topic and discuss it.

Step 2: You and your team should decide what your classmates need or would want to know. If the students will be tested on this material, your presentation must cover the main ideas. Discuss what kind of questions might be asked.

Step 3: Brainstorm the information or ideas you want to include in the presentation. Work together to set your goals for the presentation.

Step 4: Organize the information with an introduction—your main idea, your three main points, and a conclusion. Add sub-points to each of your three main points.

Step 5: Use a 3x3 chart or something similar to show this information and organization.

Step 6: Practice your presentation, but do not attempt to memorize. You'll want to speak naturally.

Step 7: Stand tall; smile; look at the listeners (not your notes or the ceiling); speak loudly enough for everyone to hear you; and show expression with your voice, your gestures, and your face. Do not smile when describing a sad situation or problem.

Step 8: Be prepared to answer questions but don't worry about questions you can't answer. A good speaker is able to say, "I don't know." There is no need to apologize or feel as if you should know. You might comment, "That's a good question but I don't know the answer."

Using a three by three

The chart below is an example of a 3x3. It has space for three main points and three details for each main point. That is the 3x3. On this chart, I added space for the introduction and conclusion.[2]

Chart 12.1 The Three by Three

Introduction – Including the three main ideas			
1. First Main Idea	Explain clearly	Example or Story	Why important?
2. Next Main Idea	Explain clearly	Example or Story	Statistics
3. Third Main Idea	Explain clearly	Example or Story	Or how to apply
Conclusion, including summary of the three main ideas			

The three main points are listed down the left side. To the right of each point are spaces for three sub-points. The sub-points often include any three of the following: an explanation, a quote, a story, or an example.

This structure is found in many sermons. Preachers are known for a simple strategy. "First, I tell them what I'm going to tell them. Then I tell them. Finally, I tell them what I told them."

Certainly, an outline with three main points, each with three sub-points, would help you organize the information, but the 3x3 chart can be drawn on an index card. Most people find it easier to visualize a 3x3 rather than a complete outline. When I speak to a group, I carry my index card but rarely need to use it.

There are two difficult parts to giving any presentation: the first several sentences and the last several sentences. Write the first one to three sentences in the upper section and the last several sentences in the lower section. You shouldn't need to read these sentences, but you can memorize them and take a last look at them just before you begin.

Many speakers include the three main points in their introduction. You might need to write only the opening sentences. You should know the three main points but, if you forget, they are on your card. This helps you start strong and end just as you planned.

If you need to make an hour-long presentation, you obviously wouldn't stop with only three points, each with three sub-points. You might use four main points, each with four or more sub-points. You can redraw the 3x3 making it a 4x4.

STRATEGY 12.3

GIVE A SPEECH TO PERSUADE

If you are trying to convince members of your organization to work on a service project, you might begin with information, though your real purpose would be to persuade. This is still a short talk. You can still use a 3x3. Assume that a nearby town has had record floods and you are suggesting your members use their weekend to go help people clean up.

Step 1: In your introduction, you might remind them of what happened and give a few statistics.

Step 2: Your first main point might be to give specific details of the damage, along with a particularly moving story to engage their interest. You might ask them how they'd feel if it was their family whose home had been flooded.

Step 3: In your second main point, you might describe what kind of help the people need, and specifically how your group could be most helpful.

Step 4: In the third main point, you might answer the question, "Why us?" Remind them of the goals of your organization. Describe what skills they have that would be especially useful in this time of natural disaster.

Step 5: In your conclusion, ask if you can count on them to help. No one wants to say no to that kind of question. Give them a way to get involved immediately:

"We need to organize three teams. Team one will plan transportation, finding out what cars are available and who will go in each car. Team two will plan meals; we need to pack a lunch, snacks, and plenty of water for each day. Team three will list equipment needed and find ways to borrow equipment from family or friends in town." Finally explain where each team will gather.

In this example you'd be giving your listeners four things. You give them information, you involve their emotions, you explain how they can make a difference and why they should be to ones to act, and you give them a way to get involved immediately.

What is the difference between a good speaker and a great speaker?

- A good speech is often generic. It could be given to many different groups. A great speech seems designed for one particular group, however large or small.

- A good speech is often based on the speaker's interests. A great speech focuses on the needs and interests of the listeners.

- When you listen to good speakers, you remember how beautifully they spoke. When you listen to great speakers, you remember how it made you feel and what decisions you made as a result.

- A good speaker wants to impress the listeners with how well he or she speaks. A great speaker wants to help the listeners understand or move them to action.

    If you don't know what you want to achieve in your presentation your audience never will. — Henry Diamond

---
Questions for Reflection:
---

1. What surprised you in this chapter? What was the most important thing you learned? How will you use what you learned?

2. Consider your lifetime goals. In what situations might you be called on to make a speech or presentation?

3. What could you do this year, perhaps even this week, to improve your skills in public speaking?

CHAPTER 13

The Never-Cram-Again System of Test Preparation

Cramming…has been likened to binge-and-purge eating. A lot goes in, but most of it comes back out in short order.[1]

J ust before the end of the semester, many students begin cramming for exams. Because everyone seems to be doing it, many freshmen assume cramming is the best way to make good grades. I've heard students say that it's smarter to study at the last minute because you'll have "less time to forget."

The truth is that cramming is the *worst* possible strategy. It does not lead to the best grades, and it certainly does not improve your understanding or memory of the subject.

Researchers agree that "Cramming is not learning. A day or two of cramming is not nearly enough time for the brain to form the permanent memories necessary to meet the neuroscience definition of learning."[2] Cramming is often done when the student should be sleeping, making the problems far worse. "A person who is sleep deprived will be 19% less efficient at recalling memories. A person who has not slept at all has 50% less memory ability."[3]

One of our Big Questions is why we work so hard—yet learn so little. Terry Doyle and Todd Zakrajsek explain part of the problem:

The practice of cramming also signals to the brain that the information being studied is not important. After you take an exam you crammed for, you usually have an exhausted, "I'm glad that is over" feeling. This feeling tells the brain that the information is no longer needed and can be purged as you sleep.[4]

What most books suggest that you do to prepare for exams

Many books on study skills begin by focusing on the test itself. Students are advised to ask questions about the test. They should try to learn how many multiple-choice, true/false, short-answer, and essay questions will be on the test. They should try to discover exactly how many points each type of question is worth so they can plan their best use of time. If the essay questions are worth 50% of the test, they reason that they should spend 50% of their time answering such questions. Another suggestion is to find and study tests from previous years.

Other strategies for the exam itself begin with skimming the test and planning how to best use your time, starting with the easiest questions, leaving plenty of time for essay questions, and always reading the directions at least twice while at the same time underlining the important parts of the questions. Then there are strategies for answering multiple-choice questions. It makes sense to eliminate answers you know are wrong, and then eliminate ones that include generalizations like *all, always, none, never, no one,* or *everyone.*

While all these suggestions can be helpful, none will help you learn anything. They might help you be a better test-taker, and they might even help you make a better grade, but they won't help you understand the material deeply or remember information longer. They will not prepare you to write essays that require serious thinking skills. This chapter is about preparing for exams in a way that also helps you learn most effectively.

Exercise: How Do You Prepare for Tests or Exams?

---

1. Do you use any of the strategies that were listed? How helpful are they?
2. Have you ever stayed up all night to study for an exam? If not, what's the latest you have stayed up to study?
3. How long before the exam do you usually begin to prepare?

4. When do you think you should begin to prepare?

Another suggestion found in many books on study skills is that students should begin preparing for exams a week in advance, instead of cramming. A few experts go so far as to suggest starting two weeks before the exams. What the authors and their readers don't seem to realize is that, though these plans are better than last-minute cramming, they are still "cramming."

In many cases, students learn part of the material earlier in the semester and then forget it. With other students, even if they did some of the reading, they never learned anything. The idea of learning or relearning an entire semester's material in two weeks simply doesn't make sense. What students should do is spend the entire *semester* learning the material, taking time to understand the material fully, and to review it regularly.

My one experience with cramming

I must confess that I did pull one all-nighter, or at least close enough. I had just transferred from a large state university to the University of Chicago. I was accustomed to multiple-choice questions and always made excellent grades on these tests. I had no idea that, in this school, I'd be expected to go beyond recognizing the best answers—that I would actually need to remember names and dates.

I joined the crowd that collected in the dormitory cafeteria to begin all-night cramming. Coffee and snacks were available. Although I never liked coffee, I decided I'd better drink some to stay awake. I think I drank about 38 cups. I "studied" until four in the morning, when I gave up and headed back to my room to get at least a little sleep. The exam was from 9 to 11 a.m. and, though my alarm clock was set, I never heard it. I woke up suddenly at 9:45, threw on my clothes, and rushed to the exam location.

I'm sure you can guess what happened. Having only half the time to take the exam, needing to know dates I hadn't studied, and feeling panicked, exhausted, and sick from too much coffee, I failed the exam. It was the only exam I ever failed.

But I was very lucky. The professor knew I'd slept late and he was sympathetic. He explained that this was a three-trimester course. The grade was calculated as your average over the three trimesters, or you received the grade you made on the final exam at the end of the year, whichever was higher. You can imagine my relief.

What might surprise you, though, is what else I discovered. After I recovered from the shock of failing the test and was able to think rationally, I realized that, even with only an hour, I had answered every question as well as I could. If I'd had a full night's sleep and arrived at the exam early, I still would have failed. The problem was that I had never learned to study for a thorough exam like this one. From that point on, I avoided cramming and began to study seriously, starting on the first day of class.

STRATEGY 13.1

USE THE NEVER-CRAM-AGAIN TEST PREPARATION

A few other books on study techniques suggest a similar strategy, but here the strategy has been revised to fit together with other strategies in this book.

Step 1: You need at least two folders for each class where you have reading notes and lecture notes. For Jane's schedule in chapter 4, on Flexible Time Management, she follows this procedure only for biology and history. These are the only classes where she has both reading notes and lecture notes. She will also do a weekly review for math.

While some writing classes might include reading and lecture notes, Jane's class involves mainly writing and critiquing each other's work. (This will be clear when you read the steps in this strategy.)

Step 2: Two-pocket folders would be best for weekly notes: Jane would label one folder "History – This Week," and another folder "Biology – This Week." For your notes for the entire semester, you might find folders that will hold at least 50 sheets of paper. Jane would label one "History – All Notes," and the other "Biology – All Notes." The All Notes folders will need to hold more material.

Step 3: At the end of each week, place 10 items in your folder: lecture notes, handouts, reading preview, reading KWL, reading questions and answers, reading notes, vocabulary list with definitions, flash cards, all verbal organizations of the material, and all visual organizations of the material.

Step 4: Condense all these notes, diagrams, and other materials into a short, well-organized 1 to 5 pages for review. These, along with your flash cards, will go into the larger folder and will be reviewed at least once a week.

You can file your original notes where you can find them if needed, but the condensed notes should be all you need to review. You will notice that, in chapter 4 on Flexible Time Management, the schedule shown in chart

4.5 has one hour each week marked for these classes, labeled "[Subject] Condense."

If you used highlighting or underlining instead of reading notes, you'd need to flip through the pages of your book for reading notes—and the process will take a great deal longer.

Step 5: At the end of each week, you will review all the material from the current week and for all previous weeks.

Note that review does not mean rereading the material; it means self-testing. When you review vocabulary, you test your memory with flash cards. When you review diagrams, outlines, or concept maps, you test yourself by re-creating the same charts or outlines by memory and checking with the original. When you review notes, you might look at the main ideas and recite mentally or aloud the important ideas in the chapter or lecture, or you might re-create the outline, concept map, or other organization based on those notes.

Again, on the Flexible Time Management Chart, chart 4.5, there is one hour a week for most classes, labeled "Review." As time goes by, you might spend 30 minutes reviewing the current week's material and use the other 30 minutes to focus on one part of the material from past weeks. One week you might review all the vocabulary; the next week, all the condensed notes, and so on. After the review, add the current week's notes to the folder of all notes. It might help to fasten each week's notes with a large paperclip.

Step 6: The day before the exam, you might take two or three hours instead of just one and review all your material again.

Be sure to eat properly and get a good night's sleep. You will go into your exam feeling well-rested and confident that you are well -prepared.

Five advantages of the never-cram-again system

1. The first advantage of never cramming for exams is obvious: You are well-prepared for exams and you'll never ever need to cram. The other advantages are not as obvious.

2. You will learn more. You may remember that, earlier in the book, research was described showing that the two most effective strategies were self-testing and distributed review. This system uses both of these strategies.

3. By reviewing the material weekly and testing yourself regularly, you'll be trying to remember what you learned and will

be relearning as necessary. This leads to long-term memory. If you'd like to remember all or part of your class material for the rest of your life, simply continue the regular review. I'd recommend reducing the amount of material you want to remember and then review it monthly at first. When it is easy to remember the information, you can review every two or three months. Eventually, you can review yearly and continue to remember what you learned.

4. By using this method, you'll get better grades.

5. The fifth advantage is especially important to students who suffer from test anxiety. Since nearly all of us experience some level of anxiety before an exam, it is actually helpful for us, too. A major part of this anxiety is due to concerns about whether or not we know the material well enough. With weekly self-testing, you should be confident that you know the material very well. This significantly reduces anxiety. Studies show that with reduced anxiety we think more clearly and make higher grades.

> *Rarely do examination questions simply require you to regurgitate chunks of information exactly in the same order that it was given to you in the lecture. Demonstrate your understanding by showing you have recognized patterns and connections within your work. — Jason Davies*

Questions for Reflection:

---

1. How have you been studying and preparing for tests?

2. What changes will you make? How will you now prepare for tests?

3. What surprised you in this chapter? What did you learn? How will you use what you learned?

You can always choose to use some of the strategies described in this book but perhaps not all of them. It's your right to choose what kind of education you want and how you plan to get it.

CHAPTER

14

Mental Processing Strategies: A Brief Introduction to Part 3

Humans are innately endowed with the capacity to compare and contrast, to classify and categorize,... to collect data through sensory pathways, to infer and generalize, to find patterns and predict, and to think spatially, numerically, and temporally.[1]

It is strange that, although most students are urged to study more, or study harder, most of the time no one teaches them *how* to study. Not only do most students not understand how to study, they have no idea what exactly is meant by "study."

New insights into how the human brain learns make it clear that many of the learning practices...that students continue to use, are highly inefficient, ineffective, or just plain wrong.[2]

Exercise: What Does It Mean to Study?

1. Describe what you actually do when you are studying. Do you use any strategies?
2. How is studying different from reading?
3. What do you think you should do when studying?
4. If you're asked to think about what you just read, what do you actually do?

What is mental processing?

You may remember chart 8.1, the simple chart called "The Empty Head. You may also remember that the information went in and the information went out, leaving nothing behind. Now, in the revised image, the input information goes to the brain for mental processing before it leads to output.

Chart 14.1 The Thinking Head

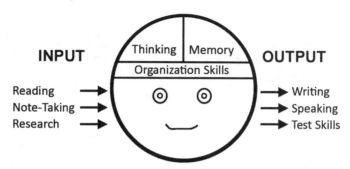

Now with information processed in the brain, something does remain. Mental processing or study leads to learning, and what has been learned is now stored in long-term memory in many places all over the brain. In the "Thinking Head," you see three new categories: Organizing Information, Thinking, and Memory.

Reflecting on the Exercise:
What Does It Mean to Study?

---

1. What do you do when you are studying?
2. How is studying different from reading?
   Many students believe that reading is studying. Reading is a way of getting information input. Even rereading is not studying; it is still reading. If, however, you use strategies like SQ3R, you combine reading, organizing information, thinking, and memory. This is a good example of studying.
3. What is study?
   Study is mentally processing learning input by organizing the information in a variety of ways, by thinking deeply about the material and by using effective strategies for memory.

4. If you're asked to think about what you just read, what do you do? Many students simply try to remember what they read. There is a big difference between remembering and thinking about something.

In chapter 16, you will learn ten different ways of thinking. Thinking is a way of taking the material that you read or learned in a lecture, reorganizing it, and then considering it from many perspectives until the material is stored in your brain. Now this material has become far more than memorized information; it is part of your own understanding of the subject.

STRATEGY *14.1*

USE MENTAL PROCESSING

Step 1: Start with input from reading or from taking notes in lectures.

You cannot study or process information until you have information to process.

Step 2: You will already be thinking as you select a few strategies to use.

Step 3: Select and use one or more ways of organizing information verbally.

You might write a summary, create an outline, or compare and contrast what you learned. These activities might use analytical thinking.

Step 4: Select and use one or more ways of organizing information visually.

Choose the strategies that will work best with your input information. With visual organization, you use different parts of your brain.

Step 5: Select and use several strategies for memory that fit well with your content.

You should always try to include self-testing and distributed practice, the two most effective strategies.

Another image to illustrate studying—or not studying

> *Some books should be tasted, some devoured, but only a few should be chewed and digested thoroughly.* — *Sir Francis Bacon*

Philosophers and essayists have expressed this idea in many ways over the centuries. Think of books you have only tasted, books you have devoured, and those you have chewed and digested thoroughly. This Zits Comic Strip appears to be based on this or one of the many similar statements.

Used with permission Zits ©2010 Zits Partnership, Dist. By King Features

Most people have a different response to a visual metaphor than they have to a verbal metaphor. Viewing this comic strip, you might almost taste the tough book covers and smell the crunchy dry pages. You might almost feel them passing down Jeremy's esophagus into his stomach where gastric acid soaks the pages. By now, Jeremy's stomach must be grumbling a bit. His books do not continue the journey in the usual way; instead, they come back up, perhaps with a sour taste. They are regurgitated onto Jeremy's test. Jeremy might get a good grade for his efforts but, unlike students who process the material well and absorb it, Jeremy will forget everything he "learned" in only a few days.

Let's take this metaphor one step further. When we chew our food well and swallow it, the partially digested food is carried to our stomach where it is thoroughly digested. From there, it moves to the small intestines where nutrients from the food pass through the intestinal walls and are carried by the blood to all parts of our body.

When you "chew" books thoroughly, the information goes to your brain, where mental processing "digests" the information or concepts. The most important ideas are then picked up by your nerves and passed along from neuron to neuron to every part of your brain. There, connections are built, linking the new ideas with prior information. These connections are stored as long-term memory until you need them again.

Too many students think professors do all the work—that they will simply pour information into students' heads. Then, when the students forget what they "learned" or do poorly on tests, they blame their professors for not teaching them properly.

The truth about learning is that professors can do little more than give you the information; you, yourself, are responsible for the chewing, digesting, and mental processing. This process isn't easy; it takes time and hard work and, unlike digestion, it's not automatic. But, just as you feel satisfied after a good meal, you should feel a similar sense of satisfaction after putting a lot of effort into studying, when you know you have learned the material well.

> *What we seek to learn shapes the thinking skills that we use to manipulate information.* — *Barry Beyer*

From introductions to life-long friendships

Imagine that you've been introduced to another person. The friend doing the introducing tells you something about the other person, perhaps that you have shared interests. You find this person interesting and want to know him or her better. You might ask a few questions and listen carefully to their answers. In turn, you should share with them your own interests and experiences, your hopes for the future, and perhaps even your values and beliefs.

If you stop here, however, you won't become friends; you will be no more that casual acquaintances. Over the years, we remember friends but forget most of our acquaintances. To develop a genuine friendship, you need to spend time together, continuing to know more about each other. You should do things together. When you participate in activities the other person enjoys, you begin to find them interesting. The more the two of you interact, the more the friendship grows. If you continue this process, you become good friends. You might even develop a life-long friendship.

Were you aware, as you read this, that the discussion about friendship was about the meaning of study—or did you think it could have been material for a different chapter, placed here by mistake?

Your professors and the authors of your textbooks are those who introduce you to new ideas. In doing so, they often tell you something about the subject they are introducing. After the introduction, they leave the rest up to you. You are the only one who can carry on the conversation and learn more about the subject. You might ask questions. This time, you might find answers to your questions in lectures and in reading your textbooks or you might need to do further research.

As with making friends, the two of you, you and the subject you are studying, need to spend quality time together. Topics you hadn't seen as important before may now seem more interesting. To truly interact with these subjects, you can analyze their structure and main ideas using outlines, summaries, concept maps, and other strategies. You can interact by thinking deeply about the subject in a variety of ways. You can use various pathways to memory to move what you are learning into long-term memory.

Some of the subjects you meet may remain mere acquaintances, subjects you will know by name and talk to from time to time while you're in college together, but that gradually, as time passes, will be forgotten. Some will be friends you remember and stay in touch with for many years. Only a few will become life-long friends.

Studying only for a test is like meeting someone you may never see again. Studying in preparation for getting a good job is like making a friend you'll want to stay in touch with. Studying to get a great education, much like building a strong friendship, takes time and effort now and for the rest of your life. This effort is worth it when we develop lasting human friendships. Is this effort worth it to get the kind of education you want?

According to James Zull, author of *The Art of Changing the Brain:*

> *If we are to learn and grow, there must come a point where we change from receivers of knowledge to creators of knowledge. Instead of reproducing the work of others, we must begin to create our own. This is where humans excel....[3]*
> *This manipulation of information in working memory is what creates new knowledge for the learner. As he organizes things in new arrangements and attaches them to networks that represent his prior knowledge, each learner creates his own understandings.[4]*

Questions for Reflection:

---

1. Of the three areas of mental processing—organizing information, thinking, and memory—which do you already do fairly well?

2. What subjects do you want as acquaintances? As short-term friends? As friends for life?

3. What surprised you in this chapter? What was the most important thing you learned? How will you use what you learned?

15

Verbal Organization — Ten Strategies

The general processes of organizing information require that the learners go well beyond the retention of isolated bits of information. Students must have the knowledge to analytically construct interrelationships so they can evaluate knowledge. This process takes mental energy, perseverance, and more; it also takes the support of focused...organizational tools that reflect different content-specific patterns of knowledge and conceptual structures.[1]

One part of effective study is organizing the information you read in your textbooks or learn in your lectures. In this chapter, we focus on organizing verbally; in the next chapter the focus is on organizing visually.

Students often ask why it's important to organize information. When you organize information, you interact with what you are learning; you make connections within the material and between the new material and what you already know. You understand more completely and remember longer. The information and concepts are internalized.

In chapter 11, you were *learning to write*—learning to write answers to essay questions on tests and to write major essays or research papers. In this chapter you will be *writing to learn*. In addition to helping you learn the content, these strategies will prepare you to answer most essay questions.

Exercise: Writing Outlines and Summaries

---

1. When do you generally use an outline? Do you ever use one to study?
2. How often do you write a summary? How would you describe the difference between well-written and poorly written summaries?
3. What is the difference between a good question and a poor question?

The ten strategies in this chapter are organized into six categories. The first strategy can be used before studying, and also during and after studying. The last strategy is to be used after studying, and the other eight (with two in each category) are to be used while studying.

The first verbal strategy: Ask good questions

In chapter 8 on reading, as you'll recall, the letters KWL stand for three questions: "What do you know?" "What do you *want* to know?" and "What did you learn?" The Q in SQ3R is for writing questions. Clearly, it is important to ask questions. You might start with simple questions, but you should continue to write better and more insightful questions as you learn more about the subject.

It's important to know the difference between good and poor questions. While teaching physics, I offered extra credit for good questions and explained it this way: If you know the answer or could easily look up the answer, it's a poor question. It doesn't require thinking. You can still begin with these simple questions if you don't know the answers.

If the question deals with a concept you don't understand, and looking it up hasn't helped, it's a good question. Occasionally you might come up with *great questions*. These are questions that involve deep understanding of the subject, questions you cannot easily look up but you can begin to explore.

My students got nothing but a frown for writing poor questions. They were wasting my time, and theirs. They earned from one to five points on their weekly quiz for good questions. But, for great questions, there was no limit. Each question was written on an index card. Soon we had index cards with questions all around the chalkboard, and they began spreading along the walls. My students learned more by writing and struggling with these questions than from reading the textbook.

One question must have earned at least 50 points. It kept us busy for several weeks: "If the moon were larger, how would it affect the earth?" This morphed into related questions: "What if the moon were larger than the earth?" and "What if the moon and the earth were exactly the same size, or the same mass?"

There are many exciting ways to look at these questions. You might consider the motions of the earth and moon. You might consider the effects on tides, weather, earthquakes, animals, people, and so much more. We could even have considered how it might affect politics or the economy in this country and around the world.

If you're studying literature, there are many kinds of interesting questions. Ask why characters behave the way they do. Ask about the underlying themes and images and their roles in the book. Ask about the author's purpose for writing the book.

Clearly, the more good questions you ask about a subject you're studying, the more you will learn. Great questions can lead to doing important scientific research, to writing award-winning books, to developing beneficial inventions, to solving difficult problems or, for students, to writing excellent research papers.

STRATEGY 15.1

ASK GOOD QUESTIONS

Step 1: Decide where to keep your questions. You might set aside space in each of your notebooks. You might have a separate notebook for questions. You might write questions on index cards and post them on your bulletin board.

Step 2: Label your questions to indicate what course they applied to or if they were personal. You could distinguish questions you wanted to answer because they might be asked on a test from ones you asked simply because you are curious. You might indicate which questions are most important or most interesting.

Step 3: As you shower, as you eat, as the professor checks attendance, or as you walk from class to class, you might do some serious thinking about your most interesting questions.

Step 4: Is it a question you can look up? Could a professor or someone else help you find the answer? Is it a question you need to answer for yourself?

When you find an answer, write it down. If the question is in your notebook, check it off. If it's on your bulletin board, take it down and store it, perhaps in a small file box.

Two strategies for studying structure: outlines and analyzing arguments

The second strategy is creating an outline. Creating an outline is an excellent strategy to analyze structure and main ideas. Many students hate outlining because they were once required to outline a chapter, but this is actually the best verbal strategy for analyzing the structure of a lecture, book, chapter, or article. You can create the outline while you're reading or taking notes in a lecture or when you're done.

STRATEGY 15.2

CREATE AN OUTLINE

Step 1: Decide the purpose of your outline and how detailed it should be.

Are the main ideas all you need or should you include a great deal of factual information?

Step 2: You can use a formal outline or a simple outline.

The formal outline includes Roman numerals and capital letters. A simple or informal outline might just number the main points or simply indents further for each level. Here, however, we are discussing how to create an outline as part of mental processing.

Step 3: Nearly all textbooks make it simple to create an outline.

The chapter title is your title. The main headings often represent the main ideas (the Roman numerals). If the book has subheadings, they're listed below the main ideas (the letters). If you have no subheadings, divide the information into several logical sections and label them yourself. If the headings ask questions, the answers to those questions are likely to be the main ideas.

Step 4: Everything you write should be brief and in your own words.

By restating the idea, you're already thinking about the idea and beginning to understand it.

Step 5: Under each subheading, list the most important information.

Don't write too much. Sometimes the material under the subheading is a single idea; sometimes it includes several related ideas. Students who do an excellent job of highlighting might include their highlighted information on their outline.

Poor outlines include random bits of information or include far too much information. Good outlines identify the main ideas and organize them to show how the information is structured.

Step 6: To review the material, test yourself.

Take a blank sheet of paper and create the outline again. Compare it to your original. Were the parts you missed important? If so, add them to your new outline. After doing this several times, you'll find it easy to remember the structure, the main ideas, and the most important details.

Step 7: If you prefer using a concept map, an outline can easily be redrawn as a concept map. If you do both, you might consider the advantages and disadvantages of each.

Step 8: The best kind of outline (requiring the most thinking) is used to condense the main ideas from both lectures and reading, structured to show the relationships as you perceive them.

The third verbal strategy is analyzing an argument.

Students are are often asked to analyze an argument. In science classes, you might identify the hypothesis, describe the evidence and how it was collected, and explain and evaluate the reasoning leading to a conclusion. In most other classes, you should identify the thesis, describe different kinds of evidence, and then explain and evaluate the reasoning or argument supporting the thesis.

By "argument," we aren't discussing a disagreement or a fight where people scream at each other. *An argument, here, is a written statement, often as part of a larger paper, that states the author's claim, hypothesis, or thesis; provides evidence; and uses logical reasoning to support his position.*

Here is some information about how important it is to drink enough water. We can use this to show implied reasoning.

1. Water keeps your brain tissues moist.

2. Water removes wastes from the brain.

3. Water cools your brain and keeps it from overheating.

4. When you don't drink enough water, dehydration makes you tired, then confused, and finally you can die.

5. Drinking enough water is important for both health and learning.

The idea that water is important both for your health and for learning seems more like a conclusion rather than evidence. Actually this is the thesis, the main idea.

The reasoning is not stated. We can, however, show that the first three statements are evidence that water keeps us healthy. The fourth statement describes results of not drinking enough water. The reasoning is implied. When we are tired or confused, we don't learn well. This proves that drinking enough water is important both for health and learning.

STRATEGY 15.3

ANALYZE AN ARGUMENT

Step 1: Your introduction might summarize the paper where the argument is found.

Step 2: Your second paragraph could identify and explain the question, claim, hypothesis, or thesis.

Step 3: The third paragraph should list and discuss the evidence. Sometimes the evidence includes examples that do little to prove the thesis.

Step 4: The fourth paragraph might analyze the reasoning and discuss the conclusions that were reached.

Step 5: Your summary might point to the strengths and weaknesses of the argument.

Note that either the outline or the analysis of the argument would prepare you to write a summary on an essay test. If you don't have time to write a complete essay on a test, just listing the thesis, evidence, and reasoning may earn you many points.

Two strategies that focus on content: summaries and explanations

How would you describe the difference between a summary and an explanation?

Sometimes, in fact, there is no difference. In a history class you could be asked to summarize the three main causes of the War of 1812, or you could be asked to explain or list causes. For all these you would do the same thing.

But if you are asked to explain photosynthesis, you must go farther than listing the main ideas. In fact, even if you are asked to summarize the steps and processes involved in photosynthesis, you would still write an explanation.

Generally, *a summary lists and describes the main ideas; an explanation focuses on understanding concepts. A summary might answer who, what, when, and where; an explanation might go on to answer how and why.*

There are many kinds of summaries. A summary of a one-page article is quite different from summaries of a chapter or book. A summary in a lab report has different, well-defined steps. A summary of a novel might include characters, setting, plot, time period, and themes. A summary of research in some specific area might be a long research paper covering the most relevant sources of information describing research in this area.

> *You don't understand a concept until, at the very least, you can define it in your own words, give your own examples of it, and explain its relationships to other concepts. — Adam Robinson*

STRATEGY *15.4*

WRITE A GOOD SUMMARY

Step 1: Identify the topic and main ideas. When summarizing a chapter, the topic is usually related to the title.

Step 2: For a simple summary, list and explain each of the main ideas.

It is important to explain them in your own words.

Step 3: For a longer and more formal summary, write a five paragraph essay.

A. Begin with a brief introduction, stating the topic and listing the main ideas. This can be a sentence or two in a short summary or a paragraph in a longer one.

B. Describe each main idea, using a single paragraph for each.

C. In the final paragraph, conclude by restating the main ideas. While a summary doesn't need an original conclusion, you might describe how the topic and main ideas are related or how they are important, closing with a sentence that pulls it all together.

Step 4: When describing the author's opinions, it is best to write them in present tense. You might write that the author *says, states, claims, suggests, argues,* or *explains.*

What is the difference between a good summary and a poor summary?

You may remember research described in chapter 8, comparing the effectiveness of the ten study strategies. Writing summaries was not among the most effective strategies. The authors commented, however, that this strategy might have been more effective if students had been taught how to write a good summary.

Too many students see the word "summary" and begin writing everything they remember on the subject, in no particular order. They focus on facts and miss the main ideas. They don't understand why they get a poor grade when clearly they remembered so much information.

You can be sure that students who have written a good summary of the chapter while studying will do better on a test where they need to summarize the same information.

A good summary focuses on the topic and the main ideas. It often explains the main ideas and shows how they fit together. It rarely includes examples or other information not directly related to the main ideas.

STRATEGY 15.5

WRITE AN EXPLANATION

Explanations can be either simple or complex. Simple explanations can include explaining photosynthesis, how to bake a pie, why Peter failed calculus, or what it means to study.

Step 1: State what you are explaining.

Step 2: List reasons or steps.

For example, to explain Peter's reasons for failing calculus, you could say that he wasn't using time management, he didn't know how to study, and he didn't realize the test would be so hard.

To explain photosynthesis, you might define photosynthesis and list the steps, in order.

To explain how to bake a pie, you might start with a list of ingredients, describe the kind of pan that's needed, and then list the steps.

Step 3: For complex explanations, do one step at a time.

    A. First describe the situation or problem.

    B. State relevant facts that are well known.

    C. Consider other related information.

    D. Use good reasoning to pull this information together to complete the explanation.

Complex explanations might include explaining why the sky is blue, why rainbows have different colors, and why a dropped rock and a folded sheet of paper hit the ground at the same time. None of these can be adequately explained with a definition and a list of simple steps. They all require reasoning.

Example: The rock and the paper: You should remember the problem my students had in understanding why the rock and the folded paper, when dropped, landed at the same time.

Describe the situation: The first time they were dropped, the rock landed first "because it was heavier." The second time, the rock and the paper landed at the same time. Because the students believed heavy objects fall faster than lighter objects, the only possible answer seemed to be that the paper got heavier. The students needed a reason and it helps if they explain the reasoning themselves.

State relevant facts: We might compare this to Galileo's experiment. We might compare this to a video of a hammer and a feather dropped on the moon where they hit the surface at the same time.

Other related information: We might discuss parachutes, asking why people fall to the ground safely while using a parachute and what happens when parachutes don't open.

Reasoning: We could ask if the folded paper was now as heavy as the rock. We could ask how information about parachutes is related to the rock and the paper. Knowing that air slowed the falling of a parachute, we might reason that air could also slow down the falling paper. The folded paper could be compared to a parachute that doesn't open.

Two strategies that show relationships

Two strategies that show relationships are compare and contrast and cause and effect. A quick reminder: If you're asked to compare and contrast or simply to compare, you describe both how the subjects are alike and how they are different. If asked to contrast or differentiate, you should describe only the ways they are different.

STRATEGY 15.6

COMPARE AND CONTRAST

Step 1: Describe significant ways in which two people, places, events, or other things are the same.

Step 2: Describe significant ways they are different, beginning by identifying the categories.

Step 3: Organize this information in paragraph form.

Notice, in the example that follows, that several differences are some-times mentioned in each sentence. You will also see that the categories can be discussed in the opening or introductory sentences. This improves the flow of the information.

Example: Compare Washington and Lincoln

George Washington and Abraham Lincoln were both well-known presidents of the United States. Both were involved in major wars, and both have been honored with monuments on the National Mall in Washington, D.C. (Note that it is never necessary to note that both were men, or that both had two legs and two arms. These facts are not significant.)

They were, however, involved in different wars and played different roles. Washington was involved in the Revolutionary War; Lincoln was involved in the Civil War. Washington was a general leading his troops into battle before becoming the first president of the U.S.; Lincoln, our 16th president, was already in office when the Civil War began and, while he discussed strategies with his generals, he never actually fought in a battle.

Their backgrounds were also strikingly different. While Lincoln was born in a log cabin to a poor family, Washington was born into a fairly wealthy Virginia family that owned slaves. Both are know for famous speeches, Washington for his Farewell Address and Lincoln for his Gettysburg Addess.

STRATEGY *15.7*

CAUSE AND EFFECT

Most questions ask you to describe either the causes or the effects. You might be asked to describe the causes of a war or another event, or to describe the effects of that event.

Step 1: State how many causes or how many effects you will discuss.

Do not describe them as "THE three causes" because it is always likely that there were many more causes (or effects).

Step 2: List and describe the causes.

You might list them in the order they occurred or in order of importance.

Step 3: Alternatively, list and describe the effects.

Start with the immediate effects and end with lasting effects.

Be careful to note that the word *affect is a verb* and the word *effect is usually used as a noun*. The war is likely to *affect* the economy. The *effects* of the war included the economy.

To remember this, think "Will Affect and The Effect." With **the effect** the e in the word "the," and the e in in the word "effect," are next to each other.

For this example, let's consider Peter again; he was planning to major in engineering until he failed his midterm in calculus. This is the event.

If you are asked for the CAUSES of Peter's failing grade, you might say:

1. Peter was not using a time management schedule and he spent much of his time playing video games.

2. Peter had made A's in high school physics and calculus with little effort and he believed he would also do well in college with little effort.

3. Peter had poor study skills and had not spent much time preparing for the midterm.

If, however, you are asked to describe the effects of Peter's new study habits, you might say:

1. Peter learned to use more effective strategies and, as a result,

2. Peter earned an A on the final in calculus and improved his grade.

3. Peter decided to continue majoring in engineering.

4. An even longer term effect was that Peter improved his grades in all his classes that semester and in later years.

Two strategies for evaluation: judgment and critiques

The two strategies for evaluation are judgment, which is more general, and writing a critique, which is more technical.

STRATEGY **15.8**

WRITE AN EVALUATION

You might be asked to judge, or evaluate, the quality or the strengths and weaknesses of poems, short stories, novels, movies, journal articles, even restaurants or bicycles. Let's assume you've been asked by the school newspaper to evaluate a new movie.

Step 1: Do research on criteria used to evaluate movies.

You might read movie critiques by several movie critics.

Step 2: Define the criteria you will use to evaluate the movie.

If you don't understand some of the criteria used by experts, that's fine. Don't use them. Different critics use different criteria.

Step 3: Some of your criteria may be more important than others.

You might give each category a number or weight. For example, the plot might be more important than the setting. So the plot could be worth 20 points and the setting only 5 points.

Step 4: You might watch several movies on TV and rate them, using your criteria.

You might want to adjust the number of points for each criterion.

Step 5: Use your system to judge the movie objectively.

Step 6: Think of your audience.

When you consider the strengths and weaknesses of the movie, think how other students might react. Take notes on what your readers would want to know. Who were the key actors, and who did an unusually good or bad job? What might students you know enjoy most in the movie? What might make students you know consider this movie a waste of time and money? Could you say that students who liked Spiderman movies would enjoy this one, or that students who liked some other well-known movie would not enjoy it?

Teachers make judgments all the time. They judge your essays or research papers. They judge your answers on tests. Whether written or not, they have their own criteria, their reasons to give one essay an A– and a similar essay a B+.

When you make a decision, you must judge the alternatives. When you choose a major or select your courses for the next semester, you must evaluate your choices.

Matthew Lipman describes epistemology as judging what is true and what is false, ethics as judging what is right and what is wrong, and aesthetics as judging what is beautiful and what is not.[2]

Writing a critique

One form of evaluation students are often required to do for their classes is writing a critique. Compare the word "critique" to "critical thinking." While critical thinking will be covered in detail later, in chapters 17 and 20, it's important to understand that using this type of thinking is an important way of organizing information verbally. Writing a critique is similar to writing an evaluation of a teacher, a restaurant, or that movie described earlier.

The four main differences are that a critique is generally about an article or other written material; it always includes an evaluation of the author's thesis, evidence, reasoning, and conclusions; it always involves critical thinking; and the writing style is more formal rather than casual or colloquial. I don't remember ever being asked in a test to write a critique. Critiques are usually written assignments where more time is allowed.

When writing a critique, the criteria are generally fairly well defined. If you are critiquing an article in science, you know it should include a clearly stated question or hypothesis as well as a detailed description of the materials and methods. Results might include data tables and charts (properly labeled). Finally, there should be a well-reasoned conclusion that considers all possible interpretations of the results.

If writing a critique of a short story or novel, you would include the plot, characters, dialogue, conflict, and other elements. Your professors might suggest the important areas to include.

STRATEGY *15.9*

WRITE A CRITIQUE

Compare, analyze, and judge the logic of arguments, the accuracy of hypotheses, and the adequacy and accuracy of evidence given in support of generalizations. Invent or discover relationships among data. Infer and then test inferences. — Barry Beyer

Step 1: You need to understand which criteria are important for the material you'll examine. Yet you don't need to actually list the criteria in the critique.

Step 2: Take one step at a time. You might first identify and discuss the thesis. Is it completely clear or is it ambiguous? How could it have been stated more clearly? Is the topic too broad or too vague? Is this something that can be proved, or is it an opinion?

Step 3: Repeat this for each area being evaluated. Describe the main ideas and evaluate them. If you are reading an article in science, pay close attention to the design of the experiment; whether the sample was large enough and representative of the entire population; whether there was an adequate control group; and how the data was collected, organized, and interpreted. In other areas, evaluate each piece of evidence.

Step 4: Pay careful attention to the reasoning and conclusions. Should the author have included other important information or looked at the information from other points of view? Could other conclusions be reached with this data?

Step 5: When writing the critique, summarize the paper in the introduction, use one or more paragraphs each to describe the thesis, the evidence, and the reasoning and conclusions. Conclude by summarizing the strengths and weaknesses in the paper. Rarely will you critique a paper that is either perfect or a total disaster.

The final strategy, journaling, can be used after studying

Throughout this book you have found exercises and questions for reflection. I've even recommended that you write your responses in a journal. Reflecting on your experiences and what you are learning is one of the most important strategies in this book.

Ronald Gross in an earlier book, *Peak Learning*, described what he called "Learning Logs." In a more recent book, *The Independent Scholar's Handbook*, he calls them Intellectual Journals. Both suggest using journals to write about what you are learning and thinking about.

I read *Peak Learning* about 25 years ago and I immediately began a habit I wished I had started earlier. With all significant books that I now read, I write the bibliography information, the date I read the book, and I take notes I can read again and again to remember the book. I also note the page numbers in case I want to find the information again – or quote it in a book. Some of the quotes in this book came from these notebooks. I sometimes refer to them as "my other brain," because they store so much important information where I can easily retrieve it.

I suggested keeping a Learning Journal in chapter 1. Now I want you to understand that this Learning Journal is more than a record of what you are learning; it is an effective strategy for learning even more.

STRATEGY *15.10*

JOURNALING TO LEARN

Step 1: At the end of each day, take time to write in your learning journal.

Step 2: Write the date. Describe what you learned that day.

Include what you learned in lectures or classes, what you learned in your reading, and what you learned while studying the material or thinking about it. You can also describe what you learned from other experiences or in conversations.

Step 3: In your reflections, describe what was most important, and why.

Sometime you can describe how these ideas are connected with other material you're learning or with questions you're asking.

Step 4: Describe what you *didn't* learn and what you still don't understand.

Some of what you don't understand, you can choose to dismiss. You might decide it isn't that important. When the material is important, plan what you will do next to better understand the material. Will you read your notes again, reread the chapter, read a different book, ask a classmate for help, talk to your professor, or what?

Journaling is like the last step, the step most often forgotten, in KWL: What did you learn? As you write what you learned, as you describe the connections and importance of what you learned, you are strengthening the neural connections in your brain, ensuring that you will remember this material longer and more completely.

Here, we have covered 10 ways of organizing information using words. This certainly does not mean that there are only 10 strategies. You can probably discover or create new and even more helpful strategies. You might make note of them here in your book.

Organizing information helps you in several ways. It helps you understand the material better, it helps you make connections between different ideas, it helps you be better prepared for tests, and it improves your memory. Extensive research has shown that organized information is learned as much as four times faster than the same information devoid of organization.[3]

In the next chapter, you will again be organizing information, but this time doing it visually. Using a combination of verbal and visual strategies is important. Verbal and visual information will be stored in different parts of your brain. Doing both can result in developing a more complete understanding as well as stronger, more lasting memories. It also makes it easier for you to retrieve your memories when needed.

> *Most of us spend very little time thinking about the purpose of our lives or seriously examining our beliefs and values. All too often, we simply repeat what we learned as children, incorporating the values and beliefs of the culture in which we grew up. Unfortunately, much of what we learn is inconsistent with our real nature, and includes contradictions, fallacies, and mistakes that often lead to cynicism, inner conflicts, and self-doubt. — Phil Nuernberger*

Questions for Reflection:

1. In which areas of verbal organization are you already most competent?

2. In which areas do you have the least experience?

3. Describe how verbal organization will help you learn.

4. What surprised you in this chapter? What was the most important thing you learned? How will you use what you learned?

16

Visual Organization — Ten Strategies

Just as cartography increased the speed and efficiency with which new lands and new people could be identified and connected, so too, do visual tools escalate the speed and efficiency with which an individual can identify new knowledge and connect it to what is already known.[1]

It is interesting to see cartography, the making of geographic maps, compared to concept maps, one of the visual tools referred to above, as both leading to new knowledge. In this chapter, you will find ten key visual tools. In addition to organizing information *verbally*, chapter 15, it is important to use strategies for organizing information *visually*. These strategies can be tools for thinking in new ways about the material.

Exercise: Visual Tools You Might Have Found Helpful

1. Are you familiar with Mind Maps or concept maps? What other visual tools are you familiar with? Which have you used and found helpful?

2. To jog your memory, what visual tools might you use in biology? In history? In statistics?

The history and value of visual tools

Tony Buzan introduced Mind Maps in the early 1970s.[2] This led to "graphic organizers" that were popular in the 1980s. Now we have a "third kind of visual tool, 'thinking-process' maps…based on facilitating well-defined thinking processes."[3]

Students who learn to use a variety of visual tools to describe, organize, analyze, and make connections might discover themselves thinking in new ways about the material. Some of these tools can be related to the verbal strategies in the previous chapter.

To answer the questions we began with, one visual tool often used in biology is the diagram, but there are certainly others like cycles and food webs. In history we use timelines and maps; in statistics we use tables and many kind of graphs.

Many of the visual tools in this chapter should be familiar; a few were developed just for this book. But don't stop with these. Create your own set of visual tools.

The ten visual strategies in this chapter include two strategies for organizing structure and content, one for organizing space, two for organizing time, and five for organizing relationships.

Organize structure and content with concept maps and branching charts

All the strategies in this and the previous chapter deal with structure and content, yet most also have another purpose. Concept maps and branching charts, however, are mainly used to show structure and content.

Concept maps are the best-known and probably the most helpful tool for organizing information visually. They can be used to show the structure of a short essay, a chapter, or an entire book. They can be used to plan an essay or a speech. I used a concept map to plan this book.

According to David Hyerle,

> *We use maps to find our way to new information, much like an evolving treasure map of the mind seeking new meaning in texts and other material…. Visual tools…enable all students to visually organize information, generate ideas and summaries of what they are reading and learning and transform information into active forms of knowledge.*[4]

STRATEGY *16.1*

CONCEPT MAPS

This strategy focuses on using a concept map to show the structure of a chapter.

Step 1: Identify the main idea or topic in the chapter. It might be the title.

Step 2: Write the topic near the center of the page inside a shape.

Most often the best shape will be a circle, oval, or rectangle, but you can use any shape you like or none at all. You can choose to use or not to use colors. I prefer to use colors only for maps or other visuals to be displayed.

Step 3: The main ideas or concepts are placed around the central topic.

In a chapter these may be the main headings. If there are more than five such headings, place those that seem related into groups. Again, these can be enclosed in a shape of your choice. Connect them to the main topic with a line.

Step 4: These ideas can be further subdivided as many times as you'd like.

A simple concept map may have only one level. A complex concept map may include many more. When doing concept maps by hand, I often carry them out to at least three or four levels. To see a more complex concept map, check the website. You will understand why it couldn't be shown on this small page.

Step 5: For the last level, it may be easier not to enclose the information in shapes.

With concept maps, though, there are no rules. Try different ways of organizing the information and choose the system that makes sense to you or works best for the information you are studying.

Step 6: If you're doing a concept map of a book, you might need a poster board.

You could place the title in the center, the main parts of the book as the second level, the chapters as the third levels, the main heading as a fourth level, subheadings as the fifth level, and perhaps important information at the sixth level. In chapter 19, on memory, you will read the story of a student who did something similar. I'd rather do a separate concept map for each chapter.

Step 7: Review your concept map by re-creating it.

For concept maps and all other visuals, it's best to start with a blank sheet of paper and attempt to redraw the map by memory. Compare your new work with the original to check what you missed or what you found confusing.

Chart 16.1 Simple Concept Map: Education

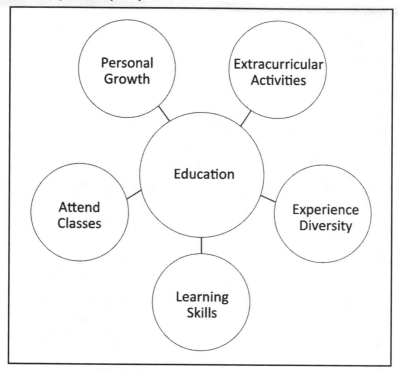

Chart 16.2 Complex Concept Map: Organizing Verbally

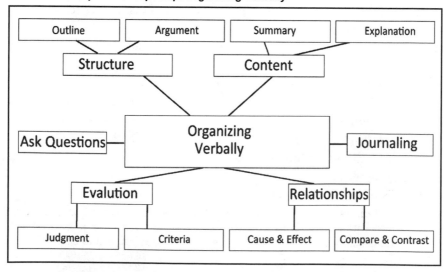

Branching charts

Two forms of branching charts are especially familiar. An organizational chart or hierarchy shows a company's president at the top level, the vice presidents and others reporting to the president at the second level, and their staff at third and perhaps fourth levels.

Another common branching chart is an upside down version of the organizational chart. In a family tree, your name might be at the bottom, possibly along with brothers and sisters. Above you in ascending levels are your parents, grandparents, great grandparents, and so on back into history.

Let's assume, however, that you choose to use a branching chart to organize the information in a chapter or in an article. Sometimes students like to use this form to create a concept map.

STRATEGY *16.2*

BRANCHING CHARTS

Step 1: Write the title or topic near the top of the page. Titles may be enclosed in a shape, or not. Placing the paper horizontally will often give you more space.

Step 2: Show the main ideas or categories on the next level down. For a chapter, these are your main headings.

Step 3: Continue, as in a concept map, to subdivide the content in further levels.

Chart 16. 3 Branching Chart of Basic Skills

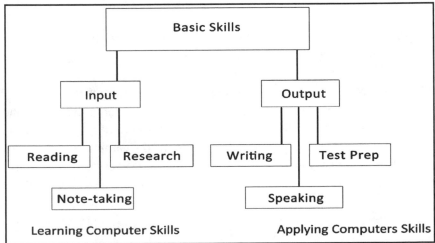

Chart 16.3 reminds us that, while they're not covered in the book, computer skills are an important part of a student's education. They are included under both input and output.

Visual strategies for organizing space

Diagrams organize space. All students should be familiar with diagrams, whether to show the planets in the Solar System, the parts of a cell, or the structure of the DNA molecule, so I have not included one here. You often copy and study a diagram from your textbook, but can also draw your own.

For organizing large spaces like a country or a state, we use maps. To see a simplified map of Africa, a major project, check the website **www. Choose-learning.com.**

For organizing more limited spaces, like a home, we can use blueprints to show the rooms, doors, windows, closets, and more. You could create a simplified chart of your dorm room to plan where to place the furniture.

This strategy shows a simplified campus map. Simplified maps are most helpful for freshmen or transfer students trying to find their way around campus or your new town.

STRATEGY 16.3

SIMPLIFIED MAPS

Step 1: Draw a rough outline of your campus.

Feel free to refer to an actual map (which you could download and enlarge), but don't try to use an exact outline.

Step 2: Divide your map into sections, preferably with straight lines.

Label the spaces. You might have areas for athletic fields, for classroom buildings divided by subject, or for dorms.

Step 3: On your map, show several important places on campus.

These might include the Administration Building, your dorm, the library, the bookstore, and buildings where you'll have classes.

It's actually easier to get a good overview of the campus when using a simplified map like this than by trying to memorize everything on a complete map.

Chart 16.4 Simplified Campus Map

Visitor Parking		Athletic Fields	Fraternities	
			Sororities	
Admin. Building	Dorms	Sciences	Humanities	Pond and Park
	Cafeteria	Classroom Buildings Business	Nursing	
Stores	Dorms	Student Union	Library	Faculty Parking	Student Parking

Visual strategies for organizing time

Flow charts are used extensively in business and manufacturing, but are rarely helpful when studying. The timeline and chain chart are more helpful for students.

The timeline is the most important tool to show how time might be organized. When you look at a timeline, check to see that time is divided into equal units. Some books or websites provide a list of dates and call it a timeline, but it's not—it's just a list.

Some books have what appears to be a timeline but, when you look more closely, the same amount of space may be used for 15 or 20 years of a person's childhood as well as for the 5 years that mark their greatest accomplishments. This is a misleading timeline.

STRATEGY 16.4

TIMELINES

Timelines are most helpful when studying history, including the history or science or other fields, but this strategy describes the creation of a simple personal timeline. The steps are the same. After the strategy you'll see two timelines, one for South Africa's great civil rights leader, Nelson Mandela, and one for a personal timeline of my own life.

Step 1: Draw a long horizontal line on a sheet of paper.

It is best if the paper is horizontal.

Step 2: For a personal timeline, start with your age.

If you are 18 years old, you need 18 *equal* spaces on the timeline (therefore, 19 lines.) You could also use 4 equal spaces, each representing 5 years.

For the chart of Nelson Mandela's life (shown in Chart 16.6), since he lived to be 95, you'd need 95 spaces if numbering with his age; or 96 spaces if using dates because the chart, like a life, usually starts and ends sometime during a year. Instead of using that many spaces, the timeline shows 11 spaces, each representing 10 years.

Step 3: Draw short vertical lines equal distances apart and label the lines from birth to your current age.

Step 4: Choose the main events or turning points in your life.

Estimate the location on the timeline and write events under the line. If many events were close in time, simply draw lines of different lengths below the line so you can continue listing events in order.

Step 5: Based on the turning point events, divide your life into several large sections.

Label each section in a meaningful and creative way.

Too many students group their first five years as preschool, the next six years as elementary school, then middle school, high school, college, and so on. This is a generic timeline; it's not really based on your life.

Step 6: A timeline can also be used for a novel.

You don't need to know precisely when an event takes place in its pages. Consider the sequence of events. You could simply divide the timeline by the chapters. When there are several main characters, you can use a separate timeline for each, possibly going down the page so you see important events in the life of one character in relation to events in another character's life.

Step 7: A complex timeline includes two or more related timelines. You might do one for the recent history of South Africa and compare events there with events in the life of Mandela.

You might do a timeline of the history of mathematics and another showing the same time period for the history of science. Such a timeline might reveal how certain discoveries in one area led to changes in the other area. A complex timeline can be found on the website, www.chooselearning.com.

Chart 16.5 Nelson Mandela Timeline

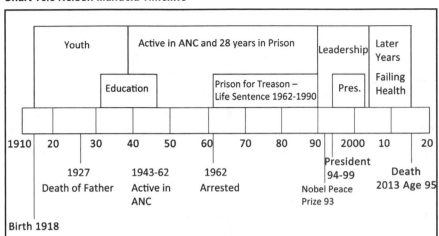

Notice that that some of these questions or turning points in the next table are key points in this book.

Chart 16.6 Judy Fishel Timeline with Questions and Turning Points

Identity	Happy Child	Eager Learner	Innovative Teacher	Inspired Writer
Age	0 10	20 30	40 50	60 70
Questions I asked	1. What will I be when I grow up? 2. Why do I forget most of what I am learning?	1. How can I get a great college education? 2. What is my role in Civil Rights Movement? 3. What is the purpose of life?	**1. How can I help students learn, understand, think?** 2. Why do students, even those making high grades, soon forget most of what they learn? 3. How can I prepare students for college?	1. How can I share what I've learned? 2. How can I help students learn more effectively? 3. How can I write more effectively?
Turning Points that changed my life	1. I was told I wasn't reaching my potential. 2. I decided **Learning is more important than grades**. 3. Advised to Question Everything.	1. Chose to sit in on extra classes in college. 2. Worked in labs with two Science Profs. 3. Married and children. 4. Eight years in Asia	1. Vice Principal at International School: Manila – doing teacher training. 2. Worked with teachers on learning strategies. 3. Went to great Workshops on teaching math, critical thinking, and brain-based teaching and learning.	1. Creating two websites on study skills. 2. Decision to write this book. 3. Reading the current research on learning. 4. Spending years creating this book.

STRATEGY *16.5*

CHAIN CHARTS

Chart 16.7 Simple Chain Chart: Creating a Time Management Chart

A chain chart involves sequential stages or steps. They can be drawn from left to right on a horizontal page or from top to bottom on a vertical one. For a simple sequence, a simple list of events is all you need. You might consider this a simple flowchart.

Step 1: Divide the information into several clear stages or steps.

Step 2: Draw shapes to represent the different stages, then label with the topic or event.

Step 3: Connect the stages with lines or arrows showing the direction from first to last.

Step 4: You might sometimes use a chain that branches. For example, if you did a chain showing what courses you need to take in biology, you might at some point make a decision to either continue as a pre-med student or become a biology teacher or, perhaps, a marine biologist.

A complex chain chart is a combination of a chain and a concept map. This is what I used as a visual image for this book.

Step 5: To create a complex chain chart, like the one in Chart 16.8, add lines to the sides showing the main ideas in each stage. This should be clear from the example.

The blank schedule

Add Courses

Meals, Sleep Work, Exercise

Study Hours

Flex-Time and Independent Study

Evaluate and Adjust Schedule

Chart 16.8 Complex Chain Chart: Straight A's Are Not Enough

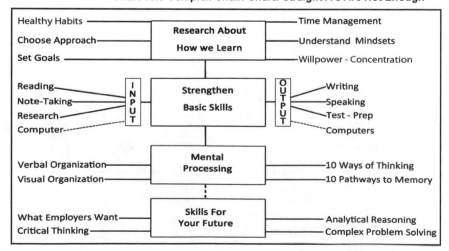

Visual strategies for showing relationships

This section includes the structural reading chart, cause and effect, compare and contrast, matrix, and web. It could also include cycles.

Structural reading charts

The structural reading chart is very similar to a timeline but, instead of organizing time, it organizes content and structure. It's included here because it requires an understanding of the timeline.

A structural reading chart is easy to create but not necessary when books or articles are clearly organized with section headings and subheadings. If this material is important, you can create the chart first, and then read the material. The chart will make it easier to see how the parts of the book are related. At other times, you can create the chart after you finish reading to help you organize the information. Studying the example will help you understand the strategy.

This is supposed to be one long chart. Imagine that the lower part of the chart is moved up and to the right so it connects with the upper section. The chapters will then read from 1-23.

Chart 16.9 Structural Reading Chart: Straight A's Are Not Enough

Book Intro	Prepare to Learn						Skills for Learning					
	Part 1: Research on Learning						Part 2: Strengthen Learning Skills					
Big Questions	Part 1 Intro	Approach, Goals, Time, Mindsets, Willpower					Part 2 Intro	Learning Input: Read, Notes, Research		Learning Output: Write, Speak, Test Prep		
Preface	1	2	3	4	5	6	7	8	9	10	11	12	13

A New Definition of Study Skills			Introduction to Advanced Skills			Conclusion
Part 3. Mental Processing Skills			Part 4: Skills for your Future			**BIG Answers to the BIG Questions**
Part 3 Intro	Organization Verbal and Visual	Think and Remember	Part 4 Intro	Critical Thinking, Analytical Reasoning and Problem Solving		
14	15	16	17	18	19	20	21	22	23

STRATEGY 16.6

STRUCTURAL READING CHART

Step 1: If the chapter is long, you might tape together two horizontal sheets.

Begin as you would with a timeline. Draw a long horizontal line through both sheets. The information below the line shows content. The information above the line shows organization, much like with timelines.

Step 2: Divide reading into sections.

In short articles, you could have a space for each paragraph. In chapters it's best to skim the chapter first and group the paragraphs in larger sections. Divide the horizontal line into enough spaces for each section. Write the topic and important information below the line.

Step 3: Identify the introduction and conclusion.

They might include an entire section or a small part of a section. Write these just above the line.

Step 4: Read your introduction and conclusion carefully.

They often provide clues to the structure of the chapter. The introduction, for example, might say, "In the chapter we will describe five cause of ...." If so, in addition to the introduction and conclusion, there should be five sections.

Step 5: Identify the main ideas.

Ask yourself what the author might have intended as the main ideas in each section. If you don't find clues, you'll need to organize the sections in a way that makes most sense to you. Label each section.

Step 6: Divide the space above the line and label to show the structure.

Read the entire book, chapter, or articles, looking for evidence of the structure and organization of ideas you've identified and for key content in each section.

Another example of a reading chart is shown on the website. It might make this easier to understand.

Another structural reading chart is the 3x3 or 4x4, first discussed in chapter 9 where it is used for preparing speaking notes. Here it can be used to show the topic and three main ideas, each with three sub-points. Obviously, the chart can be adapted to show different numbers of sub-points.

Chart 16.10 The 3x3

The topic, thesis, or argument			
1. First Main Idea	Sub-points		
2. Next Main Idea			
3. Third Main Idea			
Conclusion			

A completed example is shown on the website. This might help you understand.

Compare and contrast

Students are often asked to compare two or more items. This was described as a verbal strategy in the previous chapter. This section describes the visual version. One common image that's useful is the Venn diagram. If comparing cats and dogs, you'd list words describing both in the overlapping area, words that described only dogs on one side, and those describing only cats on the other side. You'd soon discover that there's not much room for writing in the overlapping area. The chart described here is more helpful.

STRATEGY *16.7*

COMPARE AND CONTRAST

The explanation of this chart type may be a bit confusing. Look at Chart 16.12 and it should be easier to understand.

Step 1: Draw a chart with four equal columns. Label the columns Categories, Item 1, Both, and Item 2.

The example below compares pigs and chickens, so the labels would be Categories, Pigs, Pigs & Chickens, and Chickens.

Chart 16.11 Compare and Contrast: Pigs and Chickens

CATEGORIES	PIGS	Pigs & Chickens	CHICKENS
Classification	Mammals	Vertebrates	Birds
Rel. to People		Domesticated	
Environment		Farms	
Main Use		Meat	
Secondary Uses	Skin/ Bristles		Eggs/Feathers
Sounds	Grunt Squeal		Clucking Cock-a-doodle-do
In Literature	Porky Pig Babe Wilbur		Little Red Hen Henny Penny Foghorn Leghorn
Anatomy	4 legs Hoofs Snout and teeth		2 legs Feet Bills, no teeth

Step 2: First describe significant ways in which the two are the same. Write the category in the first column and the way they're alike in the third column. Repeat until you have a good list of similarities.

Step 3: Describe how they're different. Again list the category but this time describe the two items separately.

Step 4: When preparing to write an essay question involving a comparison, you can use this chart as a quick outline. Begin the essay with ways they're the same. End by listing significant ways they're different.

Chart 16.12 Compare and Contrast: Washington and Lincoln

CATEGORIES	G. WASHINGTON	BOTH	A. LINCOLN
Historical Role		President of U.S.	
Terms as President		Two terms	
Memorials		Monuments on Mall. Cities named for them. Bills & coins show faces. On Mt. Rushmore	
Family	Wealthy		Poor
Education	Tutors – trained as surveyor		Self-taught
Presidential #	First president		16th president
Dates served	1789-1797		1861-1865
Party	None		Republican
Profession	Tobacco Farmer		Country lawyer
Major Speech	Farewell Address		Gettysburg Address

The matrix chart: an advanced compare and contrast chart

When comparing three items, you can often visualize the situation best with a Venn diagram of three overlapping circles. Even the compare and contrast chart would be hard to use. The matrix chart can be seen as a complex compare and contrast chart. While a matrix is often used to teach, I've never seen it described as a study strategy. Chart 16.14, showing classes of vertebrates, is an example of a simple matrix found in many biology books. It could be used to compare and contrast any two or more vertebrate groups.

My first use of a matrix as a study strategy was in an education class in college. The book had 50 chapters, each one discussing an important educator. I anticipated questions asking us to compare two or more educators who held different opinions on a particular issue, such as whether education should be only for children from wealthy families or for all children, whether students should study classics written in Latin or Greek, or whether it's better that they learn practical skills.

Chart 16.13 Matrix Showing Five Classes of Vertebrates

CATEGORY	FISH	AMPHIBIANS	REPTILES	BIRDS	MAMMALS
Class	Osteichthyes	Amphibia	Reptilia	Aves	Mammalia
Respiration	Pharyngeal gill slits	Skin/Gills when young Lungs as adult	Lungs	Lungs	Lungs
Blood Heart	Cold blooded 2 chambers	Cold blooded 3 chambers	Cold blooded 3 chambers	Warm blooded 4 chambers	Warm blooded 4 chambers
Surface	Scales, smooth or rough skin	Moist skin	Scaly skin Turtle shell	Feathers	Hair or fur
Fertilization Reproduction	External Moist eggs	External Moist eggs	Internal Leathery eggs	Internal Hard eggs with membrane	Internal Live birth
Appendages	Fins and tail	None or 4 legs	None or legs or flippers	2 legs 2 wings	Varied: arms, legs, bat wings, flippers
Other	Swim bladder	Metamorphosis	Some live births	Care for young	Placenta, milk

While other students started on page one, reading in the usual way, I realized I could read the book dozens of times but would never remember which educator said what. So I used a matrix.

STRATEGY 16.14

MATRIX CHART

Step 1: List the items being compared. Create a matrix with that number of columns plus one. Label the first column "categories." Label the other columns with the items being compared.

For my chart, I had one column for each of the 50 educators. I had to tape together many sheets of paper for this large a chart.

Step 2: Choose the categories for comparison and list them down the first column.

I listed the topics that were discussed by the educators. In this book there were about 40 different topics discussed so there were 40 topics listed along the left side of the chart.

Step 3: Fill in one column at a time.

With the 50 educators, I concentrated on the topics they found most important. I skimmed each chapter, finding the issues each person mentioned and the positions they took. I wrote this information under the educator's name in the row of the appropriate topic. This left most spaces blank since the short chapters only mentioned positions on one to three issues. If the educator in the first chapter supported classical education, I'd write "classic" in the appropriate row with other information on his main ideas

Step 4: Now, after entering information vertically, study the information horizontally. You might use colored markers to show similarities. Anticipate what questions you might be asked on a test.

I used a red marker to circle topics where only one educator had an opinion on a particular issue. My reasoning was that if we were asked about these people in our exam, they wouldn't be compared to any of the others. They would make good multiple choice or short-answer questions.

If there were only two educators speaking on one issue and they held radically different views, I highlighted them with the same color marker. If there were many educators speaking on one issue, I looked for the two with the strongest opinions on each side. For these educators, I anticipated essay questions asking us to compare their positions on that topic. I could almost picture the heated debates held on these issues.

Just skimming the chapters and filling in the blanks were more helpful than reading. Looking for the areas of the greatest contrast helped me prepare for the test. And yes, I definitely made the highest grade.

This strategy could also be done as a group. Each student could study a small number of chapters and fill in the information. Together, the students might discuss the comparisons and what kinds of test questions they anticipated.

This strategy should seem familiar. As an example of having a plan for every course in chapter 3, I described my matrix for a class on Invertebrate Zoology. There, the categories down the left side were the list of biological systems. Across the top were the 101 invertebrates we studied. While you may not have many situations where you'd use this strategy, when you *do* need to compare a large number of items, the matrix can be incredibly helpful.

Cause and Effect

Generally you'll be asked to describe either the causes or the effects. This topic was also described in chapter 15, on verbal strategies. Creating the chart can help you organize your ideas and prepare you to write an essay.

STRATEGY *16.9*

CAUSE AND EFFECT

Step 1: Write the event or problem. In my charts I placed the problem in a rectangle.

Step 2: If showing the causes, list the causes to the left of the problem, with lines or arrows pointing *to* the problem. If listing the effects, list these to the right of the problem with lines or arrows pointing *away from* the problem.

Step 3: Are there any long-term causes that possibly led to the main causes? Are there both short-term and long-term effects? Is it possible the long-term effects were caused by the short-term effects?

Step 4: If there are long-term causes or effects you want to include, write them farther away from the event or problem. If they led to one or several of the other causes or effects, indicate this with lines or arrows. If they weren't related to any of these, you could use a longer line or arrow, pointed to or from the actual event or problem.

Chart 16.14 Cause and Effect: Causes of Failing a Midterm Exam

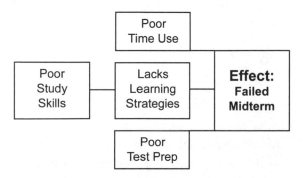

In this chart, you see the causes listed to the left of the problem. Poor study skills could be described as the root of the three main problems.

Chart 16.15 Cause and Effect: Effects of Failing a Midterm

```
                        ┌─────────────┐
                        │  Improved   │
                        │ Study Skills│
                        └─────────────┘
┌──────────┐            ┌─────────────┐       ┌──────────────┐
│ Causes:  │            │    Time     │       │ Higher Grades│
│ Failed   ├────────────┤ Management  ├───────┤ in ALL classes│
│ Midterm  │            │  Schedule   │       │ Less Anxiety │
└──────────┘            └─────────────┘       └──────────────┘
                        ┌─────────────┐
                        │ Better Test │
                        │ Preparation │
                        └─────────────┘
```

In this chart, you can see the effects to the right of the problem or event. Here, the long-term effect is that Peter made higher grades in all his classes and experienced less anxiety. Yes, these are very simple examples, but when you need to explore the causes or effects of an event or problem, you can take this idea and expand it to include far more complex causes or effects.

Webbing and networking

You sometimes see cycles in science books. When studying ecology, you also sometimes see food webs. There are many other uses for webs. One that is especially important to begin working on while you're in college shows networking.

STRATEGY 16.10

CREATE A NETWORKING WEB

Step 1: State the purpose for your networking.

Is it for getting references for an internship, for graduate school or landing a job, for finding a new apartment after you graduate, for getting advice for your research, for help starting your own business, or for something else? Writers look for contacts who have influence with literary agents or publishers, world travelers look for contacts in various countries, and politicians look for contacts with money to help fund their campaign.

Step 2: List your sources of contacts.

On Chart 16.16, you will see that Ellie started with her family, people she has worked for, her classmates, and her professors.

Step 3: While these contacts may be helpful in many ways, begin by setting a goal. Ellie is looking for a summer job related to biology.

Step 4: Speak to each main contact. Tell them about your goal and ask if they know someone who might help you.

Step 5: Contact each of these people and ask for their help or advice. Send a thank-you note and maintain contact.

Step 6: You might use social networking to form or maintain a friendship with your contacts. This means no embarassing pictures on Facebook.

Chart 16.16 Building a Networking Web
The names in bold/italics show those who offered Ellie a job.

			Boss's Sister	***Friend's Wife***			
			Joe's Boss	Boss's Friend			
			Uncle Joe	Joe's Brother			***Dr. Y***
	John's Friend		Dad		Dr. A	Dr. W	Dr. X
	John		Family		Dr. B		
Mrs. P	Boss	Work	Ellie	Professors	Dr. C	Mrs. F	Mr. G
	Jenny		Students		Dr. D		
	Jenny's Dad		Wally		Dr. E		
		Jerry	Beth	Erica			
		Jerry's Cousin		Erica's Dad			
	Mom's Boss	Cousin's Mom		Dad's Boss	***Boss's Wife***		

This chart was created to fit into this page. With a larger sheet of paper, you could certainly carry it out to many additional levels. There is no need to enclose names in rectangles as shown here. You could easily connect names with lines or simple arrows. Creating a chart like this can help you focus your attention on networking opportunities and on areas for future networking.

Using Visual Tools

Do not try to use all these visual tools all at once. Choose one or two to begin with. Use those until you can do them easily. Then add another visual tool as needed.

What's most important is that you try to use at least one verbal tool and at least one visual tool to study the same information. The combination makes it easier to store ideas in different parts of your brain. According to some research, "Studies of memory and brain processes indicate that people's memories of images are far superior compared with people's memory of words."[5]

This might not be true for all of us, but I have no doubt that it's true for most people. Even if you are one of the few people who think the visual strategies look like a waste of time, you should at least try them. You might be surprised.

To end this chapter, I want to mention the books by Dan Roam, author of *The Back of the Napkin* and *Unfolding the Napkin*. He uses a different kind of visuals, not as study methods, but as ways to solve problems and sell ideas with pictures. You might find these interesting. Roam concludes:

> *Thinking in pictures triggers more centers throughout the brain—and makes more connections across our brain—than thinking in words alone. Thinking simultaneously in words and pictures activates our whole brain—something that simply does not happen when we rely on words alone.*[6]

Questions for Reflection:

1. As you read this chapter, did you pause to try using one of the visual strategies?

2. Think about the verbal and visual versions of the same strategies. Would you find one more helpful than another? If so, why? Describe how the thinking required for each of these would differ.

3. When would you find it most helpful to use one of the verbal strategies? When would you find it most helpful to use one of the visual strategies?

4. What surprised you in this chapter? What was the most important thing you learned? How will you use what you learned?

17

Ways of Thinking — Ten Strategies

Judgment and decision making—the skills of rational thought—are at least as important as the attributes that are assessed on IQ tests. Like intelligence, rational thinking skills relate to goal achievement in the real world. Yet we fail to teach them in schools or to focus on them as a society.[1]

You often hear people say, "I was thinking about you." Or "I think I'll have chocolate ice cream." Or "Which teacher do you think is the best?" Most of the time we use the word "think" when discussing an opinion, hope, desire, or memory. These take little mental effort; serious *thinking requires hard work*.

When do you really take time to think? What do you think about? What kind of thinking do you do? Some of us would say we almost never think. Others would say we think nearly all the time. This statement from William Hughes and Jonathan Lavery (2005) expresses one view:

Virtually every conscious human activity involves reasoning. We reason whenever we solve problems, make decisions, assess character, explain events, write poems, balance checkbooks, predict elections, make discoveries, interpret works of art or repair carburetors. We reason about everything from the meaning of life to what we have for dinner.

Instead of grouping together such diverse ways of thinking, we might consider "thinking" as a continuum from the more trivial everyday thinking, such as what we'll have for dinner, to a more conscious level of thinking, like making decisions, all the way to the deep, intentional thinking that would include choosing your major or deciding what you want to do with your life. This kind of thinking starts with a decision to think deeply. It takes time to look seriously at the alternatives and struggle to find answers. It takes time to evaluate our own thinking. This kind of thinking is hard work but the benefits can be well worth the effort.

Exercise: Evaluate Your Thinking

The questions in this exercise are adapted from a book by Keith Stanovich, *What Intelligence Tests Miss*. They are designed to clarify some of the most common problems in thinking. I must warn you to be careful. These questions are often missed by intelligent people. I must admit that I missed quite a few.

1. Estimate: Make an effort to give answers you are *at least 90% sure are correct.*
    A. The age of Martin Luther King, Jr. when he died was between ___ and ___ years.
    B. The number of books in the Old Testament is from ___ to ___ books.
    C. The birth date of Wolfgang Amadeus Mozart is between the years, ___ and ___.
    D. The gestation period (pregnancy) of the Asian elephant is from ___ to ___ days.
    E. The deepest known point in the oceans is between ___ and ___ feet.

2. "A bat and ball cost $1.10 in total. The bat costs $1 more than the ball. How much does the ball cost?" Are you sure?

3. "Jack is looking at Anne. Anne is looking at George. Jack is married but George is not. Is a married person looking at an unmarried person?" Explain.
    Answers: A. Yes B. No C. Cannot be determined. Are you sure?

4. Which would be the worst disaster in a town of 10,000 people? Are you sure?
    A. A disease that kills 24.14% of the population.
    B. A disease that kills 1,286 people.

Organizing ways of thinking

To understand what it means to think, it helps to be familiar with different ways of thinking. What Stanovich describes in his book as "rational thinking" provides an interesting contrast to this book's ten ways of thinking.

Stanovich and others ask why smart people do stupid things. While many people equate intelligence with "good thinking," he suggests that intelligence is only a small part of "good thinking." Other areas of "rational thinking" include rational beliefs and behavior; intellectual curiosity; decision-making; using the scientific method; using mathematical thinking, including probability, statistics, and problem-solving; and critical thinking. All of these are in my list of ten ways of thinking.

Stanovich concludes that what is measured by intelligence tests has very little to do with our success in school, on the job, or in our personal lives. The successful person is a rational thinker who has mastered and regularly uses all kinds of thinking skills.

Many common answers to the questions in the exercise are not rational.

Answers to the Exercise

---

    a. Martin Luther King Jr. was 39.
    b. The books in the Old Testament? 39.
    c. Mozart was born in 1756.
    d. Elephant gestation is 645 days.
    e. The deepest part of the ocean is 36,198 feet.

1. If you were really 90% sure, you would miss only one out of 10. With the five questions I included in the first section, that might mean one close miss. Most people miss several questions. Our problem here is *overconfidence.*

    One example of overconfidence involves believing you can complete a project or paper in a short time, when it actually will take much longer. Overconfident people sometimes take risks, driving too fast in poor weather, making poor decisions in the stock market, and making errors in diagnosing and treating their own health problems. We must learn to be both confident and realistic.

2. Most people are sure the ball costs 10 cents. The correct answer is that the ball costs only 5 cents. If the price of the ball was 10 cents, the bat, costing a dollar more, would cost $1.10; together they would cost $1.20. Did you check your work?

This is another problem that is caused by lazy thinking and overconfidence. When questions look easy, we may not check the answers. Did my warning convince you to check yours?

3. Over 80 percent choose answer C, "Cannot be determined," but this is not true. Did you try to work it out? The problem requires two simple steps. We know Jack is married and George is not, but we don't know if Anne is married or not. This does not mean we cannot continue to solve the problem. It means we need to consider both possibilities. If Anne *is* married the answer is "Yes" because she would be looking at George, who is unmarried. If Anne is *not* married, the answer is still "Yes" because Jack, who is married, would be looking at Anne. This shows another example of lazy thinking.

4. With the disease, most people choose B. either because the number 1,286 is larger than the number in 24.24% or because the mention of actual people is more vivid than statistics. Either way, they are wrong. And it wasn't necessary to get out your calculator. 24.24% is close to 25%. One half of 10,000 would be 5,000, so one fourth of 10,000 would be 2,500, or roughly twice as many people as in the more popular choice.

Similar thinking is observed when charities ask for donations. When charities describe the millions of people who are starving to death or who die because they lack simple medicines, they don't collect as much money as when they display a photo of one appealing child who is clearly very hungry or sick, or both. Again, the reason is believed to be that the sick child whose picture you see is more vivid than a mere number. I would suggest another explanation: Millions of hungry people seem so overwhelming that there seems to be no way I could make a difference in their lives; yet I *can* make a difference for this one hungry little girl.

If you want to learn more about thinking problems like these, I recommend Stanovich's book. You will learn many practical ways of improving your thinking.[2]

Ways of thinking are closely interwoven. Some people refer to all of them as "critical thinking," though students are often asked by professors to use a specific type of thinking. They might ask students to analyze a paper, summarize (synthesize) the chapter, evaluate a method, or use critical thinking. Because these skills are closely related, we will start by understanding each one separately but, eventually, good thinkers use a combination of thinking skills.

When you were younger, you learned spelling, handwriting, and grammar separately but, as with thinking skills, you now use them together. In fact, we use thinking and many other learning skills together.

The ways of thinking resemble the verbal and visual ways of organizing information. To organize information in a summary, you must look at the big picture or synthesis. To judge a movie, you use evaluation. You really can't organize information without thinking about it. Likewise, you cannot think without having something to think about.

What are the 10 ways of thinking?

As I explored different ways of thinking, I came up with the number ten. I don't claim that ten is the correct number. I am certain other people, if asked to list ways of thinking, would come up with a variety of numbers and categories. But, since organizing ways of thinking makes it easier to develop useful strategies, we'll begin with my list of ten.

Because it's difficult to remember a list of ten items, the ways of thinking are grouped in five pairs:

- Scientific and Mathematical Thinking
- Analysis and Synthesis
- Critical and Creative Thinking
- Decision Making and Evaluation
- Problem Solving and Strategic Thinking

According to Sir William Bragg, a Nobel Prize Winner for physics,

> *The important thing in science is not so much to obtain new facts as to discover new ways of thinking about them.*

The same thing could be said about all other subjects.

Scientific thinking

Scientific thinking and mathematical thinking are closely related to their subject areas. You could also add thinking in other fields, such as historical, geographical, literary, artistic, medical, legal, philosophical, or business ways of thinking.

My first image of scientific thinking would be the scientific method I learned in seventh grade: Observation, Hypothesis, Experiment, Data Collection, and Conclusion. Our science book described this as *the* scientific method. As I got older, I began to notice that experiments we did in class and those we read about didn't all follow this method.

> *There simply is no fixed set of steps that scientists always follow, no one path that leads them unerringly to scientific knowledge. There are, however, certain features of science that give it a distinctive character as a mode of inquiry. Although those features are especially characteristic of the work of professional scientists, everyone can exercise them in thinking scientifically about many matters of interest in everyday life.*[3]

STRATEGY 17.1

SCIENTIFIC THINKING

Step 1: Learn to observe. Observe nature, business trends, and human behavior.

Step 2: Ask questions about what you observe.

Step 3: Start with an open mind that is free of bias or prejudice. Don't simply look for proof that your own ideas are correct.

Step 4: Collect evidence. Look for factual information from reliable sources.

Step 5: Consider information from different points of view.

Step 6: Create a hypothesis about what you observed.

Step 7: Evaluate the evidence for and against your answers.

Step 8: Sometimes you can actually prove your hypothesis.

Most of the time, you will find evidence to support your hypothesis, or another one, without actually proving it true or false.

Mathematical thinking

Many students who make excellent grades in math classes have never experienced mathematical thinking. Solving problems without discovering your own strategies isn't likely to involve real mathematical thinking. I'll share two examples I used with students from fourth grade through high school seniors.

Problem 1: One farmer raises only pigs and chickens. There are 18 animal heads and 50 animal legs. How many pigs and how many chickens are on the farm? There are at least three mathematical ways of solving the problem. Give it a try. Can you find another method? How could a fourth grader solve it?

Problem 2: In an even greater problem, assume that you start with one penny and double it every day for 100 days. You don't need to do the work. Without calculating the answer and without calculating it on a computer, look for a pattern that will allow you to calculate the total amount of money you'd have after 100 days. If you give up, the answers are on the website www.choose-learning.com. A seventh grader discovered this method and taught me how to do it.

Most students are frustrated by such problems because no one taught them methods for solving them. But, when they create a method on their own and discover a pattern, they get excited. Following directions to solve problems can be boring; *thinking mathematically is exciting.*

STRATEGY 17.2

MATHEMATICAL THINKING

Step 1: Be aware of numerical data around you. Observe numbers, sizes, shapes, angles, speed, and other relationships.

Step 2: Look for patterns. For example, you might have looked into a kaleidoscope and noticed the triangles. You might even count the triangles.

Step 3: Try to explain the patterns you observe. Can you tell by the patterns in the kaleidoscope how many mirrors are inside and at what angles?

Step 4: Test your hypothesis (sounds like science, doesn't it?). For kaleidoscope questions, you might take small mirrors and test what you see with mirrors at different angles.

Step 5: Sometimes you'll be able to reach a conclusion. Yes, if you count the number of images in a simple kaleidoscope, you *can* tell the number of degrees in the angle of the mirrors.[4] If you're stumped, the secrets are on the website.

Analysis

You might know the word "analysis" in other contexts. A chemical analysis uses certain procedures to identify the substances in an unknown sample. A psychiatric analysis looks for experiences in your past that might cause problems now. A student may be asked to analyze a novel, poem, scientific paper, argument, or other written material. You might also analyze math problems, business situations, or decisions. Analysis basically means dividing material into its parts and then describing them individually in order to make sense of the whole.

STRATEGY 17.3

ANALYSIS

Let's assume you are analyzing a short article.

Step 1: Divide the article into parts and identify the main ideas.

Step 2: Examine each of the individual parts. What's the purpose or function of each?

Step 3: Describe how the parts are structured or related.

Step 4: Describe what you've learned, your conclusion. Describe your reasoning.

Synthesis

Many people are quite clear about synthetic materials: They are manufactured materials such as polyester. To a chemist, "synthesis" means combining two or more substances to make something new. But synthesis as a way of thinking may not be as clear.

Synthesis simply means making something or putting parts together to create something new. We might describe synthesis as seeing "the big picture." For students, synthesis means taking all the parts— everything they know about a subject or topic—fitting the pieces together to understand it in a new way. Writing an essay or research paper is a good example of synthesis. We'll use a research paper in the strategy.

STRATEGY 17.4

SYNTHESIS

Step 1: Collect all the data you need on the topic.

Step 2: Organize the data in several different ways.

Step 3: Choose the method of organizing the information that appears to give you the best view of the big picture or the most complete understanding.

Step 4: A statement of the big picture will be your thesis. You can then support your thesis with evidence from the data.

Critical thinking

To some people, the word "critical" is related to "criticism" and therefore seems to be negative. Actually, critical thinking means evaluating thinking—yours or someone else's. Critical reading involves evaluating what you read. Critical writing can mean writing a critique, preparing an evaluation of someone else's writing, or thinking critically as you write. Critical listening means evaluating what you hear.

The term "critical thinking" is often used to describe a combination of all these, and sometimes more as well. Since critical thinking is discussed at length in chapter 20, it's covered only briefly here. But, because you must always have something to think about, we'll assume you're reading an article.

STRATEGY 17.5

CRITICAL THINKING

Step 1: Evaluate the sources and the person who wrote the article.

Are they reliable? Is the writer known as an expert in the field? Evaluate the sources used as evidence. If this is a scientific article, you should also evaluate the methods used.

Step 2: Evaluate the statements.

Are they clear or ambiguous? Do they express facts or opinions? Do they make it clear whether a statement is a fact or opinion? Do they make unwarranted generalizations such as *everyone, always,* or *never*?

Step 3: Evaluate the fairness of the positions the author holds.

Is there any bias? Do the positions reflect only one point of view or do they take the opposing points of view into consideration?

Step 4: Evaluate the data.

Are they accurate and precise? Is the evidence relevant and adequate?

Step 5: Evaluate the reasoning. Is the reasoning logical?

You must begin by evaluating the paper step by step. Eventually, you will find yourself doing this automatically, focusing mainly on areas with problems.

Creative thinking

> *Why does education inhibit creativity?... In school you are taught to define, label, and segregate what you are learning into separate categories. — Michael Michalko[5]*

We often recognize that, while children are usually creative, as the years pass they become less creative. Sometime this is explained as a result of their fear of failing or of being laughed at for having crazy ideas. Michalko, quoted above, has an interesting new explanation. He suggests that *schools* are the problem. Instead of praising creative answers to questions, teachers often seem to want only the one right answer. In college courses, too, creativity may not appear to be valued—but think again.

The most exciting new areas of scientific research are the result of asking creative new questions and suggesting hypotheses no one else has considered. In any essay or research paper, teachers look for original approaches or ideas. In business, in engineering, in almost every area, creative ideas lead to new procedures and products.

> *Creativity is the quality that enables us to generate novel approaches to situations and to discover new and improved solutions to problems.*[6]

STRATEGY 17.6

CREATIVE THINKING

Here, as our example, we'll consider a business looking for an improved or new product.

Step 1: Start with the facts. Understand the situation.

Study the problems with our current products. Why aren't customers buying them? Do research if necessary to understand the problems.

Step 2: You might find ways to improve current products or find new uses for them.

You might develop improved or totally new products. Brainstorm. List many ideas. When you run out of ideas that seem to make sense, add ideas that seem crazy, more like a fantasy, and some that are completely impossible.

Step 3: Take ideas suggested by others and find ways to combine them.

Consider the opposites. Consider changing the sizes, the materials, the shapes, or the purposes.

Step 4: Never criticize ideas, whether your own ideas or those suggested by others.

Even the wildest ideas may lead to a new idea that will work and produce results and profits.

Step 5: Take a break now and then.

Let the ideas incubate, blend, or simply bounce around in your brain. Don't rush to choose the best suggestion. This is the most important step.

Step 6: Look around.

Imagine a variety of objects or activities as clues to an innovative answer. The best answers may come when you least expect them, like while lying in bed for a time before getting up, while taking a shower, while doodling with nothing on your mind, or while watching children at play.

Step 7: Narrow down the answers.

Choose those that seem most exciting, most creative, and most interesting. Ask how they might be applied.

Step 8: Choose the best idea and try it.

If it doesn't work out, try something else. Keep testing ideas until you find one that works.

The most important step in creative thinking is often ignored. It's the incubation period. Only when you learn to use this time effectively, when you allow the ideas to incubate, will you be likely to come up with the most creative and productive ideas.

Think about incubation. It often involves a bird sitting on eggs to keep them warm. Eventually, the eggs begin to crack and a baby bird is hatched. Our early ideas are like those eggs. They aren't quite what we want but, when allowed to develop slowly, they might hatch an exciting new idea.

Another metaphor I like is taking time for ideas to percolate. Imagine starting with coffee grounds. They might smell good but they aren't good to eat or drink. Add water and they're even worse: You have soggy coffee grounds. But just let the water boil and pour back through those grounds and something totally new is created. You have a steaming cup of hot coffee.

This is why you take that break. It isn't because you need to rest. Rather, it gives you time to allow the brainstormed ideas to be transformed into wonderful new ideas.

Taking time to incubate ideas is also helpful when writing a paper or for decisions like choosing a major.

Creativity, as has been said, consists largely of rearranging what we know to find out what we do not know. Hence, to think creatively, we must be able to look afresh at what we normally take for granted. — George Kneller

Decision making

> *It's actually very surprising how little we think about the quality of our decision-making and how we could improve it. How absent decision-making classes are from educational curricula. How little we think about how it is we think. — Noreena Hertz[7]*

We all make decisions. You decide to have a salad rather than a sandwich for lunch. You decide to see one movie rather than another. You decide to learn French instead of Spanish. But most of these events don't involve serious decision-making. They are simple choices. Little thinking is involved. Certainly, there's a place for simple choices like these, but too many people make *serious* choices with little more thought than what to eat for lunch.

STRATEGY 17.7

DECISION-MAKING

Step 1: State the question clearly.

Are you deciding to take Spanish or not take a language at all, or are you making a choice between Spanish and French? Are you deciding if you want to get married or if this is the person you really want to marry?

Step 2: List all the alternatives.

Even the question "Should I marry this person?" has more than two alternatives. They include "yes," "no," "we need to know each other better before making this decision," or "maybe we could just live together." For many questions such as choosing your major, there are dozens of alternatives. Sometimes we need to learn more about the alternatives before we make a decision. Before you decide to get married, it would be helpful to learn more about yourself as well as more about the person you might marry.

Step 3: For each alternative you consider, list the possible consequences.

You might also list pros and cons for the most likely choices.

Step 4: Consider your goals, beliefs, and values.

Consider what advice your parents or guardians would offer. You don't need to do what they'd want, but you should certainly consider it. Think of others you respect and what advice they'd give you. For a serious decision, you might actually ask their advice!

When choosing a major, you might think about how your choice relates to your long-term goals and whether you want to spend many years of your life working in that field. Will you enjoy it? Will you make enough money to live on? You might also consider which courses are required. Some biology majors change their plans when they realize they must take calculus and organic chemistry.

Step 5: None of the previous steps will make the decision for you.

Just because you can think of more pros than cons doesn't mean that alternative is the best. Some factors are more significant than others. In the end, after considering all the relevant information and arguments, you still must make the decision, yourself—but now it will be a well-informed decision.

Evaluation

Decision-making and evaluation are similar. Decision-making is about choosing the best thing to do. Evaluation is about deciding what you like. The word "evaluation" is based on the word "values." We make our values clear by identifying criteria to use in evaluation.

Food critics might begin by using their own criteria, perhaps based on the presentation and taste of the food, as well as the service and the décor of the restaurant. But, even then, they make a judgment about taste and presentation of the food. They still end up making a judgment based on what they liked.

Your professors probably wish they had well-defined criteria to use when grading your essays, your creative writing, or your poetry. Even if all professors used the same, well-written criteria, they would still interpret them differently. They must use their best judgment. They give the highest grades to what they feel is the best.

When choosing a college, choosing a major, or deciding on a person to marry, no matter how many criteria you set, no matter how many alternatives you list, no matter what the consequences might be, you will still make a judgment based, at least in part, on intuition—on how you feel about the alternatives.

Strategy 17.8

Evaluation

Step 1: Define your criteria.

Some may be fairly objective. Others, like "beauty," are subjective. The food critic might look at her watch to see how long it takes to be served, but can't objectively measure how beautifully the food is arranged or how delicious it tastes.

Step 2: Prioritize your criteria. Which are most important? Consider giving each criterion a weight or number of points.

Step 3: Test your criteria and point system.

Use them to evaluate several examples. Are you satisfied that, with your criteria, you're identifying the best examples?

Step 4: When the evaluations are important, work with a team.

Consider the staff whose task it is to read and evaluate college applications. One individual might make the decisions to reject applicants who are obviously not qualified, or to immediately accept those who are clearly among the best.

But, for that large number of applicants who meet the qualifications, a team often works together to discuss reasons for and against accepting each of these students. Working as a team means relying on the judgments of many people rather than those of a single person. It's not an easy job to make decisions that will make such a huge difference in the lives of those students.

Problem solving

This thinking skill is not about solving math problems; it's about solving problems in your own life, in your business, in your family, in your neighborhood or in the world. Again, this is an important area and will be discussed at length in the next part of the book. Here, I will give only one example at the end of the strategy. The example describes a very complex well-known problem.

STRATEGY *17.9*

PROBLEM SOLVING

Step 1: State the problem clearly.

This is often more difficult than you might imagine. It's important to distinguish the situation—that which cannot be changed—from the problem, where change is possible.

Step 2: Ask why this problem exists.

Is there a deeper problem that's the cause of the more obvious problem? Sometimes, you need to ask "why" several times to find the actual root of the problem.

Step 3: When you're clear on the problem, brainstorm possible solutions.

Step 4: Choose the best solution and create a plan for implementation.

Implementation is described in the 10th and last way of thinking: Strategic Thinking.

This example deals with a very complex problem that many people have tried to solve.

The Problem: Children in economically deprived areas often do poorly in school. Many eventually drop out before high school graduation.

The Root Problem: This problem has been studied intensely. One explanation is that parents who never got much education don't encourage their children to do better in school. But the fact that the parents never got an education is the situation. It cannot be changed. The fact that they don't encourage their children to do better in school *can* be changed.

If this problem had only one cause, a solution would already have been found and implemented. But this, like many complex problems, has many different causes. Because many parents don't read to children, the children aren't familiar with books. Because many parents don't talk as much to their children, some children enter school without knowing the alphabet, numbers, the names of common animals, and more. Because the children are often hungry, they have problems paying attention in class. We could list dozens of other reasons why these children do poorly in school.

Brainstorm Possible Solutions and Implement Your Plans: The government and many organizations and individuals have done this, and have come up with a variety of solutions. Head Start programs were begun to help children start learning earlier in life. Free lunch programs and summer feeding programs were set up to see that these children get more food and healthier food. In some places, every new mother goes home from the hospital having learned how important it is to read to her children. Often they're given a book to take with them. In other places, children are sent free, age-appropriate books for their first three to six years. We must continue to identify further parts of the problem and develop new programs to make improvements in those areas.

Strategic thinking

When you set goals, it's important to create a plan for reaching them. When you identify a problem and choose a solution, you need a detailed plan for implementing that solution. These plans involve strategic thinking.

STRATEGY *17.10*

STRATEGIC THINKING

Step 1: State your goal or solution clearly.

For our example, we'll consider a campus organization that decided to do a work project at an orphanage in Haiti.

Step 2: Create a plan.

The members worked on the details. Students in this organization decided to send 20 students to Haiti over spring break to make repairs to the orphanage, paint the children's classrooms and, since they learned that what the children want most are shoes and soccer balls, they'd bring these with them. The main problem would be raising $20,000 to pay for the trip. They needed a strategy to raise that much money.

Step 3: Brainstorm a list of possible strategies.

The students brainstormed ways to raise the money. Out of the list of over 30 suggestions they chose 5 strategies:

1. Hold a huge yard sale, renting spaces for $20 each. Their goal is to rent 100 spaces. This would raise $2,000. For those members that wanted to do a bake sale, they could sell baked goods. Others could sell cold drinks and other snacks.

2. They'd have a "Rent-a-Student" weekend. People on campus or in town could rent a student to do odd jobs for $20 an hour. With 40 members in the organization, if each one worked for 10 hours, they'd earn $8,000 total.

3. They could visit local churches and other places of worship and describe the work they planned to do. They could promise to return to report what they had accomplished. If they visited 50 congregations and if each congregation averaged $100 in donations, they'd raise $5,000.

4. This would give them a total of only $15,000. They finally calculated that if the 20 students who were going could each raise $250, this would add the necessary $5,000. These students could easily find 25 friends or family members to each donate $10.

5. To get shoes to take to the children, they'd ask for donations of gently used children's shoes. For the soccer balls, they'd ask people who hired them to do a job if they had a few items to donate to the giant yard sales. They could use this extra money to buy soccer balls.

Step 4: For each strategy, you plan to use, you must develop a detailed plan—sometimes called tactics.

Each of the 40 members of the organization chose one of the five strategies to work on. They listed materials they'd need, created a schedule, planned publicity, assigned jobs for the actual events, and divided up the work leading to the event.

To be able to make presentations at 50 churches, temples, or mosques, they could divide the group into 10 groups of 4 students. The groups would visit 10 places of worship each Saturday or Sunday for five weeks. Several students would need to start contacting the institutions. They'd likely need a list of at least 100 places of worship to get 50 to agree.

Someone else in that group would plan transportation, making sure that at least one person in each group had access to a car. Another person would write thank-you notes. Each of the groups had similar plans to make.

Step 5: Plan the schedule and assignments.

After students worked on individual plans, they needed to coordinate the plans, starting with a calendar. It wouldn't be a good idea to do "Rent-a-Student" and the giant yard sale on the same weekend. Doing "Rent-a-Student" earlier allowed students to ask for items they could sell themselves at the sale. They could also ask about children's shoes. They decided to do the presentations to religious groups first. They'd tell these people about "Rent-a-Student," the massive yard sale, and the shoe collection.

The group would meet early each week to plan that week's work and be sure each member knew what they'd be expected to do.

Step 6: Put all plans on a schedule.

The students put the main ideas on the calendar first. Then they added steps that needed to be taken earlier in preparation.

What's important is not what these students did to reach their goals but the steps they took—starting with setting their goals, identifying the problem (raising the money), brainstorming possible strategies, and developing a detailed plan for each strategy they decided to use.

> *Doing anything better requires effective thinking—that is, coming up with more imaginative ideas, facing complicated problems, finding new ways to solve them, becoming aware of hidden possibilities, and then taking action. What is a surprise is that the basic methods for thinking more clearly, more innovatively, more effectively are fundamentally the same in all areas of life—in school, in business, in the arts, in personal life, in sports, in everything. The other surprise is that these methods of effective thinking can be described, taught and learned.[8]*

A comparison of the 10 ways of thinking

The table, or matrix chart, in Chart 17.1 compares the 10 ways of thinking. Notice that we can visually organize most types of information—even about ways of thinking.

The best way to improve the way we think is to use our mind with increasingly complex material. Like getting to Carnegie Hall, getting to better thinking takes "Practice, Practice, Practice." And this brings me to a favorite quotation. Jean Houston said this, referring to the brain:

> *We are given as our birthright a Stradivarius and we come to play it like a plastic fiddle.— Jean Houston*

Questions for Reflection:
---

1. Which ways of thinking do you use most often and most easily?

2. Which ways of thinking are new to you, or seem more difficult?

3. Which ways of thinking are most important in the courses you're taking, or for reaching your long-term goals?

4. What surprised you in this chapter? What was the most important thing you learned? How will you use what you learned?

Chart 17.1: A Comparison of the Ten Ways of Thinking

Way of Thinking	Thinking about	Looking for	Methods	Questions
Scientific Thinking	Nature	Explanations	Scientific Methods: Experiment Statistical	Are there alternative hypotheses? Can the experiment be replicated? Is the experiment fair? Adequate controls? Does it show correlation or prove the hypothesis?
Mathematical Thinking	Numbers	Patterns	Proofs Logic	What is known? And unknown? What are constants? And variables? How can it be stated mathematically? How can it be solved? And applied?
Analysis	The Parts	Relationships	Contrast Cause & Effect Relationships	What is the thesis and the argument? What are the main ideas and the structure? How can I organize it differently? What is the purpose and function of each part?
Synthesis	The Whole	The Central Idea	Compare Connections Combine Synthesize	What do different sources have in common? How do they agree and disagree? What are the facts and opinions? What are the different points of view?
Critical Thinking	Thinking	Reasonable Thinking	Examine Questions Evaluate Reflect	Is it a fact, opinion, belief, or wishful thinking? How reliable are the sources? Is there bias or an unwarranted assumption? Is it clear, reliable, logical, and fair?
Creative Thinking	Innovation	New Ideas	Brainstorming Prediction	What is the real problem? How can we approach the problem in new ways? Can we blend ideas to create something new? How can I learn to let ideas incubate?
Decision-Making	Choices	Alternatives	Pros and Cons Predicting Consequences	What are all the alternatives? What are all possible consequences? How do alternatives relate to values and goals? What are the pros and cons?
Evaluation	Values	Strengths & Weaknesses	Set Criteria Evaluate	What are characteristics of the ideal? What are appropriate criteria? What are the strengths and weaknesses? How could it be improved?
Problem-Solving	Problems	Solutions	Analyze Cause Set Goals	What is the situation and the problem? What are the possible causes of the problem? What are the goals or vision? What is blocking us from reaching our goals?
Strategic Thinking	Goals	Strategies	Steps to Goals Timeline Evaluation	How can the goals be stated practically? What are the steps to reach the goals? What materials and skills are needed? Create a timeline and list of assignments

18

Pathways to Memory — Ten Strategies

The more ways something is learned, the more memory path-ways are built.... The more ways the material to be learned is introduced to the brain and reviewed, the more dendritic path-ways will be created.[1]

We'll begin with a story, a true story—one that changed my life. In the early 1980s, I found a little book in the library, *Use Both Sides of Your Brain* by Tony Buzan.[2] I've bought later editions of this book several times since then and, while it's an old book, it is still an important one and I recommend it highly. What is most amazing is that this book suggests study skills that are now considered some of the newest ideas and the most effective strategies.

The book begins with a story referred to as an "Impossible Dream." While my brief summary is not as powerful as the full story, it will give you the main ideas. I hope you will find it as inspiring as I did.

The story of Edward Hughes

Edward Hughes was a mediocre British high school student who, when he was 15, took the "O" level exams and made his usual B's and C's. He had dreamed of being accepted at Cambridge, but his scores were not nearly high enough. It was then that his father gave him a copy of Buzan's book, published in 1974. Reading this book led Hughes to believe he could change his study habits, that he could make all A's, and that he could be accepted at Cambridge.

When his teachers and others laughed at him, Hughes didn't give up. He knew he could do it. Now, as he read his textbooks, he began creating "Mind Maps," Buzan's term for images similar to concept maps but often based on creative thinking. Hughes gradually created giant Mind Maps containing the concepts and information for an entire course or book.

To review this material, he used three more of Buzan's strategies: He used self-testing, he studied in 45-minute blocks followed by breaks, and he used scheduled reviews, now called distributed practice.

Instead of rereading his Mind Maps, he re-created them from memory, checking to see what he'd missed. Later, he went back to study material he should have learned in earlier years. He also read other important books in the field, using the same strategies.

In addition to his studies, Hughes began eating healthy food and getting regular exercise. He said it helped him improve his concentration. He also recognized that, since the Cambridge entrance exam consisted of four essays, he would need stronger writing skills, so he set about improving these skills with the same firm determination.

As a result of his efforts, Hughes not only did well on his exams; he made the highest scores on three of the four tests, and the highest score ever made on the fourth. He was accepted at Cambridge and, while he was there, he continued using these strategies. He also participated in several sports, and gained leadership positions in several organizations to meet his new goals.[3]

Exercise:
Comparing This Story to
What You Have Read in This Book

---

1. What did you find in this story that is similar to what is in this book?

2. How is this story different from the material in this book?

3. What questions do you have? What do you wish you could ask Edward Hughes?

While Buzan's book covers many important topics, people who read this story often came to the conclusion that there was some sort of magic in using Mind Maps. I spent plenty of time doing them myself but never found them quite as helpful as Hughes did. Still, I could never forget this story.

After rereading the book many times, I finally began to understand. Mind Maps are *not* the secret. If you read the story again, you will find much more was involved. This is how I summarize the important points in the story:

1. Something happened to Edward Hughes that changed his life. Actually, two important things happened. First, he made poor scores on a test, making him think he might never reach his goal of going to Cambridge. The second event was getting a book that gave him hope and provided practical strategies. He knew what he had to do.

2. He already had a goal. Now he developed a plan. He would do exactly what Buzan recommended. And, while he was clearly motivated to make excellent grades, he was also focused on deep learning.

3. In addition to using new study strategies, he made changes in his health habits and improved his writing skills.

4. While he didn't use a time management schedule like those in this book, he studied in 45-minute blocks, followed by breaks, as suggested in Buzan's book.

5. He would never have heard of "mindsets," but he clearly had a growth mindset. He *knew* he could succeed. He also demonstrated incredible self-discipline and willpower.

6. He used Mind Maps to organize information. Although Hughes does not agree with me, I firmly believe that students could use an outline, a series of summaries or, even better, a combination of both verbal and visual strategies for organizing information and learn just as well. The Mind Map or concept map, however, is still an excellent choice, especially for visual learners. What matters most is putting a good deal of thinking and hard work into organizing the material and self-testing by re-creating Mind Maps.

7. Hughes spent time thinking deeply about what he was learning.

8. He used both of what we are told are the two best strategies for learning: self-testing and scheduled reviews (distributed practice). A third strategy that he used, taking breaks, has only recently been recognized as an important strategy. We used to think we took breaks simply to relax for a while. Now we know that we take breaks to give our brain a

chance to strengthen its neural connections and store our new knowledge for later retrieval.

What is most amazing to me is that Buzan, using the brain research of the 1970s and earlier, was able to identify strategies that today's research is proving most effective.

Edward Hughes answers my questions

To be certain that I had my facts right, I asked Hughes a few questions. When I asked whether he would agree that learning is more important than grades, he responded,

> *The ability to learn and think is something that you carry with you for life. Grades are purely a snapshot of a moment in time.*

I asked if he'd been working mainly for grades or for deep understanding, and he replied,

> *I was studying academic material for the purpose of getting a great grade in order to achieve my goals and ambitions. However, the real value is the ability to think, to be creative, and to analyze situations in life long after you stop taking tests and getting grades.*

Finally, I asked if he went back to college today, whether he'd do anything differently.

> *I would use the same study techniques but would make sure that I had an equal focus on networking—as, frankly, most of what you learn at school and college is not that useful.*

Our main point of disagreement was on point 6 above, where I suggest that Mind Maps (or concept maps) might be especially helpful for visual learners but that a simple outline or other strategies might work just as well for others. Instead of seeing Mind Maps as being related to visual learning, Hughes relates them to *thinking*, which I believe is an important insight.

> *Mind Maps make you think about a topic as you are not copying someone else's writing but rather creating your view of it. They also enable you to make connections between related materials and are easily memorized. Linear writing is not intuitive, contains a tremendous amount of redundancy, and does not force thinking.*[4]

While I agree with much that Edward Hughes says above, I continue to believe that other visual and verbal strategies can also force you to think and I still recommend using a combination of several strategies.

The ten pathways to memory are organized in four categories: two traditional pathways, three sensory pathways, and five pathways for new strategies based on research. We'll begin with two of the most familiar strategies, those I call traditional. The first of the traditional pathways is rote memory or memorization.

The first pathway is rote memory

With some people, rote memory or memorization has a bad reputation. Actually, this is the best method for learning certain kinds of information. For other kinds of learning, though, there are far better strategies. The main problem with rote memory occurs when students have a list of randomly selected pieces of information that looked important. They memorize these facts, without connecting them or giving them meaning. As a result, the information is soon forgotten.

> *Memory without understanding is useless unless you want to hire yourself out as a talking parrot.[5]*

STRATEGY 18.1

ROTE MEMORY

As you'll discover, research has shown a more effective way to use flash cards.

Step 1: Create your own flash cards. I preferred index cards cut in half. They're easier to carry in my pocket. When learning new vocabulary, write the word on one side and the definition on the back. If you're learning the pronunciation, add that on either side.

Step 2: Write definitions in your own words. This forces you to think about the meaning.

Step 3: You can also use flash cards with questions and answers for many different classes.

Step 4: Use the cards to test yourself. Self-testing is far more effective than repeatedly reading or saying the definition.

What surprised me is that research now shows it is better to use one larger pack of cards rather than several shorter packs. I used to divide my cards into easy, medium, and difficult material. It turns out that this wasn't a good idea. With a large pack of flash cards, there's more time between your first and next times viewing a given card. This means you have more time to forget—and having time to forget is now understood as helpful. The experience of struggling to remember or actually forgetting and relearning the information helps strengthen the memory.

This is one of several reasons why it's better to practice in many shorter periods rather than in one long period. You have more time to forget. You remember far more in ten short periods, or study sprints, than with an equal amount of time in one long period.

Step 5: Another way to improve memorization is to find a way to make what you're learning personal. Connect the words you are learning with words you already know. Make connections between the information you're learning with the flash cards and other material in the course. Use words you're learning to describe yourself and your own experiences. Use the terms repeatedly over the next several weeks, even if you use them only when talking to yourself, your dog, or your teddy bear.

Step 6: *Never* memorize definitions or answers to questions if you don't understand them.

Step 7: *Never* throw away your flash cards. Wait a few weeks and test yourself again. Test yourself before every test, midterm, and final.

Although you might not intend to take further classes in this area, you might change your mind. Review your flash cards again and you'll be better prepared for that next class. Even when you graduate, you might review them once a year and remember them forever.

The second pathway is mnemonics

Even if you aren't familiar with the word "mnemonics" (pronounced nuh-MAH-niks), you may have used some of these methods. Can you remember the names of the Great Lakes? Can you name the planets in order? How many digits in pi can you remember?

Mnemonics is a creative way of memorizing facts.

For the Great Lakes, use the word "HOMES." For the planets, I like the phrase "My Very Excellent Mother Just Served Us Noodles." (She used to serve nine pizzas before Pluto was demoted.) And, to remember the first

15 digits of pi, you can use "How I want a drink, alcoholic of course, after heavy lectures involving quantum mechanics."

That last sentence uses a different system. You can't use first letters for numbers because numbers in English include the numbers 2 and 3 starting with T, 4 and 5 starting with F, and 6 and 7 starting with S. With T, F, or S, you'd have no way of knowing which number was intended. So, instead, we count the number of letters in each word. "How" has 3 letters. "I" has 1 letter. "Want" has 4 letters. With these words, we already have 3.14, the first three digits of pi.

You could also use this method to remember important dates in history. To remember the date when the Declaration of Independence was signed, try "O Declare Freedom People" where the numbers of letters in the four words are 1, 7, 7, and 6. It takes time to find appropriate words with the right number of letters but, for those with problems remembering dates, it could be useful.

Some people have the idea that if they use mnemonics they'll be able to remember anything. The sad truth is that, though mnemonics can be marvelously helpful in remembering certain kinds of things, they are of no help at all in other areas. Mnemonics are useful mainly for lists. Dates are lists of numbers.

Another misconception is that you need to search for an existing mnemonic to fit your needs. This is nonsense. The best strategy is to create your own. I was once asked by a Mexican student if he needed to use the English words in his mnemonics. The answer should be obvious: Any strategy is far more helpful when using the language you know best.

STRATEGY *18.2*

MNEMONICS

Step 1: Try using an acronym.

A few mnemonics, like HOMES for the Great Lakes, are so good that you'll want to use these rather than creating your own. Many acronyms have become words, like Radar, Sonar, Laser, and Scuba. One you might have learned in physics is "Roy G. Biv" which names the colors of the spectrum in order.

Step 2: Create your own acronym.

Take the first letters of the words on your list and try to combine them to form a word. Most of the time, there won't be any way to do this.

Sometimes you can use synonyms for the words on your list and this might help.

Step 3: Use acrostics or first-letter mnemonics.

You might at some time have listed the letters of your name or someone else's name. The example shown here uses the word "study."

Chart 18.1 The Acrostic for Study

S	trategies
T	ime management
U	nderstanding
D	ecisions
Y	ields results

To use an acrostic for memory, start with the first letters of each word in the list of terms you want to remember. Choose words starting with these letters that make sense, sometimes forming a memorable sentence. One example for the notes of the treble clef in music is "Every Good Boy Does Fine." You might have an easier time remembering "Eat Green Babies During Famines."

Another example of acrostics include "King Phillip Came Over For Green Sneakers" to remember taxonomy: Kingdom, Phylum, Class, Order, Family, Genus, and Species. You might use "My Very Excellent Mother Just Served Us Noodles" to remember the planets, starting with Mercury and ending with far-distant Neptune. Acrostics or "first letter" mnemonics are much easier to create and use than acronyms.

Step 4: When you create your own acrostics, make an effort to include the first several letters instead of just the first one. This makes it easier to remember the word you want.

For example, if you want to memorize the stages in mitosis—Prophase, Metaphase, Anaphase, Telophase, and Cytokinesis—you could try "Please make apples turn corners." But consider how much more helpful it would be to use "PROgram METAPHysical ANimals TELephoning CYnthia." This is especially helpful when you have several words starting with the same letter.

Step 5: None of these strategies will work unless you're already so familiar with the terms that the letter will quickly remind you of the related word.

If you don't actually know the names of the Great Lakes, HOMES cannot help you. Practice using your acronyms and acrostics many times before you use them in a test. If you don't know the names of the planets, It would be a waste of time to learn "My Very Excellent Mother Just Served Us Noodles."

The mnemonic I found most useful in college was for the geological time periods. My geology professor considered this information the one thing all students absolutely must know. For the first several weeks we were quizzed on this in every class. Then it appeared on every test, including the final exam. I created my mnemonic the first day and never had any problems. Other students simply used rote memory and had problems all semester. I'd share it with you, but the geological time periods today have more and different categories, so my mnemonic would now be useless. You can easily find newer mnemonics for this and other lists on the internet. You might simply Google "Geological Time Periods mnemonics."

The next three memory pathways involve using your senses. Since auditory and visual senses are often used together, they're combined here.

The third pathway is audiovisual memory

You remember, of course, how you learned the letters of the alphabet. Nearly all children learn the alphabet song. Singing the letters made them easier to remember. I have found it fascinating in my travels to find children singing the same tune, Twinkle, Twinkle Little Star, for many different alphabets.

As you know, if you're asked to speak the words to any song you know well, even the national anthem, you might have problems. But, if you're allowed to sing the song, the words come to mind more easily. While it isn't easy, you can sometime put the information you're trying to memorize into a song based on a familiar tune. If you put new words to a familiar tune, humming or singing the tune might help you remember the words. You would need to sing the song over and over to memorize the new words. It isn't easy.

There are many easier ways to use what we hear and see to remember new information.

STRATEGY *18.3*

AUDIOVISUAL MEMORY

Step 1: Most people find it helpful to use rhyming words:

"In fourteen hundred and ninety-two, Columbus sailed the ocean blue." The problem with this rhyme is that your only clue is that "two" rhymes with "blue." You still must remember the "fourteen hundred and ninety –."

Some students learn names, events, and dates by creating similar rhymes about what they're studying. Try this: "The divided nation he was fixing, Lincoln president number sixteen." "Sixteen" and "fixing" don't rhyme perfectly but they're close enough to help you remember.

I learned a helpful rhyming rule as a child. "Red and black: friend of Jack. Red and yellow: kill a fellow." Anyone living in a part of the country where the sometimes-deadly coral snakes are found should recognize this one. We repeated this when we saw a snake with brightly colored rings around its body. When I first saw a snake in my backyard that fit this description, I realized the red and yellow rings were next to each other. It was a coral snake.

A similar reminder is "Righty Tighty, Lefty Loosey." To tighten a screw or a jar lid, turn to the right. To loosen the lid, turn it to the left.

Step 2: You might use an audiovisual strategy for learning a foreign language.

In Spanish, for example, "pajaro" means "bird." I divided the word into parts: pa –hah – ro. This sounds like Pa is laughing and rowing a boat. The problem with this is the missing bird. My improved approach was to think "Pa-Hair-Oh. Pa is very hairy, and Oh my goodness, a bird has built a nest on his hairy head." You don't have time to learn all your new vocabulary this way, but it helps with words you have trouble remembering.

Step 3: You might also create a little story using the sounds.

My son and I created many of these mini-stories to help him learn vocabulary words in high school. Our favorite was for the word "stentorian," which means speaking in a loud voice. We pictured a man – a Tory – standing on a table in an inn filled with people. He needed to speak loudly so they could hear him. This was shortened to "Standing Tory in the Inn," which sounds a lot like "stentorian." The fact that this involves both a picture and sounds—truly audiovisual—made it easier to remember. To this day, neither of us has forgotten the word.

I often use this strategy to remember words that seem to fade from my mind. For a few weeks during the summer we have beautiful, deep-red

Crocosmia blooming in our garden. Because I haven't needed the word Crocosmia for a year, I often have trouble remembering the name. I finally broke the word into cro – cos – me – ah, which then transformed into "crow caws me at." I picture a large, shiny-black crow perched next to the beautiful red flowers. The crow is cawing at me to come and look at the flowers. This audiovisual image solved my problem.

Step 4: Think about the charts for visual organization.

You have the visual and can always add the audio. Add sounds.

Look at the chart and describe each part of the diagram in a different way. Think of words that rhyme with some of the terms. You might even use the chart as your notes for giving a "lecture" to an imaginary audience.

Step 5: Don't just look at diagrams; copy them.

Color the parts. Then create the diagram several times from memory. Name the terms as you look at them and describe what that part does. When taking a test, you might be able to close your eyes and picture that diagram in your mind.

Step 6: Use audiovisual memory to remember people's names.

First listen carefully to the name. Repeat it to be sure you have it correctly. If you aren't quite sure or you soon forget, ask them to tell you again. People are flattered that you care.

Use the name in a sentence or, better yet, in several sentences.

"Janice, I like that name. My little sister had a doll named Janice." As you speak, emphasize the name, "Janice." At the same time, picture your sister's doll sitting on this girl's head, perhaps pulling her hair—something outrageous or silly is most helpful. This visualization helps you remember her name. If you don't have a sister or she didn't have a doll named Janice, you might have a cousin or friend named Janice. If not, you might think about rhyming words or words that come close, like vanish or atlantis or even bananas.

At the same time, you need to focus on what you see. Remembering her name is useless if you don't recognize Janice when you see her again. Look at the shape of her face, eyes, nose, mouth, ears, and chin. Study her hair, its color, length, and style, but remember that hair can be cut or restyled. It might be in a ponytail next time. Study her smile. Observe her mannerisms. You'll then recognize her the next time and you can greet her by name, earning points and possibly a new friend.

Another way to remember names is to think what they sound like. I used to make it easy for people to remember my name. My last name was Ruhnke, a name no one had ever heard. For many years, I'd introduce myself, saying, "Hi. I'm Judy Ruhnke—rhymes with 'monkey.'" They didn't just hear a rhyming name; they had a strong visual image: "This girl is like a monkey. Maybe she climbs trees!" (Actually, I did.) People never forgot. Weeks later I'd meet them again and they'd say, "Hello, Judy Ruhnke-rhymes-with-monkey." They could pronounce the name but most never learned to spell it.

With almost any name, you can find a way to create a visual image. Mrs. Blake might make a delicious chocolate cake, or remind you of a fat red snake, or you can picture her holding a large lobster at a clambake.

Mr. Knight certainly looks powerful in his imaginary chainmail. Jimmy Keith is not a thief…or perhaps he has a strong belief or, when he leaves, you breathe a sigh of relief. Hank Pinkerton could be pictured at a bank whose walls are painted pink. (No, the rhymes are not perfect, but they work.)

The fourth pathway is kinesthetic memory

Kinesthetic memory involves "hands-on" learning. It might involve manipulating objects or moving your own body. While it can't be used in all areas, it adds another dimension to memory.

STRATEGY 18.4

KINESTHETIC MEMORY

Step 1: Moving your body sometimes helps you remember.

When someone gives me directions, I use my body. They say, "At the next traffic light, turn left." I hold out my left hand. "Go four blocks and take a right." My hand moves up and down four times to count the blocks and then moves right. "It will be the third house on the left, a corner house." My finger counts three houses to the left and forms a corner. Without doing this, I find it much harder to remember the directions.

Step 2: Act out the important moves.

I've watched many golfers hitting an imaginary ball to prepare for the real play. If you're preparing to do a lab, practice the steps by acting them out before you begin. If studying literature, act out the most important scenes. For a moment in history, you could role-play several incidents, taking the roles of key players.

Step 3: Create movements or even a dance to illustrate a concept.

One creative strategy I developed was to help students understand the kinetic theory. This theory explains the changes in the states of matter based on the movement of the molecules.

We began with all of us standing in lines in the back of the room. We were water molecules. First, we'd pretend the temperature was absolute zero. At that temperature molecules don't move. We were a solid. It's is funny how hard it is for students to stand totally still. Then the temperature slowly warmed up and the molecules began moving a little but staying in the same place because we still formed a solid. We'd wiggle and shake faster and faster.

Then at 32 or 33 degrees, something strange happened to us. First, those on the outside began to move out of place. They were melting. Then another layer melted, and another. Before long, all of us had become a liquid. We could now move anywhere in the back of the room—in our imaginary container.

As the temperature rose, we moved faster. What happened when we moved really fast? We bumped into people. Sometimes we'd even get bounced out of the container. We evaporated. We continued until all of us finished evaporating and became a gas.

When we reviewed for a test, someone always begged to review the kinetic theory. We'd all stand quietly, without moving at first. The students then copied my movements, waving back and forth, slowly warming, then melting and evaporating. No words were necessary.

Step 4: Review your visual charts by redrawing them in the air.

Describe them as you "draw".

"The central idea here is memory. There are three kinds of memory. Here is traditional memory with two sections…"

You might even try to *be* the visual image. Try being the complex chain chart for this book. Your feet can be the early chapters on preparing to learn. Think of them as a firm foundation. Your body is the next part, strengthening basic skills. You might use one arm for input skills and wiggle three fingers to represent reading, note-taking, and research. The other arm would represent output, with three fingers for writing, speaking, and test-preparation. Your head, of course, represents mental processing.

You could even use your ears for organizing verbally and visually, your eyes for thinking skills, and the top of your head for pathways to memory. If you want to add the fourth section of the book, wear a hat. You might point to each part as you describe it.

Step 5: In some courses, you use kinesthetic activities in class.

You dissect a frog. You demonstrate the Heimlich maneuver. You make your own microscope slides. You practice athletic skills. You paint, sculpt, or create pottery.

But in most courses, you'll need to find ways to add movement on your own. Children sometimes have tiny plastic soldiers to act out great wars. They use action figures to reenact movie scenes. You can do the same things. Find small objects and let them reenact a historical scene or critical moment in a story. I can see two stones with faces drawn on them that play the roles of Romeo and Juliet.

Step 6: Build a model.

When I began learning about the brain, I had a hard time visualizing the different parts. I got some clay and little odds and ends, including kidney beans and colorful beads, and slowly built my model of a "brain." With this, I could easily picture the relationships between the different parts of the brain.

Step 7: Play with your food.

This is my favorite strategy. Play politely, of course. I don't want you throwing tater tots at each other. Imagine you're studying the cell. Find something on your plate that can be the cell. A slice of bread works fine. Or you might use two slices: one for the plant cell and one for the animal cell. Add bits and pieces of food for the parts of the cell. You might use peas or small pieces of lettuce for chloroplasts, use a thin slice of hotdog as a nucleus, or tear out a hole for a vacuole, and so on.

At first, your friends will laugh a little, but all too soon, they'll want to help. "Why not use the crumbs from my chocolate cookie for the ribosomes?" "I've got some okra that would make beautiful mitochondria." You'd be reviewing kinesthetically but, on a test you'd remember visually: "I remember the okra. What was it they represented?"

You can also do something similar to review the digestive system and other major body organs, the parts of an engine, or to compare different types of bridges.

The fifth pathway to memory is association

The fifth pathway to memory is association. We will include association with prior knowledge, association with experience, and association with emotion. Memory is strengthened when you make connections between what you are learning, what you already knew, and your personal experience.

STRATEGY 18.5

ASSOCIATION AND MEMORY

Step 1: Associate new information with what you already know.

Think about KWL. The reason you start with what you know and want to know is that this brings prior knowledge to mind. Recalling what you already know makes the memory stronger. As you read or listen to lectures, you're more likely to compare what you are learning with what you knew (or thought you knew). The new information helps you better understand what you already knew and, at the same time, makes the new information more meaningful and complete. The better you make connections with prior learning, the more quickly new information is moved to your long-term memory.

Step 2: Start with a concept map showing what you already know on the topic.

Try to add the new information you are learning to this concept map. You might need to reorganize the concept map based on the new information. Again, as you think deeply about the connections between prior information and new information, they will be forming strong connections in your brain.

Step 3: Relate what you are learning with you own experience.

When your physics teacher discusses centrifugal motion, picture the clothes in the washing machine all sticking to the outside when they spin dry or remember how, when you're in a car taking a sharp curve, you're pushed into the door. You are associating new information with personal experiences.

Step 4: Ask how you could apply what you are learning.

Now that you understand centrifugal force, how could you use that information?

Step 5: Compare a character's experience to your own.

In literature, find ways a character's experiences or concerns are similar to your own. What would you do in their place? What did this story teach you about yourself? Again, you're associating what you are reading with your own experience. Neurons are connecting the new information with the experience, making both of them easier to remember.

Step 6: Imagine yourself as part of the event.

History may seem to have no connections with your own experience. That's why many students find it boring. Ask what situations and issues in earlier times are similar to present-day situations or issues.

Ask what you'd have done if you'd been there. What would you have done if you'd been a German teenager when Hitler took over? What if you'd been a Jewish teen? What would you have done if you'd been a teenager living in the South during our Civil War? A black teenager whose family had been sold?

Step 7: Involve your emotions.

Think about the times in your life you remember most clearly. They're usually very bad or especially happy times. The stronger your emotions, the more you remember the events. With learning, we remember the information we're most interested in or find most surprising or even shocking. Find something exciting in each course you take.

Take it a step further and find something exciting in every lecture and every chapter. Starting with good questions can help. Doing a little research on your own is also helpful.

Step 8: In each chapter or lecture, find something you feel deeply about.

Associate this information with experiences when you felt strong, positive emotions.

Step 9: Decide what is most exciting.

As you finish each lecture and each chapter, write in your notes, "The most exciting thing I learned is…." Take it a step further; tell a classmate what you found so exciting. Sure, they might think you're weird. That's OK. Ask them what they found most interesting, or surprising. You'll be doing them a favor.

The sixth pathway to memory is distributed practice

As I suggested earlier, some of the "newest" and most important strategies were first suggested 40 years ago by Tony Buzan. They are never cited in the research, because Buzan didn't do the research himself. He studied the research and recognized the implications for learning.

Buzan called this next strategy "Scheduled Reviews." It simply means that you practice or review in many short periods distributed over a long period. Distributed practice is part of the Never-Cram-Again Test Prep Strategy described in Chapter 13.

STRATEGY 18.6

DISTRIBUTED PRACTICE

Step 1: After a lecture, check immediately to see how well you understand.

In SQ3R, this means "reciting" what each section is about. In KWL, this is writing 'what you learned.' You might do this while reading or while still in the lecture room. You might wait 15 or 20 minutes. An immediate review helps you remember what you learned.

Step 2: Later that day, do another review. This time you might write an outline or summary or create a concept map. You might also reorganize and rewrite your lecture notes.

Step 3: Before sleeping, review mentally, and check your notes.

Sleeping after rehearsing the information seems to strengthen neural connections.

Step 4: Soon after you get up in the morning, do another quick review.

Step 5: Create your own review schedule.

You might review once a day for the first week or only twice during the week. "The simple act of spacing out study and practice and allowing time to elapse between them makes both the learning and the memory stronger."[6]

Step 6: And after exams are over?

What then? If it is possible that you'd take a related course or use this information in any way, continue to review, perhaps twice a month, then once a month, until you get it down to once a year. This isn't too much to ask to be able to remember the material you worked so hard to learn.

The seventh pathway to memory is Self-Testing

Edward Hughes used self-testing as he re-created his Mind Maps from memory. And again, research shows that this is one of the two most effective learning strategies.

STRATEGY 18.7

SELF-TESTING

In a *New York Times* article, one of the researchers describes a study showing how effective this strategy can be.

> *Students were asked either to study a passage four times, study it three times and take a test, or study it one time and take a test on it three times. They were then retested after five minutes and after a week. Those who studied—O.K., crammed—did slightly better after five minutes but a week later the three-time test takers outscored the other groups significantly. Just repeatedly looking at something doesn't mean you own it. The act of retrieval is a very active memory enhancer.*[7]

Self-testing may seem, at first, to lead to little immediate improvement but, after a week or more, students who used self-testing made significantly higher scores. Rereading is one of the most commonly used and least effective strategies, while self-testing is one of the least used and most effective strategies.

Step 1: When you recite—the first R in SQ3R—you're using self-testing.

Step 2: When you use flash cards, you're using self-testing.

Step 3: When you study using questions and answers, you're using self-testing.

Step 4: When you rewrite an outline or summary by memory, you're using self-testing.

Step 5: When you re-create a concept map, you're using self-testing.

Step 6: When you write practice essays, you're using self-testing.

> *The finding that rereading textbooks is often labor in vain ought to send a chill up the spines of educators and learners because it's the number one study strategy of most people—including more than 80% of college students in some surveys.... Rereading has three strikes against it. It is time consuming. It doesn't result in durable memory. And it often involves an unwitting self-deception, as growing familiarity with the text comes to feel like mastery of the content...but the amount of study time is no measure of mastery.*[8]

The eighth pathway to memory is using Varied Strategies

Most of us remember being taught that students should study in the same place every day, preferably sitting at a desk, studying alone, and working in silence. We always finished working on one subject before starting another, and usually kept working until our work was done. According to current research, every one of those practices is wrong.

Strategy 18.8

Use Varied Strategies

Step 1: Try interleaving different subjects.

Picture a stack of leaves with a layer of oak leaves, then layers of hickory, maple, poplar, and birch leaves, and then imagine repeating the sequence. Instead of changing from one kind of leaf to another, change from one subject or one topic to another.

The most effective examples rotate related topics in a single subject, like rotating between different kinds of math problems. Doing ten or twenty problems using the same method is boring. Switching between different kinds of problems is harder, but it helps you learn more about solving the problems. In biology, you might spend ten to fifteen minutes reading, then practice vocabulary, and go on to redrawing diagrams.

It is important to realize that interleaving subjects can often cause students to feel like they are learning less. It really is harder to remember information. This is intended! When you need to keep relearning, you are strengthening the connections in your brain.

Step 2: Study in many different places.

Research has shown that most students learn more effectively if they study in a variety of different locations. You might study one day in an empty classroom, next while sitting on a park bench, in a garden, in the library, or in a cafeteria.

Step 3: Try studying with different background sounds.

While some students do better work in silence, many others work more effectively with familiar music (without words.) You might work well with the noises in the cafeteria, but nearby conversations are nearly always distracting.

Step 4: Spend time studying in groups.

While it was once thought that effective study required working alone, we now know that many students do better when they work with a study pal or with a small study group.

I found working with a study pal especially helpful for calculus, and I worked with a fairly large study group for an advanced physics class where we needed to cooperate to master incredibly difficult problems. Teaching each other helps both students learn more. I also found that I learned more when working with another student who needed my help. For practical reasons, in most other subjects, I generally worked alone. It seems likely that different students might prefer different ways of working.

Step 5: You might even study while moving.

While students have traditionally been told to sit still and stop squirming, we now know that squirming may be helpful. Actually, what was tested was moving feet. Students who moved their feet while reading remembered more. When students were allowed to walk around the room to study a poster, they remembered more.

Reading a book while walking down a busy sidewalk is still a bad idea but, if you feel like getting up to stretch while you study or you like moving around the room while flipping through your flash cards, it might be helpful. Then again, some of this research may be related to the "novelty" effect. Doing something a little differently might help you learn more just because it's different.

The ninth pathway to memory is Taking a Break

According to Buzan, students should work for no more than 45 minutes and then take a break. I'd suggest, though, that each student is different. Some might need a short break after only 15 or 20 minutes. With some kinds of work, you might work effectively for two hours and then take a longer break. A number of studies show that being interrupted while studying can actually be helpful. According to one of these studies:

> *Even brief diversions from a task can dramatically improve one's ability to focus on that task for prolonged periods.... This study is consistent with the idea that prolonged attention to a single task actually hinders performance.... Brief mental breaks will actually help you stay focused on your task.*[9]

STRATEGY *18.9*

TAKE A BREAK

Step 1: Work in short periods.

If you have an hour for study, you might find it helpful to work for 20 minutes and then take a short break before working another 20. The timing will vary, according to what works for you, the time of day, and the difficulty of the material.

Step 2: Give your brain a break.

If you've been concentrating especially hard, you may need a study break to give your brain a rest. Sometimes taking a break, just like sleeping, gives your brain time to finish making connections.

Step 3: If you feel stressed, give yourself a break.

If you feel overwhelmed by the material you're working on or stressed, or you just can't concentrate any longer, the wise choice is to take a break.

Step 4: When you work hard, you need a break.

If you have one class that's particularly challenging, your brain might recover more easily if you don't schedule another class immediately afterward. Taking a good break after a difficult class is a fine use of your time.

"Taking a break" does *not* mean checking email and Facebook or texting your friends. It's far better to simply relax. Taking a long walk outside is one of the best ideas. Exercise can also be helpful.

The tenth pathway to memory is Using Multiple Pathways

Do not simply choose one of these pathways to memory and stick with it. Your memory will grow far stronger if you use a combination of several pathways to memory, just as when you chose a variety of ways to organize information.

If you want to follow a healthy diet, you wouldn't decide that spinach was healthy and eat nothing but spinach. You'd include a variety of foods, including protein, fruits and vegetables, whole grains, and even healthy oils. Your memory strategies should also include a variety of effective strategies.

> *The more regions of the brain that store data about a subject, the more interconnections you make.... This cross-referencing of data strengthens the data into something we've learned rather than just memorized.*[10]

STRATEGY 18.10

USE MULTIPLE PATHWAYS

Step 1: Use several strategies together.

When you're studying, choose two or more memory strategies that are appropriate for the material you are learning.

Step 2: Include Sensory pathways.

In many situations, you might use one or more of the sensory pathways, along with association and some of the other pathways.

Step 3: Always try to include the two most effective strategies: distributed practice and self-testing. Vary the other strategies you use.

You might soon find that it would be hard not to use multiple pathways.

Questions for Reflection:

---

1. Which pathways to memory have you used for many years?

2. What surprised you in this chapter? What's the most important thing you learned? How will you use what you learned?

3. What new strategies are you looking forward to using?

CHAPTER **19**

What Employers Want Most: A Brief Introduction to Part 4

Internships occupy an awkward place in our labor market. Many of them are indistinguishable from jobs but while unpaid jobs are considered immoral, unpaid internships are considered common.... Even desirable internships can resemble worthless months of servitude.... Yet employers will eventually consider these agonizing periods of numbing boredom to be the most significant professional moments of our college career.[1]

This statement, on The Atlantic.com (2014), might surprise many students. Even more surprising was the graph that went with it. The graph showed eight work areas: Business, Health Care, Manufacturing, Government/Nonprofit, Education, Service/Retail, Science/Technology, and Media/Communications. *In every single area listed, internships were rated as most important in deciding who to hire.* It was followed fairly closely by "employment during college."

What were the areas considered least important? These were college GPA, relevant coursework, and volunteer experience.

In a different survey, according to employers who were surveyed, 94% say it's important to provide a liberal education for students.[2] A liberal education was defined as one that:

helps students develop a sense of social responsibility, as well as intellectual and practical skills that span all areas of study, such as communication, analytical and problem solving skills, and a demonstrated ability to apply knowledge and skills in real-world settings.[3]

For students who are concerned about getting a good job after graduation, understanding what employers want most is critical. If you're a freshman and need to focus on your studies, go ahead and skip this section of the book for now and read the conclusion. This part of the book will make good reading over the summer. But you should certainly read this before your sophomore year, because you may want to look for your first internship.

Don't let that opening quote discourage you. While some internships may be a waste of time, many students report that their internships were some of the most rewarding experiences in their college years.

Exercise: What Employers Want

---

1. List at least five personal qualities you think employers want most.
2. List at least five experiences you think employers wish students to have.
3. List at least five skills you think employers consider very important.

You might think, with dozens of surveys done each year, there would be some agreement on what employers want. But either the surveys on what employers look for involved different kinds of employers (quite possible) or the questions employers were asked were totally different. When comparing results, we find not only different responses, but different kinds of responses.

What personal qualities do employers want?

One survey claims that employers are looking for people who are warm, friendly, easy-going, cooperative, and good-looking. Another list claims they want students who are honest, reliable, hard-working, and highly motivated. I found only one list that mentioned job seekers' majors or their grades as important.

Every employer wants to work with someone who is friendly, cooperative, honest, and hardworking. But aren't they also looking for something more important?

One very thoroughly done survey listed these three personal qualities as most important:

1. "Ethical Integrity" was judged important by 96% of employers.

2. "Intercultural Skills" were also judged important by 96%.

3. "The capacity for professional development and continued learning" was judged important by 94%.[4]

What experiences do employers want students to have?

In several surveys, employers emphasized experience above all. What seemed most important to them was finding candidates who had either relevant job experience or internships in the field, had actively participated in campus organizations or done volunteer work, had spent time studying abroad, and had completed a significant project in college.

The survey described above listed the following priorities:

1. "Developing research questions in their field" was important to 83% of employers.

2. "Completing a major project" was important for 79%.

3. "Completing internships or community-based field projects" was important for 78%

4. "Developing skills to conduct research collaboratively" was important to 74%.[5]

Over the years, experiences like these have become more and more important to employers. Students might look for internships, paid or unpaid, doing the kind of work they'd like to do after graduation. An internship where you do no more than run the copy machine has little value. Look for experiences where you learn new skills and accomplish something significant.

Do not wait to see which companies advertise internships. Identify companies that would give you experiences that would help you get a job in your field. Visit these companies early, tell their recruiters you'd like to work in their field, and ask if there's a possibility you might do an internship with them. An unpaid internship this year might lead to a paid internship next year, and sometimes to a great job offer when you graduate.

Which skills do employers consider most valuable?

In the survey I found most helpful, the critical skills were discussed in detail. These skills are similar to those that colleges and universities describe in their own goals for students. On this list, the percentage includes employers who described the skills as either important or very important.

1. 82%: "Critical thinking and analytical reasoning."

2. 81%: "Complex Problem Solving and Analysis."

3. 80%: "Written and oral communication." In some surveys this is described as being able to write or edit company reports. Some recommend that students take a course in technical writing.

4. 78%: "The application of knowledge skills to real-world settings."

5. 72%: "The ability to locate, organize, and evaluate information from multiple sources."

6. 71%: "Innovation and Creativity."

7. 67%: "Teamwork skills and the ability to collaborate with others in diverse group settings."[6]

Preparing for the Collegiate Learning Assessment

The CLA or Collegiate Learning Assessment is a test created to help colleges and universities evaluate how well their students were improving in four areas: critical thinking, analytical reasoning, problem solving, and written communication skills. Starting in 2014, students at some 200 schools were allowed to take this test, at a cost of $35, so they could show evidence of these four skills when interviewing for a job.

Several problems must be considered. In past years, many college students "only minimally improved their skills" and "at least 45% of students show no statistical gains."[7] Unless you take classes that help you improve your skills in these areas, or learn on your own, your scores aren't likely to impress your employer.

Another problem is that current methods of scoring the CLA don't actually evaluate critical thinking. Students have been given credit for giving reasons even if their reasons were not logical. Several articles on the Internet have critiqued this scoring system. Fallacies have been discovered in the reasoning of students' answers that had been judged to be excellent. The problem is that these tests cannot be scored by computer, and those scoring the test individually gave full credit for any effort to defend an answer—even if the reasoning was poor. I would hope that changes will be made in this area.

If you choose to take the CLA, you might find this section of the book helpful. As far as I can tell, as this book goes to print, there are no other books that help students prepare for the CLA. But, having said this, I wrote this section not to prepare you for the CLA, but to prepare you for the kind of jobs you really want.

STRATEGY *19.1*

BE THE PERSON EMPLOYERS WANT MOST

Step 1: Speak to people in the fields you are interested in.

Ask them which of the skills listed earlier are most important.

Step 2: Take the chapters in this book seriously.

Find opportunities to apply some of what you're learning. Choose the topics you believe will be most useful for your own future, and go on to learn more about them.

Step 3: Take courses that will help you do your job.

Study technical writing, statistics and probability. If you can find courses in analytical reasoning and problem-solving, take these, too. Check out your college's business department. Its faculty may offer helpful courses. It doesn't matter what you're majoring in; courses like these will prove helpful on nearly all kinds of jobs.

Step 4: Do your best to get several internships.

Try to get them in fields you're most interested in. Use these experiences to learn as much as possible and to assume responsibilities that will improve your résumé.

STRATEGY *19.2*

DEVELOP NETWORKING SKILLS

To get internships, to land a job, or to have someone to consult with about a specific job or industry, you need to create a network of contacts. You might remember that Edward Hughes said he wished he had focused more on networking.

Step 1: List your career goals or interests where contacts might be helpful.

If your main interest is in getting an internship now and a job later in a particular kind of industry (perhaps computer software for hospitals), you should list the four to six companies you'd most like to work for. You'd want contacts with influence in these companies.

Step 2: List 100 people you know who might be part of this network or who could introduce you to helpful people.

Start with your parents. Which of their friends would be a helpful part of your network or might have friends who would be helpful? Ask for an introduction. Think of your friends and their parents. Even consider high school teachers as well as college faculty and staff. They all might know people with connections.

Step 3: Attend conferences.

One helpful way to make contacts with people in your field is to attend conferences. When you meet people you'd like to have in your network, ask their advice or discuss important issues. Don't rush into the fact that you want help finding a great internship. Later, send them a handwritten thank-you note saying how helpful they were. Stay in contact perhaps every two to three months by email or letters. Everyone likes to think their advice has been helpful.

Step 4: Think about other fields for which you'd like contacts.

If you plan to start a small business, you could really use contacts in real estate, website building, accounting, advertising, and many other disciplines. A paleontologist could use contacts with people in geology, history, biology, and chemistry.

Step 5: Use social networking to build further contacts.

Check to see whether your target companies or key contacts have a presence on Facebook, Twitter, LinkedIn, Google+, Pinterest, or other social or professional networking sites. Choose contacts that seem most helpful and follow them on their preferred sites, thereby building a relationship that later can become a personal one.

Step 6: When you read a helpful book or article, contact the author.

Email the author and ask a few pertinent questions to begin the conversation. Continue the conversation over the years.

Step 7: Use these contacts when you need help or advice.

When you really need help, these contacts can suggest where you might get a great internship, or offer you one working with them. They might have insights into the different companies and suggest people who might be helpful. When they do help you, be sure to let them know how much you appreciate their help.

STRATEGY *19.3*

FIND A GREAT INTERNSHIP

Step 1: Start with your goals, including career goals and other interests.

Step 2: Choose the company or organization that could help you reach your goals.

Do serious research about the company.

Step 3: Approach the company early.

Don't wait for them to advertise their internship; approach them first. Ask to speak to someone fairly important who could make this decision. Explain why you want to work with their company, how it will be helpful to you, and what you can do to help them.

Step 4: If invited to an interview or presentation, be prepared.

Dress professionally, arrive on time, and take your résumé and relevant work samples (especially if in the arts or advertising). Do your research. Learn about the company.

Step 5: Make a good first impression.

Use a firm handshake, maintain eye contact, don't cross your arms or gaze around the room. Do your best to look and sound both confident and enthusiastic.

The importance of collaboration and innovation

For years, employers have valued both collaboration, also described as teamwork, and innovation. A book that has just been published ties the two of these together and describes their role in the digital revolution. Walter Isaacson points out in the introduction to his book that

> *Most of the innovations of the digital age were done collaboratively…. It [his book] is also a narrative of how they collaborated and why their ability to work as a team made them even more creative. The tale of their teamwork is important because we don't often focus on how central that skill is to innovation.*[8]

To prepare for collaboration, you should begin building your network and start looking for new ways to share and mix your insights, abilities and creativity to create something new and exciting.

The titles of the next three chapters may sound rather intimidating, and some books on these topics are quite difficult. But these chapters are meant to offer a simple, easy-to-understand introduction to these topics. You might discover that you enjoy the challenges of critical thinking, analytical reasoning, and complex problem-solving. You might want to learn even more.

> *Colleges and universities, for all the benefits they bring, accomplish far less for their students than they should. Many students graduate college today...without being able to write well enough to satisfy their employers...reason clearly, or perform competently in analyzing complex problems. — Derek Bok, former president of Harvard University*[9]

Questions for Reflection:
---

1. What kind of work would you really like to do?

2. What would you especially like about doing that kind of work?

3. What skills do you already have, and what skills would you need for that type of work?

4. What surprised you in this chapter. What was the most important thing you learned? How will you use what you learned?

20

Critical Thinking, Reading, Writing, and Listening

Economists who have studied the relationships between education and economic growth confirm what common sense suggests: the number of college degrees is not nearly as important as how well students develop cognitive skills, such as critical thinking and problem-solving ability. — Derek Bok

Over and over again, you may hear how important it is to become a critical thinker, but many colleges offer no courses in critical thinking. Even students who have taken a course in critical thinking may have difficulty using what they learned. According to Stella Cottrell,

> *Students are expected to develop critical thinking skills so they can dig deeper below the surface of the subject they are studying and engage in critical dialogue with its main theories and arguments.... Students need to develop the ability to evaluate critically the work of others. Whilst some find this easy, others tend to accept or apply the results of other people's research too readily, without analyzing it sufficiently to check that the evidence and the reasoning really support the main points being made.*[1]

This chapter summarizes the steps in critical thinking, provides an example, and goes on to discuss critical reading, writing, listening, and reflection.

Exercise: Are You a Critical Thinker?

---

1. How would you define critical thinking?

2. Do you often recognize deceptive methods in television commercials, print advertising, and websites?

3. Do you ever accept a statement simply because it's made by someone of your own political party? Do you automatically reject all opinions made by members of a different party?

4. How often do you question or disagree with information in a lecture or in a textbook?

What does it mean to be a critical thinker?

Stephen Brookfield, in the preface to his book on critical thinking, gives this common sense explanation of what it means to be a critical thinker.

> *When we become critical thinkers, we develop an awareness of the assumptions under which we and others think and act. We learn to pay attention to the context in which our actions and ideas are generated. We become skeptical of quick-fix solutions or simple answers to problems, and of claims to universal truth. We also become open to alternative ways of looking at and behaving in the world.[2]*

Later in the prologue he adds what seems to be addressed specifically to college students:

> *When we think critically, we come to our judgments, choices, and decisions for ourselves, instead of letting others do this on our behalf.[3]*

Common errors in thinking

One common error that is often intentional is attacking the person rather than the person's thinking. For example, "Sally's idea is terrible. How could someone who's been divorced twice understand this issue?"

Another error involves predicting terrible things that will happen if this idea is accepted. For example, "If medical marijuana is legal, it won't be long till even our children will be addicts."

A common error, often used in advertising, is expecting to you agree with an idea because "everyone knows it's a good idea." Just because something is a popular opinion doesn't make it true.

A special case of this error involves people who label others as "traitors" or no longer accepted in a political party or other group when they disagree on some issue that others consider important. The term "RINO," for Republicans In Name Only, is one example. We should understand that there are good Republicans who hold very different beliefs, just as there are good Democrats or Independents or Tea Partiers who may share some of those beliefs. Critical thinkers should never claim that their way is the only way.

Another common error, often intentional, is when someone takes a comment out of context and claims that this is what their opponent thinks or supports. They distort what the other person says or believes in order to argue against them.

Some people even use a distorted statement of statistics to support their own position. For example, do you ever question the results of a poll? What about a "survey" that claims that four out of five dentists surveyed recommend a certain product? A critical thinker should think, "Right. Maybe they only surveyed five dentists—dentists who were their friends or who worked for the toothpaste manufacturer." Until they give us the total number of people surveyed and describe how these dentists were selected, the results are questionable.

Another problem found in some surveys is that biased questions are asked. Compare these two questions: "What do you think about the president's misguided efforts in the war in Iraq?" and "What do you think about the president's attempt to bring democracy, markets, and freedom to the Iraqi people?"[4]

Another common error is making the assumption that there are only two choices. "What are you doing tonight? Will you come with us to the party and have a great time, or do you plan to stay home and study all night?" This question not only assumes there are no other alternatives, it also adds emotional content. It implies that if you decide to study, you don't want to have fun with your friends.

Another error is using a one-sided argument providing all the good reasons for believing one position but not including the equally good reasons for an opposite position.

Finally, there are arguments based on a few isolated examples. "Eating more salt is good for your health. I know this because my grandmother and three of my cousins all salted their food and they all lived until they were in their 90s." You might hear this sort of argument when someone urges you to try a drug, arguing that it wouldn't hurt you. After all, they took it and it never hurt *them*.

STRATEGY 20.1

UNDERSTAND CONTENT DEEPLY

Step 1: Put the material in your own words.

Can you do this without changing the meaning in any way? Can you explain what the author is saying? You cannot critique material fairly if you don't understand it.

Step 2: Identify the issue. What question is being asked and answered?

Step 3: Study the conclusion. What is the thesis or main idea?

Step 4: Examine the argument. What evidence, examples, or reasons are given?

STRATEGY 20.2

EVALUATE CLARITY

Step 1: Are the statements clear or ambiguous?

Is there any possibility of misunderstanding? How could they be more clearly stated?

Step 2: Is the information complete?

What important information has been left out?

Step 3: Do the statements include overgeneralizations?

Look for words like *all, none, everyone, nobody, always,* or *never.* Some of these statements can be true, like "No one from Earth has ever traveled to the planet Jupiter." As you probably know, many statements with such generalizations are not true.

Step 4: Is the material oversimplified?

Stating something in a simple way is good; over-simplification can be a problem. It's important to understand that saying something is oversimplified is a judgment just as much as saying that one movie is "better" than another.

Step 5: Does a statement include emotionally laden words?

This is often true in religious speeches or statements and in politics. Words such as *treason, traitorous, killing babies, believing in the one true faith,* and *illegal foreigners* all communicate a strong personal opinion, usually taking the place of logical reasoning.

Step 6: Is the statement deceptive in any way?

Are apparently logical statements intended to persuade you to agree with someone else's beliefs?

STRATEGY *20.3*

EVALUATE BIAS

Step 1: Can the author's statements be trusted?

Is the speaker or author a highly respected authority in the field? If not, are the sources of information used reliable, accurate, and precise?

Step 2: Does the statement take into account conflicting points of view? Does it treat each way of looking at the issue as important?

Step 3: Is there any evidence of bias?

Speakers who work for a certain company may argue for a decision that would, in the long run, be profitable for their company.

Step 4: What assumptions are made?

Is it assumed that you have certain information or experience or that you share their beliefs or values? Some beliefs and values are so commonly believed that they can be assumed, such as the importance of honesty, kindness, and reliability.

With other beliefs and values, however, there may be little agreement. The ongoing battles between the pro-life groups and those who believe in a woman's right to choose are based, not on facts or logical reasoning, but on different values. Arguments based on values are generally useless.

STRATEGY *20.4*

EVALUATE DATA

When information is based on a survey or experimental data, it is important that you evaluate both the procedure and the data.

Step 1: Was the sample large enough, and was it representative of the entire population? What is surprising is how many respected scientists do not calculate the size of the sample needed for significant results.

Step 2: How was the data recorded?

Were precise measurements made or were personal opinions used?

Step 3: Are the statistics clearly displayed?

Are they properly labeled, and without deceptive techniques?

A common deceptive technique is showing only a small portion of a graph, making very small changes appear significant.

STRATEGY 20.5

EVALUATE CONCLUSIONS

Step 1: Is the evidence relevant?

For example, in stating the main causes of the Civil War, an author might mention the opinions of a number of slaves. While this might be interesting, it probably had no effect on why the war was fought.

Step 2: Is the evidence adequate?

For example, Ben smoked three packs of cigarettes a day and now has colon cancer. He thinks smoking caused his colon cancer. While it is commonly known that smoking causes some kinds of cancer, the evidence that Ben smokes might be relevant but clearly it isn't adequate.

Step 3: What additional evidence is needed?

To prove a relationship between smoking and colon cancer, we'd need to study a huge sample of smokers and nonsmokers whose ages, weight, diets, medical problems, and other factors were similar. Only then could we have a chance of actually showing a relationship. To be more convincing, we'd need to trace how smoking could have an effect on the colon. The effect of smoking on the lungs is easier to explain.

Step 4: What evidence could prove the conclusion false?

Step 5: Does the available evidence actually prove cause and effect?

Sometimes it shows only a correlation. Just because people who chew gum frequently are more likely to play video games would not prove that one caused the other.

STRATEGY 20.6

EVALUATE REASONING

Step 1: Look for the argument and evaluate the reasoning.

In some arguments, as in many political arguments, there is very little reasoning to be evaluated.

Step 2: Does the argument attack a person rather than the issue?

Step 3: Does the argument exaggerate or misrepresent an opponent's viewpoint?

This is sometimes done in order to convince you the other person is wrong.

Step 4: Does this argument use statements by celebrities to convince you to believe it?

Step 5: Do the writers or speakers respect those they disagree with or do they refer to such people as stupid, unreasonable, or even as traitors?

Step 6: Is the reasoning logical?

Does the evidence really prove something is true or is it only used in an attempt to change your opinion?

Thinking critically about research on study skills

You may remember this study from the chapter on reading. Read it again, critically.

John Dunlosky and four other researchers studied hundreds of previous studies on the effectiveness of 10 common learning strategies considered most effective. The strategies that were studied are:

1. Explaining why something is true
2. Relating new information with what is known
3. Summarizing information
4. Highlighting and underlining main ideas
5. Comparing information with sounds
6. Using mental images
7. Rereading the book
8. Testing yourself
9. Distributed practice
10. Interleaved practice (studying two or more subjects in rotation)

Before you read any further, write any problems you see in this study. I found seven important problems.

You may remember the results. The two strategies rated as *most* effective were numbers 8 and 9: self -testing and distributed practice. The five strategies rated *least* effective were numbers 3, 4, 5, 6, and 7: **summarizing, highlighting and underlining,** relating information with sounds, using visual imagery, and **rereading.** The three most commonly used study methods are in bold. They're all in the group of least effective strategies.[5]

Using critical thinking to write a critique: seven problems in this research

First, I should say that Dunlosky and his fellow researchers are all well respected in the field. Dunlosky, for example, is a professor of Psychology at Kent State University and also the Director of Experimental Training. Even the best researchers sometimes do not see the problems in their own work.

1.   We are not told what methods the previous researchers used.

Later, in a part of the paper you didn't read, the researchers pointed out that, with several of these strategies, the problem may have been that students never learned to use the strategies effectively. This would imply that previous research methods were not adequate. They should have done studies comparing three groups: students taught to use the strategy well, students using the strategy with little or no instruction, and students not using the strategy.

2.   We cannot tell whether any of the studies compared all ten strategies.

It is unlikely that this was done. The earlier researchers were more likely to look for the difference between students who used a particular strategy and those who did not. Just because students who used self-testing made higher scores than those who didn't and students using summaries did not score much higher than those not using summaries does not logically prove that self-testing is more effective than writing summaries. Imagine that Carlos and Adam are taking different math classes. Carlos makes an A on his test and Adam makes a C on his test. Would this prove that Carlos is better at math than Adam?

3.   Many students use a variety of different learning strategies.

The students told to write summaries might normally have used other strategies. Using an unfamiliar strategy, might have resulted in lower scores. It is difficult to test the effectiveness of a new strategy compared to using more familiar strategies.

The length of time that a strategy has been used would also make a difference. Students using a new strategy over a period of several months might find it much more effective than students who used it only for a single experiment.

4.   Most disturbing is that they compare "apples and oranges."

While this appears to be a list of learning methods, it actually lists at least four kinds of methods: three reading strategies, two for organizing information, one thinking strategy, and four memory strategies.

Reading strategies include highlighting and underlining, rereading, and interleaved practice (alternating reading for different classes). Interleaved practice is also used in math and for other purposes. The two strategies for organizing information are summarizing and explaining. The only strategy for thinking was relating new information with what is known. Four strategies are mainly related to memory: comparing information with a sound, using mental images, self-testing, and distributed practice.

Comparing different kinds of methods is like comparing a professor and a guitar player. It doesn't make much sense.

5. The researchers left out many of the most effective strategies.

For reading, they should have included taking reading notes, previewing the book and chapter, writing and answering questions, KWL, and SQ3R. For organizing information, they should have added outlining, as well as visual strategies such as diagrams, concept maps, or compare and contrast charts. For thinking, they could have added critical thinking, creative thinking, analysis, and more. For memory, they forgot the two most frequently used strategies: memorizing and mnemonics.

6. While self-testing and distributed practice are definitely outstanding learning methods, we must recognize that, for students to use these, they would first need to read and understand the material.

They probably took notes, organized the information and thought about it, before going on to self-testing using distributed practice. It doesn't make sense to compare students learning at this level with students who are simply reading a chapter.

7. Self-testing and distributed practice are typically used together.

Using two powerful strategies at the same time will lead to improvement in both. Students also use these after having used other strategies. Obviously students working this hard will learn the most.

If you found other problems in the study, please let me know.

This was a brief example of using critical thinking to write a short critique. A full critique would be based on reading the researchers' full paper, of course, and would be considerably longer. In most critiques, it will be hard to find this many problems. But, in spite of these problems, I would still conclude by describing this as a helpful study and I would still agree with many of its findings.

Critical reading

There are many definitions of critical reading.

> *Critical reading requires you to focus your attention much more closely on certain parts of a written text.... As it involves analysis, reflection, evaluation, and making judgments, it usually involves slower reading than that used for recreational reading.*[6]

I found this next explanation of critical reading especially helpful.

> *To the critical reader, any single text provides but one portrayal of the facts, one individual's "take" on the subject matter. Critical readers thus recognize not only what a text says, but also how that text portrays the subject matter. They recognize the various ways in which each and every text is the unique creation of a unique author.*[7]

STRATEGY 20.7

CRITICAL READING

Step 1: Identify the author's goals or purpose.

Go further and identify their thesis, facts, opinions, evidence, and reasoning.

Step 2: Understand what the author says.

Step 3: Think about the information.

Consider how it is related to what you're learning in class or to information you already knew.

Step 4: Decide what you find most helpful or informative.

Critical reading involves thinking about what you read, asking what other opinions might exist on the subject, and deciding for yourself what makes sense.

Critical writing

When writing, it is your own ideas, your own words, and your own reasoning you must study. As you write, take time to look back at your work and ask whether it's clear, unbiased, and logical, with evidence added that's both relevant and sufficient.

*Most of the text is dedicated to presenting a case through pro-
viding reasons, using relevant evidence, comparing and evaluating alternative arguments, weighing up conflicting evidence,
and forming judgments on the basis of the evidence.*[8]

STRATEGY 20.8

CRITICAL WRITING

Step 1: With critical writing you use critical thinking as you write.

You must begin with careful thinking as you decide what you want to say.

Step 2: Identify the purpose of your writing.

Are you writing to inform or explain, to influence or persuade, to express your
ideas or tell a story, or to entertain?

Step 3: Create an outline that will help you reach your goals.

Step 4: As you write, ask if your writing is clear, fair, and logical.

Critical listening begins with understanding

Critical listening does not mean telling the other person that their evidence isn't adequate or that their reasoning is illogical. That would be arguing rather than listening. Browne and Keeley suggest that "critical thinking
is a "friendly tool, one that can improve the lives of the listener and the
speaker, the reader and the writer." They suggest seven helpful techniques,
of which I include only four (quoting from their book).

STRATEGY 20.9

CRITICAL LISTENING

Step 1: "Be certain to demonstrate that you really want to grasp what is being
said. Ask questions that indicate your willingness to grasp and accept new
conclusions…

Step 2: "Restate what you heard or read and ask whether your understanding…is consistent with what was written or spoken….

Step 3: "Voice your critical questions as if you are curious. Nothing is more
deadly… than an attitude of 'Aha, I caught you making an error'….

Step 4: "Convey the impression that you and the other person are collabora-
tors, working toward the same objective—improved conclusions."[9]

Critical reflection

Reflecting critically is sometimes called metacognitive thinking. It involves examining your own beliefs, opinions, and goals, asking whether they're clear, honest, unbiased, and supported by good reasoning. Critical reflection also includes questioning and examining your assumptions, likes and dislikes, and deepest values.

"People who are outstanding at critical thinking tend to be particularly self-aware. They reflect on and evaluate their personal motivations, interests, prejudices, expertise and gaps in their knowledge. They question their own points of view and check the evidence to support it."[10]

When practicing critical reflection, it's best to choose one topic to focus on at a time. I find it particularly helpful to write my questions and then my answers to those questions. This is the reason why each chapter in this book ends with questions for reflection. If the questions you find here aren't quite right for you, write your own questions.

> *Once learners begin questioning the assumptions underlying conventional wisdom in academic subjects, they are likely to apply the same critical habits to analyzing their own lives and the political structures in which these lives are lived.*[11]

STRATEGY 20.10

CRITICAL REFLECTION

Step 1: Examine your beliefs.

Select something you believe or have a strong opinion about, something that cannot be proved with evidence. Ask yourself how you arrived at this belief.

Step 2: Ask why you believe this.

Ask yourself what it would take for you to change your belief or opinion.

Step 3: How important is this belief or opinion in your life?

Step 4: Reflect on your own thinking.

What are you thinking about when you think most clearly? When or on which topics should you learn to think more clearly and objectively?

Step 5: In what ways may your thinking be biased?

When do you accept information without questioning? Which ideas or beliefs are most difficult for you to examine, and why?

The importance of asking deep questions

The most valuable advice I was given when I was young came from my pastor, Rev. Goddard Sherman. He encouraged me to question *everything*. He said it was good to question what your parents say, what your teachers and textbooks tell you, even what you learn in church.

As a child, growing up in the 50's in the segregated South, I was taught that segregation was the best system for both black and white people. I dared to question that idea. Arguing for integration at that time in history did not make me very popular, but I knew it was the right thing to do.

Some students today are taught by parents or religious leaders that being gay or lesbian is a choice and leads to a sinful lifestyle. In recent years, many people have dared to question that belief and have come to different conclusions.

When you dare to question your own beliefs, you may arrive at conclusions that are not comfortable, but they will be *your* beliefs, not your family's beliefs. As more people are brave enough to question and reflect on their own thinking, the easier it will be to create positive changes in the world.

Questions for Reflection:

1. What opinions or beliefs do you need to examine critically?
2. What are some of the Big Questions you need to explore?
3. What surprised you in this chapter? What was the most important thing you learned? How will you use what you learned?

21

Analytical Reasoning: Interpreting Numerical and Verbal Data

Interpreting data involves probing the data for their meaning within the context of the inquiry and inquiry question. In this process you will be making assumptions, adding meaning and moving to conclusions about possible actions. The data may raise as many questions as it answers.[1]

As you move on to more difficult courses, as you begin doing serious research, and as you launch your career, you may need to organize and interpret large amounts of data. This chapter is, of course, only a brief introduction to the topic. To learn more, you should read a book or take a course on the subject.

Interpreting numerical or quantitative data

You probably learned the basic information about graphs in elementary and middle school and, with any luck, improved those skills in high school. You might even know how to use a computer program such as Excel to create a variety of graphs. What many students find most difficult, however, is interpreting the graphs.

Exercise: Understanding and Using Tables and Graphs

1. Explain when it's appropriate to use a pie graph, column graph, bar graph, line graph, or histogram.

2. What kind of information usually goes on the x-axis and on the y-axis of a graph?

3. Explain mean, median, and mode. How are they similar? How are they different? Why might you choose to use one rather than another?

4. In what classes have you used tables? In what classes have you created them?

5. How is a graph different from a table? What's the advantage of each?

Starting with the basics: Understanding Line Graphs

Let us begin with a very simple series of examples, possibly too easy for some of you but still difficult for others. Consider Graph 21.1. What data is shown on the x-axis? On the y-axis? If you have trouble remembering which is the x-axis, think of the x-*axis as a place where roads cross*. They go across (horizontally). The *y-axis goes up high—it aims at the sky* (vertically). Note that for each graph in this chapter, you are first shown the table used to organize the data.

Table 21.1 and Graph 21.1 Distance Over Time #1

Hours	Miles
10	600
9	540
8	480
7	420
6	360
5	300
4	240
3	180
2	120
1	60
0	0

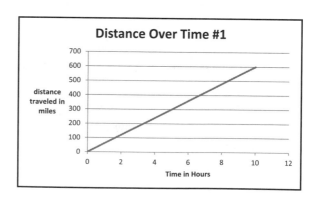

Can You Answer These Questions?

1. Why does the line on the graph go up?

2. At what speed is the car traveling?

3. How far did the car travel in one hour? In two hours? In 10 hours?

4. How far do you think the car will have traveled in 11 hours?

A Similar Graph Based on Different Data

Table 21.2 and Graph 21.2 Distance Over Time #2

Hours	Miles
10	540
9	530
8	500
7	420
6	340
5	260
4	220
3	180
2	180
1	120
0	60

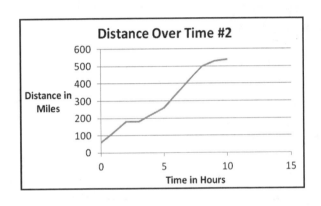

1. Do you find the information easier to understand on the table or on the graph?

2. How is Graph 21.2 the same as the previous one, and how it is different?

3. What does this graph show at two hours? What does this mean? What might have happened?

4. Explain what happened and what the graph might show at three hours, at five hours, and at eight hours. Suggest a possible explanation for the entire pattern.

In line graphs, the x-axis generally shows something that is set or changing in a regular way like time. The y-axis shows the variable. Here the variable or what is changing is distance. If someone put the distance on the x-axis. It would be like upending this graph and it would be very difficult to understand.

Reflecting on the Two Line Graphs

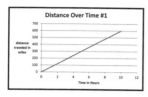

Some students assume that when the line in Graph 21.1 goes up, the car is going up a mountain. Others believe the car is accelerating. Both answers are wrong.

In this case—check the y-axis—it's the distance that is increasing. You should recognize that if the car travels the same distance in an hour, the car's speed is constant. If the y-axis showed speed instead of distance, then this same line would show change in speed which is acceleration.

It is hard to estimate the distance traveled in the first hour but, after checking the second hour, it should be clear that the car is traveling at 60 miles per hour. This is particularly easy to calculate when you see that in 10 hours it covered 600 miles. If it continued at this speed for another hour it will have gone 660 miles.

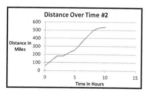

Graph 21.2 is more interesting and more challenging than the first one. Notice that the first graph begins at 0,0. The car had not begun to move yet. Therefore it needed to go a little faster than 60 mph to average 60 mph for the first hour. The second graph starts at 0,60. The distance traveled is already 60 miles. It simply continues at the speed. At about two hours, the line suddenly stops moving up. It goes flat for a bit. Notice that the distance is no longer changing. The car isn't moving. Several things might have happened. The driver and passengers might have stopped for lunch. The gap seems too long to be just a restroom break. There might also have been a bad accident, leaving traffic totally blocked for an hour. This car probably wasn't seriously involved since it soon speeds up.

At about the third hour, the car begins moving again, but the slope or angle of incline is a little less; the car is moving more slowly. The change in speed is hard to notice because of the break between the two parts of the line.

Why might a car go more slowly? There could be traffic problems, perhaps road construction, or they might be traveling on a secondary road with a lower speed limit. They could also be going through a city with a much lower speed limit.

At about the fifth hour, the line becomes even steeper than before; they're going faster. Perhaps they were trying to make up for lost time.

From the eighth hour to the end, the slope gradually becomes less steep and nearly goes flat. They are slowing down. Again, they may be in a city where the speed limit is lower, and they may be further slowed by traffic lights. They apparently slow down even further as they approach their destination, perhaps watching for street signs or asking for directions.

Notice that each description above began with a description of the graph itself, followed by the meaning of the changing slope, and finally a possible explanation.

STRATEGY *21.1*

CREATING A SIMPLE GRAPH

Step 1: Know what types of graphs should be used for different information.

Step 2: Consider your data and form a clear question.

Step 3: Select the appropriate type of graph.

Step 4: Create a simple table to display the data in an organized way.

Step 5: Create the graph from the data.

Step 6: Label the x-axis and y-axis properly.

Step 7: Write a title that describes what is shown in the graph.

Step 8: Label the x and y-axis to describe what is shown on the graph. When it makes sense, include the general category and specific units such as time in hours, time in weeks, age in years, height in inches, weight in pounds, or speed in miles/sec.

STRATEGY *21.2*

INTERPRETING A SIMPLE GRAPH

Step 1: Read the title carefully.

Step 2: Read the labels on the x-axis and y-axis.

Step 3: Describe what you see on the graph.

Step 4: Interpret what you see on the graph. What does it mean?

Step 5: State the purpose of the graph. What does it show?

Step 6: Evaluate the graph.

Does the graph make sense? Is there really a relationship between the information on the x-axis and the y-axis? Would another type of graph have been a better choice? Should it have been labeled more clearly? Could the title have been more helpful?

Reflections on the Earlier Exercise

A pie graph (also called a pie chart, circle graph, or circle chart) is always used to show parts of the whole.

A column or bar graph shows a comparison of information by category. Nothing is changing over time.

A line graph usually shows how a variable changes over time.

A histogram is similar to a bar or column graph but shows information for a range of data such as ages 10-20 or prices from $50-$100, or speeds from 30-50 mph.

The information on the x-axis is set or independent. Information on the y-axis is dependent or variable. This is the information that changes. The speed of the car can change. The number of people who like a flavor of ice cream can also vary.

A table shows the numbers clearly but may be hard to interpret. The graph may not show the numbers as clearly but it presents the big picture. It gives us a way to interpret the data.

Understanding Pie Graphs

The two most important things you need to know if you create a pie graph are that all numbers must be stated as percentages of the whole thing and therefore the numbers must add up to 100%. Some strange pie graphs appear now and then in newspapers or even on TV where the numbers added up to 135% or something equally weird.

Table 21.3 U.S. Four-Year Title IV Colleges

Kinds of Colleges	Percent
Public	22.70%
Private nonprofit	52.30%
Private for profit	25.00%

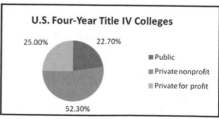

What do you find surprising on this graph?

Many people who simply read the numbers don't see the comparison quite so clearly. I would have expected private for profit colleges to be the smallest group, certainly not the largest.

Column and Bar Graphs

Column graphs and bar graphs show the same information. You've probably never heard of column graphs unless you've used Excel or a similar computer graphing program. Most people call both of them bar graphs. Both compare information in categories rather than across time. On a column graph, the bars are vertical; on a bar graph, like Graph 21.4, they are horizontal. With bar graphs you have more space to identify each item.

You might use column or bar graphs to show the numbers of people who prefer different ice-cream flavors, different types of music, or different sports. None of these include ordered categories. The choices can be listed in any order. Some people prefer to list the categories from most popular or most common to least popular or least common. Creating a line graph for this kind of information makes no sense. Nothing is changing over time.

Table 21.4 Favorite Flavors

Ice Cream Flavors	
Flavor	# of people
Moose Tracks	7
Maple Walnut	10
Cookies and Cream	5
Strawberry	17
Vanilla	37
Chocolate	24

Graph 21.4 Bar Graph: Favorite Flavors of Ice Cream

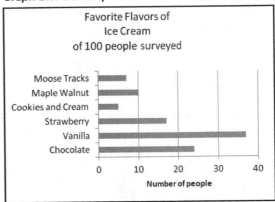

If the x-axis lists a category like ice cream flavors, the graph should be a bar or column graph.

Histograms

If the x-axis lists intervals such as ages 0–9, 10–19, and 20–29, it's best to use a histogram like Graph 21.5 (similar to a bar graph but with bars touching).

Table 21.5 Reunion Participants

Age	0-9	10-19	20-29	30-39	40-49	50-59	60-69	70-79	80-89	90-99
Number	17	6	22	34	28	25	29	32	16	7

Graph 21.5 Histogram Showing Reunion Participants

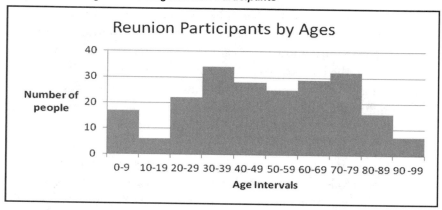

We see that most people at the reunion were in the 20-80 age group. It is easy to explain the lower numbers at older ages, but the reason for the small number in the 10-19 age group is not so clear.

Understanding the three measures of central tendency

Most students are familiar with averages, but less certain about mean, median, and mode. The mean is what we commonly call the average. When professors calculate your grades, they add up your test grades and divide by the number of tests to get your average. This is the mean.

The median is simply the number in the center of the list. Think of the median strip in the road. It is right in the center.

The mode is the number that appears most often. Here's an example showing grades on a biology test:

14, 17, 24, 24, 24, 24, 24, 24, 48, 50, 73, 79, 80, 80, 81, 83, 83, 83, 84, 85, 100

The average or mean is 57.7 although no students made that exact grade. The mode is 24. Six students made this grade. The median grade is 79. This is the number right in the center.

If you were thinking of getting a job in a company that tells you the average annual salary is $150,000, it might sound great, but the CEO might be making $6 million, thus skewing the average. There might be no one making this "average salary." It would be helpful to know what salary is made by the largest number of people—the mode. But, you might object, those are the factory workers and you'd expect to earn more than that. In that case, the median might be more helpful. You might anticipate a starting salary somewhere between the mode and the median.

Presentation and Use of Data

Good data presentation skills are to data-based analysis what good writing is to literature, and some of the same basic principles apply to both. Poor graphical and tabular presentations often lead both readers and writers to draw erroneous conclusions from the data and obscure facts that better presentations would reveal. Some of these practices involve deliberate distortions of data, but more commonly they involve either unintentional distortions of data or more simply ineffective approaches to presenting numerical evidence.[2]

Deliberate distortions of data are often used by politicians who interpret data to their own advantage. Debates rage on in Congress and state legislatures about what the evidence proves with regard to global warming, about changes in the crime rates, and about why American students score so poorly on international tests. Some public figures argue opposing positions, all the while appearing to prove their positions with carefully selected, nonrepresentative statistics.

Interpreting complex tables

Small tables are usually easy to understand but, with extensive research, the tables can be extremely large and complex. To interpret the data, you need to understand the main ideas, list specific questions you'd like to answer, and organize the information. At this point the information may be clear. If not, a graph of the data might be helpful.

Table 21.6, though less than one quarter the size of the original complex table, is still overwhelming. And, believe it or not, I looked for a large data table that was fairly easy to understand.

Table 21.6 STEM Occupations
Among employed 25-34-year-olds with a bachelor's degree in a science, technology, engineering, or mathematics (STEM) field, percentage with STEM and non-STEM occupations by sex, race/ethnicity, nativity, and citizenship status: 2011.

	TOTAL	STEM total	Computer Math	Engineers Architects	Sciences	Medical
Total*	100	47.8	12.5	8.8	5.5	21.1
Sex						
Male	100	48.9	19.6	14	5.2	10.1
Female	100	46.7	5.4	3.6	5.8	31.9
Race/ethnicity						
White	100	47.1	9.5	9.3	5.7	22.6
Black	100	39.5	10.1	4.5	3.8	21.1
Hispanic	100	38.2	7.7	8.8	4.8	16.9
Asian	100	59.3	27.2	9.1	5.9	17.1
American Indian/Alaska Native**	100	40.3	7.6	6.7	3.7	22.3
American Indian	100	33.7	6.4	3.9	3.9	19.5
Two or more races	100	46.8	14.6	6.3	6.1	19.9
Race/ethnicity by sex						
Male						
White	100	46.5	15.9	15.3	5.4	10
Black	100	39.7	18.3	8.5	2.7	10.1
Hispanic	100	39.5	12.2	14.3	4.1	8.9
Asian	100	63.8	35.2	11.9	5.6	11
American Indian/Alaska Native*	100	37	15.4	16	‡	‡
American Indian	100	27.2	‡	10.7	‡	‡
Two or more races	100	48	20.3	9.6	6.3	11.9
Female						
White	100	47.7	3.3	3.6	6	34.8
Black	100	39.4	4.7	1.9	4.6	28.2
Hispanic	100	36.9	3.6	3.7	5.4	24.2
Asian	100	53.2	16.2	5.4	6.2	25.4
American Indian/Alaska Native*	100	42.2	‡	‡	‡	35
American Indian	100	37.3	‡	#	‡	30.1
Two or more races	100	45.5	8.1	2.6	5.8	28.9

* Total includes other racial/ethnic groups not shown separately.** Includes persons reporting American Indian alone, Alaska Native alone, and American Indian and/or Alaska Native tribes specified or not specified
# Averages to zero.
‡ Reporting standards not met. Either there are too few cases for a reliable estimate or the coefficient of variation (CV) is 50 percent or greater.
SOURCE: U.S. Department of Commerce, Census Bureau, American Community Survey (ACS), 2011. Note: This is about 1/6 of the original chart; Table 505.30.

To see the entire table, go to http://nces.ed.gov.programs/digest/d13/tables/dt13_505.30.asp (retrieved August 21, 2014).

As you take a quick look at the table, begin by trying to answer two simple questions:

1.   How many men and how many women work in STEM and non-STEM occupations?

2.   Are there more men or more women working in STEM occupations?

Write down your answers. These questions will be discussed later.

You'll see that the main categories in the title are areas of STEM occupations (Science, Technology, Engineering, and Mathematics). Continuing to the right was the list of non-STEM occupations. These were removed so the table would fit on the page.

If you're very observant, you might notice that the categories on the actual table are not the STEM categories listed in the title of the table. Instead, they include Math (and computers), Engineers and Architects, Sciences (including social sciences), and Medical. Many areas with incomplete data or information you wouldn't need were also removed, making this table comparatively simple.

STRATEGY 21.2

INTERPRETING A COMPLEX TABLE

For this strategy, I will demonstrate the necessary thinking for each step.

Step 1: Describe what the table is about.

Reading the title usually gives you a good idea. This title tells us the table is about college graduates from 25 to 34 years old who are employed in a STEM field. There will be information about males and females and about several races or ethnicities. If you don't take the time to read titles carefully, you'll often miss some of the main ideas.

From this, you know that people who did not graduate from college or people older than 34 years or younger than 25 years, even if they work in this area, are not included in the statistics.

Step 2: Ask questions you should be able to answer by using this table.

Start with simple questions before asking more complex ones.

My first question was: "How many men and how many women work in STEM and non-STEM occupations?"

Step 3: Create a smaller table, using only the data you need to answer the question.

Step 4: Use this data to create a graph.

Step 5: Interpret the data, using either the table or the graph, or both.

This involves writing a brief explanation of what can be learned from the data. Generally, this focuses on the most interesting or most surprising information or perhaps the greatest contrasts.

Beginning with two simple questions

Let us begin with the two "simple" questions asked earlier.

How many men work in STEM occupations? Did you think the answer was 47.8? Did this make any sense? To begin with, you can't have eight tenths of a man. And then, wouldn't you think there are a lot more than 47 men working in these areas? What does this number mean? If I had created this table, I would have made it clear.

One clue is the "100" written in the first column. You are expected to understand that the number of men in STEM occupations are 47.8 out of each 100 men surveyed. This means the table shows percentages, not actual numbers.

The correct answers to the question could be either "47.8% of the men surveyed" or "There is no way to know because we don't know the number of men surveyed."

The second question seems easier, but is it, really? The percentage of men in STEM occupations is 47.8%. The percentage of women is only 46.7%. Doesn't this mean there are more men than women?

Think again. If 47.8 % of the workers in this area are men and 46.7% are women, that would add up to 94.5%. Something is wrong here. Who are the workers who are *not* men or women?

You need to be cautious when discussing percentages. We should ask, "percent of what?" The researchers who prepared the chart weren't talking about percentage of the total number of people in STEM occupations. They were talking about the percentage of the men who were surveyed and the percentage of the women who were surveyed. It makes no sense to add these percentages or compare them.

Are the total number of employed men and women ages 25–34 with degrees in STEM areas the same? If they are, you would be right. You could compare them. But I've seen statistics showing that many more women are getting college degrees. It is possible that, if more women fit this description, that 46.7% of the women might be more than 47.8% of the men.

If this isn't clear, ask yourself which is greater, 46% of 200 or 48% of 100.

Let's take this insight one step further. When you realize that you're looking at percentages of employed men or women, you should also realize that percentages of different-sized populations can be confusing.

We can probably assume that there are far more white males than Hispanic males with a bachelor's degree in STEM areas. This would mean that 30% of white males and 30% of Hispanic males therefore represent very different numbers. The 30% of white males would be a much higher number.

If you are clear about these distinctions, you probably know more about statistics than most college students.

The first simple graph

My first question was "How many men and how many women work in STEM and non-STEM occupations?" This question should be rewritten as "**What percentage** of men and **what percentage** of women work in STEM and non-STEM occupations?" These questions can be answered.

With this simple table, there is no need for a graph. But if you wanted a graph, you would need two of them, one to show the percentage of women and one to show the percentage of men.

Table 21.7 Men and Women in STEM and Non-STEM Occupations

	STEM	Non-STEM
Men	47.80%	52.20%
Women	46.70%	53.30%

How did we know the number of men and women with this background working in non-STEM occupations?

Graph 21.7-A Men in STEM Occupations

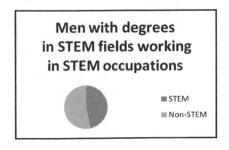

Graph 21.7-B Women in STEM Occupations

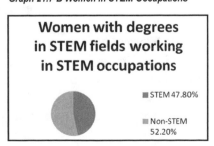

To answer the last question, the percentage of men in non-stem occupations is found by subtracting the percentage in the area from 100%. *My interpretation:* While a slightly higher percentage of men have STEM jobs, the percentage of men and women who are employed in STEM jobs is surprisingly similar.

Answers to the third question and the graph based on this table

My third question was "What are the percentages of men and women in each of the four categories of STEM occupations?" I needed to look in different parts of the chart for the male and female statistics. Again, you might not need a graph to interpret this data. Since this involves categories, a bar graph is more appropriate.

Table 21.8 Percentages of Men and Women in Four STEM Occupation Areas

	Medicine	Science	Engineering	Math
Men	51.1	5.2	14	19.6
Women	53.3	5.8	3.6	5.4

Graph 21.8 Percentages of Men and Women in Four STEM Occupation Areas.

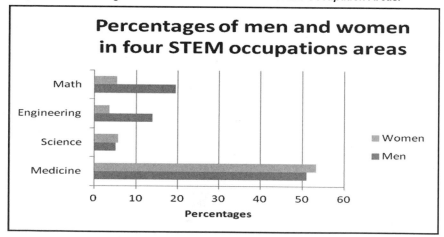

My interpretation: It's clear that men and women in STEM fields tend to work in different areas. Men choose math and engineering far more often than women; women choose science and medicine slightly more often than men. It might also be noted that by far, the largest number of people surveyed work in the medical field.

The Fourth Question

My fourth question was to ask how this information varied in the different racial/ethnic groups. Table 21.9, my choice for organizing this information, is more complex than in earlier tables but still can be understood fairly easily. Again, all this information is found on the complex table.

Table 21.9 Men and Women of Different Ethnic Groups in Different STEM Jobs

		Math	Engineering	Science	Medicine	Non-STEM
Asian	Men	35.2	11.9	5.6	11	36.2
	Women	16.2	5.4	6.2	25.4	46.8
Hispanic	Men	12.2	14.3	4.1	8.9	60.5
	Women	3.6	3.7	5.4	24.2	63.1
Black	Men	1.83	8.5	2.7	10.1	60.3
	Women	4.7	1.9	4.6	28.2	60.6
White	Men	15.9	15.3	5.4	10	53.5
	Women	3.3	3.6	6	34.8	52.3

Graph 21.9 Men and Women of Different Ethnic Groups in Different STEM Jobs

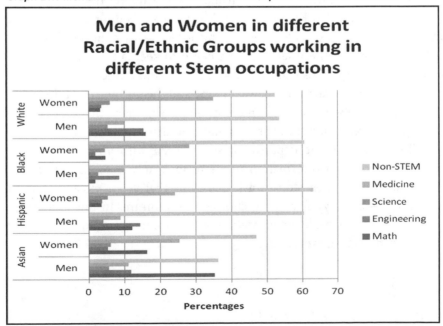

Interpretation: Write this one yourself.

The Interpretation of Verbal or Qualitative Data

Imagine that you're doing anthropology research in a small village in Kenya. What kind of information would you collect? Imagine that you're working in a department store. Your boss brings you a dozen file boxes of reports, budgets, minutes taken in meetings, emails, and other data. Or imagine that you're writing a thesis on the behavior of different species of monkeys, as observed both in the zoo and in the wild. How would you organize and interpret these kinds of data?

> *In much qualitative research, the analytical process begins during data collection as the data already gathered is analyzed and shapes ongoing data collection.*[3]

Organizing quantitative or numerical data is fairly straightforward. You begin by putting the numbers in data tables. You make it easier to interpret the information by organizing the data in a variety of graphs, each designed to answer a particular question.

With verbal or qualitative data, you must also start with questions and then organize the data to try to find the answers. The question is how you organize the data. You should ask your questions early in the process and focus on collecting the data that will allow you to answer these questions.

The researcher in Kenya might ask what work is done most often by men or by women; by elderly people, by adults, or by children. With this question in mind, the researcher can begin to keep a record of who did each kind of work. This will change verbal data into numerical data.

If researchers wait until they get home and then want to sort the information, their job will be much more difficult. You make the job easier by listing questions you want to answer and collecting appropriate data.

The person in the department store, faced with an unmanageable amount of random information needs to look at a small sample of the information and then stop to ask questions that seem most important and most necessary for making choices in the future. In this case, these questions act as a guide for separating out the information that is relevant rather than reading everything.

Sex in red maple trees—a true story of interpreting verbal data

When working on my master's degree in biology, I did my thesis on red maples. (The sex came later.) One day I was looking out a window with the professor who taught my class on "Trees and Shrubs." I knew that the trees in the distance with the deep-red flowers were red maples. My books said red maples, *Acer rubrum*, had red stems and red flowers in the spring and red leaves in the fall. I had no idea which trees had orange flowers, and the professor didn't know, either.

That afternoon, I checked the trees and I was amazed. The trees that appeared to have orange flowers were *also* red maples. The flowers were still red, but they had so much pollen, they appeared to be orange. The red flowering trees had no pollen, no stamens. They had pistils. I had no idea that red maples had male and female trees. Neither did the professor or any books I could find. It was a fascinating discovery, yet not enough for a thesis.

Over the next several years I kept records on several hundred maple trees. I noted the colors of the flowers (ranging from yellow to dark red), if the trees were males or females, the color of their leaves (the same range of colors plus leaves splotched with several different colors) and the environment. I hoped to find some relationships between some of these factors, but had no success.

Then, finally, I discovered something really shocking. I found one tree, an old female tree, with one branch that had a few male flowers. I first decided it must be a strange mutation, but I looked for others and I found them.

This time my question was what might cause this to happen. My hypothesis was that when trees were stressed, possibly about to die, they might produce some chemical that stimulated the growth of male flowers. This would give these trees an evolutionary advantage. Since female trees can't tell if there are male trees nearby, having male flowers on the same branch would ensure reproduction.

I surveyed a large group of trees, including what I called my "multi-sex" trees, for anything that might cause stress: flooding, construction that might damage the roots, being hit by a car, or severe infestation by gypsy moth caterpillars. I could use numbers for the many causes of stress: one meant no obvious stress and five meant serious stress.

My data tables included male trees and female trees, with and without male flowers, each with the various levels of stress. Male trees, even those with a great deal of stress, showed no female flowers. Female trees with a higher stress level had the largest number of male flowers. There *was* a definite relationship between stress and having both male and female flowers.

I thought it would be fun to call my thesis "Sex in the Maple Tree," but my professors were not amused. The final title was "A Study of Variation in *Acer rubrum*."

STRATEGY 21.3

INTERPRETING VERBAL OR QUALITATIVE DATA

Step 1: Identify your goals.

Step 2: Start with questions.

Step 3: Based on the questions, collect appropriate data.

Step 4: Sort the data, using numbers where relevant. Look for data that can be ordered, or rated, such as *excellent, good, satisfactory, fair,* or *poor.*

Step 5: Evaluate data as relevant and not relevant. If dealing with an unwieldy amount of data, select samples of data from each category.

Step 6: Search for potential relationships.

Step 7: Where possible, create data tables and create graphs.

Step 8: For each question, list possible answers and sort the data that supports each answer.

Step 9: Summarize information, the methods you used, what you learned, and your level of certainty.

Errors in interpretation of data

Many errors are made in interpreting data. One of the most interesting is called "Rooster Crowed: the Sun Rose." This type of error assumes that, because one event occurred before another, the first event caused the second one. Taken to the point of absurdity we have: "Rooster crowed; the sun rose; therefore the rooster made the sun rise."[4]

While we know this is absurd, we commonly hear that a person was elected mayor or police chief or governor; the crime rate went down or education scores went up; therefore, the newly elected official deserves the credit. This makes as little sense as the rooster making the sun rise. Notice that these same people will not claim the credit if the crime rate went up or student scores went down. In your work, there must be a clear explanation of how one thing actually caused the other.

Sometimes, when there really is a relationship between events, it might be because both were caused by something else. If you learn that people who brush their teeth more often are less likely to be obese, it clearly isn't because brushing teeth will cause you to lose weight. It could be because people with good health habits might brush their teeth more often, eat healthier foods, and get regular exercise. These habits could lead to less obesity.

Returning to the rooster example, this might be an instance of reverse causation: Before the sun rises, the sky gets lighter, which might cause the rooster to wake up and crow.

A similar example is this one: "Death penalty states…actually have higher murder rates than non–death penalty states. We should ask if this is because the death penalty fosters more violence in society, or is it that more violent states tend to adopt the death penalty?"[5]

Another common error in data interpretation might be due to changes in sample sizes. Check out Table 21.9. In fact, this table puzzled so many people that it's called a Simpson's Paradox.

Table 21.9 SAT Verbal Scores by Race and Ethnicity

	1981	2002	Gain
White	519	527	+8
Puerto Rican	437	455	+18
Mexican	438	446	+8
Black	412	431	+19
Asian	474	501	+27
American Indian	471	479	+8
All Students	504	504	0

Source: Gerald Bracey, "Those Misleading SAT and NAEP Trends," 2003.

What do you notice about this table? First, you must notice that these are average scores on the SAT verbal test, from two different years, 1981 and 2002. You should then notice that the last column shows the average scores and gain for six ethnic groups. Most people who look at it notice the greatly improved scores for every ethnic group on the chart. They conclude that the average scores on the SAT are going up, but they are flat wrong. Look at the last category. When they consider all students taking the test, the average score both in 1981 and in 2002 was 504; the two scores are exactly the same.

Can you explain how this could be true? How could every ethnic group show improving scores while the averages stay the same?[6]

This time, it isn't the percentages that cause a problem, but another important number is missing.

You might say this is one of those situations where there's good news and there's bad news. After the questions for reflection, you'll find the explanation. First, try to explain how it is possible that scores improved for every group taking the test, but that the average score did not change.

Edward Tufte: Best known expert in this area

Edward Tufte is sometimes described as a pioneer in the field of data visualization. His books are among the best known in the field. If I were to recommend one book in this area, it would be his book *The Visual Display of Quantitative Information,* in which he writes:

> *Excellence on statistical graphics consists of complex ideas communicated with clarity, precision, and efficiency. Graphical displays should…induce the viewer to think about the substance rather than about methodology….*[7]

Questions for Reflection:
---

1. What information in this chapter did you already know well?

2. What surprised you? What was the most important thing you learned? How might you use what you learned?

3. Considering your future goals, should you learn more about interpreting data?

What really happened with those SAT scores?

The explanation for Table 21.9 begins with the fact that we simply don't know the numbers of students in each group who took the tests. Second, the numbers are average scores for that particular group. If there had been little or no change in the number of students taking the test in each group, this wouldn't be a problem.

Here are two hints that might help you

1. What would you guess might have taken place with the numbers of students over those 20 years?

2. Which group had the highest average score both times?

Another two hints if you really need them

1. The number of white students taking the test probably increased.

2. I don't know the numbers, but I do know the number of minority students increased at a much greater rate.

Even though the minority students were making better scores than in the past, they were still making scores that were lower than the white students' scores. The larger number of minority students lowered the overall averages, while the increasing scores in each group raised averages. They just happened to raise and lower the scores by the same amount. How can we explain why the new average is exactly the same as the earlier average? That happened strictly by chance.

Complex problem solving: the five levels of complexity

Problem solving is puzzle solving. Each smaller problem is a smaller piece of the puzzle to find and solve. Putting the pieces of the puzzle together involves understanding the relevant parts of the system. Once all the key pieces are found and understood, the puzzle as a whole "snaps" together, sometimes in a final flash of insight.[1]

Imagine that you're about to begin working on a jigsaw puzzle. If the puzzle has only 500 pieces, you can probably solve it by yourself but, if it has 50,000 pieces, you probably want others to work with you.

Just as there are different levels of difficulty in jigsaw puzzles, there are levels of difficulty in problem-solving. While you can solve some problems fairly quickly by yourself, solving monumental problems like world hunger or climate change would require the creative thinking, resources, and commitment of large numbers of people and countries around the world.

The goal of this chapter is to help you solve problems more effectively now, and to encourage you to develop your skills so you can contribute to the solution of problems in your work, in your communities, and in the world.

Recognizing the problem is more important than recognizing the solution since an accurate representation of the problem leads to its solution. — Albert Einstein

---
Exercise: Problem-Solving
---

1. Name five problems you'd like to solve, including some that could be solved in less than a day and others that might require weeks, months, or years.

2. When you decide to work on a problem, how do you go about it?

A level one problem is a choice

You might solve a level one problem in less than an hour. You don't need to explore the problem; it is likely to be obvious. You don't need to list alternatives; they might already be clear. Still, making a decision isn't always easy. As you read these examples, take notes on what each of these students could do.

1. Winter is coming and Belinda needs a winter coat. Should Belinda pay more for a blue coat that is extra-warm, or buy the less-expensive red coat that looks more stylish but isn't as warm? Or should she simply have the broken zipper replaced on the jacket she wore in high school? Belinda really can't afford either of the coats she likes.

2. Spring break is coming and Diego would love to go to Florida with friends but the trip would be expensive. He was offered a short-term job—substituting for a student who's going to Ft. Lauderdale—for which Diego could earn close to $800. He needs the money, but going to Florida sounds like fun.

Level two problems are more than just decisions

For level two problems, you might need to understand the problem and think seriously about the alternatives. You might need to ask for advice or help.

3. Keisha can't find her cell phone. It's the third time this week she's had this problem. She doesn't just need to find her cell phone; she needs to avoid losing it again.

4. Sam's roommate likes to study late with music playing but Sam needs his sleep. They should have discussed the issue when they first met, but several months have gone by. What can Sam do?

5. Paula's 20-year-old car has had several minor problems that she had fixed, but a new problem will cost her over $500. Is it worth paying this much to fix an old car?

While it is easy enough to understand these problems, these students must still consider the consequences of each possible decision.

Level three problems are more complex and may affect other people.

Level three problems are more complex. They require a deeper analysis of the problems and solutions may not be easy to define.

6. Patrick didn't realize his bank account was so low. His check bounced— the check for this semester's books. He doesn't have money to pay the bill and he cannot call his parents for help.

7. You know you are gay or lesbian, but never told anyone. You are tired of living a lie but afraid of how your friends or family will respond if you tell them. What are your alternatives? Others might think this is simply a matter of making a choice, but you know it will affect your parents, grandparents, and your brothers and sisters. It might affect your relationships with new friends you've made on campus as well as your high school friends with whom you've kept in touch. It might even affect your ability to get a job. You should certainly find someone to talk to before making a decision. You might be wary of approaching your pastor after hearing that others who talked to their pastors were no long accepted in the church.

Level four problems are complex and involve a large team working together

The most complex kinds of problem you are likely to experience are level four problems. These might involve solving problems in your job, or in an organization you're part of, or in a political campaign you're working for (or even running for office yourself). In most cases, the decisions are made by a large group.

8. Your college has too few parking spaces. Juanita has been late to one class three times now and actually missed the class once because she couldn't find a parking space. Other students are having similar problems. This isn't just Juanita's problem; it's a college-wide problem. Juanita would like to work with other students to find a solution.

9. Jamar is president of his own company, which has a number of problems. The price of raw materials is going up. The competition is selling similar products for less. The labor unions insist that the workers need higher salaries. The government wants the company to pay more for their health care. Jamar doesn't want to lay off workers. What else can he do?

10. Zelda feels strongly about the next presidential election. She took off time from her job to work in the campaign. Over the years, Zelda held important positions in her city and state government. Now, people in her state want her to run for the U.S. Senate to help support the president. Zelda doesn't like the current senator and knows she could do a better job. What problems will she need to solve? What strategies will be most effective?

Level five problems are national or global problems

Monumental problems that a single organization cannot solve working alone can be categorized as level five problems. Such problems are often a combination of many related problems, so they require a massive, coordinated group of solutions. They require the cooperation of many national and global organizations working together. You can probably name several such problems:

- Global warming/climate change
- World hunger
- Preventing wars
- Curing cancer and other diseases and dealing with Ebola epidemics
- Providing a good education for all the world's children
- Developing alternative sources of energy before the current sources are depleted

Even in much-discussed areas such as these, I found an insight I had not heard before. It is an example of how important it is to rephrase questions from many perspectives.

In a discussion of global warming and climate change, the main question that is asked is "How can we reduce the amount of greenhouse gases?" This is a difficult task.

Some groups have rephrased the question and now ask "How can we prevent the greenhouse gasses from being released into the atmosphere?" They suggest that we could collect these gasses and dispose of them where they will do the least damage, far below the surface of the earth or at the bottom of the ocean. This solution might reduce the current problem but it creates a new problem: paying for the collection and disposal of these gases.

But the problem can be rephrased again, this time asking "How could we use these gases in productive ways?"[2]

This discussion offers more than just an exciting option for dealing with global warming. It provides an example of how we might turn a problem into an asset. This is a good example of a positive problem-solving strategy.

> *We fail more often because we solve the wrong problem than because we get the wrong solution to the right problem. — Russell Ackoff*

STRATEGY 22.1

PROBLEM-SOLVING

Step 1: Identify the problem or problems.

Step 2: Clarify the problems.

Restate the problems in different ways. Understand the difference between the situation and the problem. A situation cannot be changed. Ask questions. What is causing this problem? Why is this problem important? What is the *real* problem?

Step 3: Identify the goal or goals.

Step 4: List possible solutions or strategies.

What can you do to solve the problem and achieve your goal? Sometimes we should begin by asking how we might reduce the problem. Don't stop with the obvious solutions. Look for many alternatives. According to Morgan Jones, "Failure to consider alternatives fully is the most common cause of flawed or incomplete analysis."[3]

Step 5: List the advantages and disadvantages of each strategy.

For some problems, you need to do research. You might want to discuss the problem with others. Decide which advantages are most important and which disadvantages would be most difficult to deal with.

Step 6: Make a decision.

Step 7: Develop a plan.

What will you do first, and when? Will you need anyone to help you?

Step 8: Create a schedule

List each major step you need to take. At regular periods, you might need to evaluate your progress and make adjustments to your plan. Occasionally, you might need to go back to the beginning to restate the problems, based on new insights, and to look for more effective alternatives, to make new decisions, and to create new and more effective plans.

The best resource I've found on problem-solving is the website www.thwink.org:

> The fundamental premise of Thwink is that only an analytical approach can solve difficult social problems. The world's problem solvers are failing to solve problems like global environmental sustainability and the corporate dominance problem because they are pushing on low instead of high leverage points. Activists are presently running blind. They are like a blind bull stumbling around in a china shop. They can't see the difference between what resolves root causes and what does not due to an instinctual problem solving process rather than an analytical one.[4]

Example: Level one problem-solving

Belinda wants a winter coat. She listed three alternatives. One coat is extra-warm, one is more stylish, and then there's her jacket that needs a new zipper. She also needs to consider her budget. If Belinda needs to go without eating or without buying her books to purchase the coat she wanted, she'd be better off fixing the zipper on the old jacket.

But Belinda is a problem-solver. She decided to ask for advice and look for other alternatives. A girl down the hall tells her about a great thrift shop not far from campus. The two girls go together to check out winter clothes. They find several dozen winter coats to choose from, and Belinda finds a beautiful red coat that fits perfectly for only $8. She can afford to buy boots, three warm sweaters, a wool hat, and leather gloves for less than $20.

Example: Level two problem-solving

Let's consider Sleepy Sam. He needs more sleep, but his roommate studies late with music playing. There are at least two problems. First, Sam needs his sleep. The second problem might be the roommate. We don't know yet if the roommate's habits are a real or assumed problem. He might change his habits to make Sam happy.

Sam decides to raise the question on Monday afternoon when he and his roommate are both in the room for at least an hour before dinner. He will explain that he has a problem and needs his roommate's help. Asking for help is more likely to get a favorable response than complaining about the problem. Sam will say, "You probably aren't aware that this is a problem…. I really need your help." He plans to suggest several alternatives. "Would you be willing to study somewhere else? You could study in the lounge or in Mark's room. He enjoys the same music." Or "Maybe you could use earphones or an iPod to listen to your music. That would help me a lot."

If this doesn't work, if Sam's roommate declares that this is *his* room and he can listen to music whenever he wants to, then Sam's roommate *is* the problem. Sam might ask the resident assistant to talk to his roommate, but this might only make his roommate angry.

A better solution would be to find another student with the same problem and switch rooms so the two students who want sleep can get their sleep. This switch will work best, of course, if the music-loving night owls enjoy the same music and the same study hours.

Example: Level three problem-solving

Poor Patrick didn't realize his bank account was so low. The immediate problem is clear: Patrick needs to get at least $200 to make good on the check he used to buy his textbooks. What are Patrick's alternatives? He could ask his family to send money. Last year when this happened, he called home and his dad had sent him an extra $1,000. Now, since his father lost his job and was having a hard time paying his own bills, Patrick couldn't ask for more money. Not only that, but his father had warned him not to let this happen again.

So if Patrick can't find someone to give him money, could he borrow some? He couldn't think of a single person who'd be willing to loan him $200. Maybe he could find 10 friends who would each let him borrow $20. But he'd need to find a way to pay them back. That wasn't much of a plan.

Could he sell anything to get the money? He could sell his video games, maybe for half-price. He might get $50 dollars for his TV. Maybe he could return the textbooks and get his money back. But he needed his books. Could he earn some money? The best solution would be to get a job and earn enough to cover this bill *and* his expenses for the rest of the year.

His final statement of the problem was this: "I need money immediately to cover the bounced check. If I borrow money, I will need to pay it back. I also need money to live on for the rest of the year. This means I need to do two things: I need to get a job and I need to keep track of my money."

Patrick took his new textbooks back to the store and got his money back: $850. He took the money to the bank to take care of the bounced check, paying the bank $250. Then he returned to the bookstore and paid cash for used textbooks, something he hated to do. But the used books cost only cost $375, leaving him with just over $200.

The next day, he began looking for a job. Since he was a math major—believe it or not!—he found a good job in the Tutoring Center, helping students with math. He actually enjoyed his job as well as making some much-needed money.

Patrick began thinking about the next school year. He talked to the people in the financial aid office and will get more aid next year. He is also applying for scholarships like he did in high school and hopes to get enough in scholarships to cover the rest of his expenses so his parents won't need to pay any of his bills.

Example: Level four problem-solving

Let's consider the parking problem. Juanita put up posters. A total of 23 students and 2 teachers showed up for a meeting to discuss the problem. They listed these alternatives:

1. Since there was no area for expanding parking nearby, they decided it would help to have more parking some distance away. They identified two places where parking lots could be added.

2. They could ask for a parking garage to be built on the present parking lot, but that would be expensive.

3. They could put parking meters in the parking lot so students wouldn't leave their cars there all day long. They might limit student parking to just two hours.

4. They could allow free parking for high-occupancy vehicles holding three or more students.

5. They could use the large parking lot near the football stadium if there was a regular bus to carry students to different parts of the campus.

6. They could move the classes with the largest number of students to a building close to a parking lot that's usually half empty.

Juanita's group asked the two teachers and two students to take the problem and possible solutions to the administration, suggesting that, at least as a temporary solution, the classes with the largest number of students be moved. A group was formed to study the long term problem and the suggestion of moving the larger classes was accepted.

Example: Providing a good education for all the world's children

Actually, this example was not an effort to solve this problem around the world. That problem is a long way from being solved. This dealt with the problem in only one small village in Guatemala. I worked with a team in this village to help the villagers identify their own problems, to list realistic alternatives, to choose solutions they thought most likely to work, to create a plan, and then to work together to reach their goals.

Of the many problems they identified and worked on, I want to concentrate on a single problem. Very few girls in this village went to school. We asked the people "Why don't the girls go to school?" The girls were at home helping their mothers. "Why did the mothers need their help?" They needed the girls to get water for cooking and washing. "Why did getting water take so much time?" The nearest source of water was five miles away. Girls carried heavy jugs, walked five miles to the river, and five miles back. They repeated this several times a day to get the needed water. On laundry days, they carried the dirty clothes to the river, washed them in the river, and laid them on bushes to dry while they carried water back and forth. As the villagers said, "There's nothing you can do about it. That's just the way it is."

The real problem, therefore, wasn't that girls didn't go to school. The situation they were dealing with was that the closest source of water was five miles away. We restated the question: "How can we get water to the village?"

The group thought about digging a well, but it might need to be deep and the ground was rocky. They considered getting a truck to haul in large containers of water, but that would be expensive. Finally, after much discussion, it was decided that the best solution was getting water into the village from the river.

While most villagers doubted this could be done, they all helped build a plan. They could lay pipes from a high point along the river going to the village. The water would flow downhill, so no pumps were required—important, since there was no electricity. The pipes could be attached to a faucet. If the women took turns getting water, there would be plenty of water for everyone. The mothers wouldn't need the girls to help get water, so the girls could go to school.

The biggest problem would be getting the pipes. The people in this village couldn't afford to buy pipes. The solution came with the information that a group of American college students wanted to do a work project. The students would provide pipes and shovels.

While waiting for the arrival of the students, a few villagers laid out the path where the pipes should go with strips of colored cloth on sticks. Others worked together to list all the tasks and to plan who would do what. Everyone was assigned a task. Villagers donated food from their gardens for meals. Older women volunteered to cook the food. Children would help carry pipes or take water to the workers.

When the day arrived, the college students, along with all able-bodied villagers, began early to dig shallow ditches to hold the pipes. A few, with more technical skills, attached the pipes to a faucet. With help from everyone but the youngest children, the work was finished in less than a week. The village had running water. The girls could go to school.

Not all problems are solved as easily as this one. Problems dealing with the economy, employment, global warming, and war require a great deal of planning and resources as well as innovative solutions. But this was a problem no one in the village thought could be solved. With a little outside help, the people in the village came up with a solution, and they did most of the work.

The best part of this kind of solution was that when people in nearby villages saw what had been done here, they might decide they could do the same thing. They could make it possible for their girls to go to school.

You can help solve some of the world's problems

Go to www.InnoCentive.com and look at some of the many challenges and some of the problems that have been solved by its participants. You might even find a problem there that *you'd* like to work on. The staff on this site describe themselves this way:

> *We crowdsource innovation solutions from the world's smartest people, who compete to provide ideas and solutions to important business, social, policy, scientific, and technical challenges.*
>
> *Our global network of millions of problem solvers, proven challenge methodology, and cloud-based innovation management platform combine to help our clients transform their economics of innovation through rapid solution delivery and the development of sustainable open innovation programs.*

The companies or organizations that want these problem solved offer awards ranging from $5,000 to over $1 million and the problems are solved by people from all parts of the world. What is most interesting is that many of those who solve these problems work in different fields. "Solvers were actually bridging fields—taking solutions and approaches from one area and applying them to different areas."[5]

> *In times of increasing globalization and technological advances, many problems humans have to face in everyday life are quite complex, involving multiple goals as well as many possible actions that could be considered, each associated with several different and uncertain consequences in environments that may change dynamically and independent of the problem solvers' actions. — Joachim Funke[6]*

Questions for Reflection:

1. Consider the problems you listed in the exercise. If one seems particularly important, look for its causes. Is this a decision you need to make, or do you need to find possible solutions?

2. Are there problems on campus or in the community that you'd like to work on?

3. What surprised you in this chapter? What was the most important thing you learned? How will you use what you learned?

CHAPTER **23**

Big Answers for Big Questions

One of the great benefits that a college student today has over previous generations of college students has come from the development of neuroimaging tools that allow…scientists to look inside the human brain and see how it operates. As a result, today's students have accurate, scientifically proven information about how their brains learn and remember information and skills. — Terry Doyle and Todd Zakrajsek[1]

We began this journey together with some important questions —questions that all students should be asking, questions for which we have learned many answers. The main questions were:

1. **Why do so many students work hard, make good grades, but quickly forget what they "learned"?**

2. **How can students learn more, understand deeply, and remember longer?**

3. **What can students do to get the great education they want and need?**

We began with the assumption that, even if colleges made major changes in their ways of teaching, this still would not solve the problem. It would still be important for students themselves to set their own goals, to change their attitudes, and to become serious students.

The goals of this book are

■ to enable you to rediscover the excitement of learning

- to share information about the most effective learning strategies
- to challenge you to take charge of your own education

This conclusion does two things. It will summarize the main ideas in the book and it will answer the three Big Questions.

The Problem and the Solution: The first two questions

1. **Why do so many students work hard, make good grades, but quickly forget what they "learned"?**

2. **How can students learn more, understand deeply, and remember longer?**

It only makes sense to answer the first two questions together. The first question asks about the problem; the second asks about the solution. The first question asks about the approach that results in learning very little; the other asks about the approach that leads to deep understanding and lasting memory.

It would be easier to define two kinds of students, but this would be a mistake. Students can't be divided neatly into shallow learners and deep learners. You can't separate them into the students who have no interest in learning and those who are eager to learn, or into the students who use the least effective strategies and those who use the most effective strategies. We don't fit neatly into such categories.

All of us are intentional learners in some ways. But none of us, and I include myself, are ideal learners, intentional in every way. We can all become more intentional in our approach to getting an education.

We conclude, instead, by considering our habits, those that are less intentional and those that are more intentional. Perhaps you will select a few areas where you choose to use the more intentional habits. You may then discover that you learn more, understand deeply and remember longer.

Comparing six learning habits

The first poor habit is taking a shallow approach to learning and letting yourself be motivated by other people's opinions. When our motivation is extrinsic we believe that grades are more important than learning and we often have no real interest in learning.

Better habits—those of students who want a great education—begin with a deep and intentional approach to learning. When we understand that learning is more important than grades, we are more likely to be intrinsically motivated with a strong desire to learn.

The second poor habit is accepting the common idea that students who get better grades must be smarter. When we don't believe that, even if we worked much harder, we would be any more successful, we are even less likely to work hard. With this approach, we may have little willpower, have trouble concentrating, and be less likely to get enough sleep or regular exercise. As a result, it's even harder to focus on what we read or hear.

More intentional habits, based on the confidence that we can succeed if we work hard enough, increase our willpower and concentration. With strong willpower, we are more likely to eat healthy meals, get enough sleep, and exercise regularly, all of which make it easier to learn.

The third poor habit is assuming that it's the responsibility of our professors to give us an education. With this way of thinking we are less likely to set our own goals or develop plans for learning. Without clear goals we have little or no interest in time management. We might find ourselves getting further and further behind until we seem to be lost.

With more intentional habits, we should realize that our professors can't pour an education into our empty minds. We should know that we have to decide what kind of education we want, and we should create a plan for getting that education. With goals like these, we are more likely to create and use an effective time management plan, and we will finish assignments and still have time to focus on independent learning and other activities.

The fourth poor habit is believing the basic skills we used in high school are good enough for college. Even when we sense that other students are stronger readers or more skillful writers, we are tempted to say we wouldn't know how to improve these skills and that we just don't have enough time. We are convinced that reading an assignment is what is meant by "studying" or that the only further study we need should be to memorize some of the information for tests.

A more intentional habit starts with the understanding that college really *is* harder than high school and that it's important to strengthen our basic skills. Based on this belief, we can improve our skills by taking classes, by working on our own and asking for help when we need it, and by practicing these skills. We understand that, while memorizing is helpful for some material, it's all too easy to "memorize and forget," so we look for more effective ways to study.

The fifth poor habit is using the most common strategies for learning, the strategies that are the least effective. We might prepare for tests by cramming and, when the exam is over, breathe a sigh of relief, thinking "That's over. Now I can forget it all."

A more intentional habit is to find and use the most effective learning strategies. We can begin preparing for exams starting with our first class so we will understand more and remember longer.

The sixth poor habit is not thinking about the future or about what skills employers might want. We might hear about critical thinking and even take a class on the subject but still not be interested enough to use what we learned. We might see college as an extended period between high school and getting a job when we can have a good time.

A more intentional habit would be thinking seriously about the future, about the skills we might need and experiences that will prepare us to get the kind of job we want. We might even decide to learn and practice skills in critical thinking, analytical reasoning, and problem solving.

Students who practice more of the intentional habits will learn more, understand deeply, and remember longer. They will get an excellent education and go on to become lifelong learners. No one is likely to become perfectly intentional.

You must choose the kind of education you want and determine how hard you are willing to work to get that education. You must decide which of these habits and which strategies you will use to help you reach your goals.

There is always hope

If you, like so many other students, have had little or no interest in learning, you can still break out of this mind-numbing pattern. You can rediscover the excitement of genuine learning and take charge of your own education. You can expand your interests to include subjects long considered important for a well-rounded education, sometimes even finding these subjects so interesting that you go on to learn more than what's assigned. You can learn to think deeply and access many of the pathways to lasting memory. When you do these things, you will then get that great education—the kind that can change your life.

> *Success isn't a result of spontaneous combustion. You must set yourself on fire.*— *Arnold Glasgow*

What can students do to get the education they want and need?

To answer the final question, we will use a strategy. There really are no answers to this question but your own answers. Each student will have a different image of the kind of education they want and need. **The last Big Question should really be "What can I do to get the education I want and need?"**

STRATEGY 23.1

GETTING THE EDUCATION YOU WANT AND NEED?

Step 1: Think about what it means to get a great education.

Discuss this with friends and with adults whose opinions and advice you respect. Even discuss this with a few of your professors. Understand that a "great education" for these people may be different from the kind you want and need.

Step 2: Define the kind of education you need and want.

Step 3: List what you want to learn while you're in college.

Step 4: List the skills you want to develop while you're in college.

Step 5: List the Big Questions you want to explore while you're in college.

Step 6: Develop a plan to get the kind of education you want.

List courses you want to take and topics you plan to study on your own. List campus activities, jobs, internships, and other experiences that will add to your education and help you reach your goals.

Step 7: Use a journal to reflect on what you're learning and what you need to work on.

Step 8: Evaluate your progress on a regular basis, and change your plan as needed.

When you and other students choose to get the kind of education you both want and need, colleges and universities might respond by offering *all* students better opportunities for meaningful learning.

Only when you practice, read, write, think, talk, collaborate, and reflect does your brain make permanent connections. Your teachers cannot do this for you, and at times this work will make you tired. When you are worn out from learning, rest a bit and reflect on the fact that you are changing the neurochemistry in your brain. That is pretty amazing.[2]

Questions for Reflection

1. Describe the education you want and need. What must you do to get that education?

2. What is the most important thing you learned in this book?

3. Since you began reading this book, how have you changed?

4. What new goals have you set for yourself?

5. What decisions are you considering?

6. What Big Questions do you plan to explore?

7. What surprised you in this chapter? What was the most important thing you learned? How will you use what you learned? Try asking these now familiar questions at the end of every lecture you hear and and the end of every chapter you read.

8. Who will you tell about what you learned in this book?

ENDNOTES

*Good **Very Good ***Excellent for helping you understand the main ideas in this book

Preface: Why I Had to Write This Book and Why You Need to Read It

1. Peter Brown, Henry Roediger III, and Mark McDaniel (2014). *Make It Stick: The Science of Successful Learning*. Cambridge, MA: Belknap Press, p. 159.***

Chapter 1. Eight Giant Steps: A Brief Introduction to Part 1

1. Terry Doyle and Todd Zakrajsek (2013). *The New Science of Learning: How to Learn in Harmony with Your Brain*. Sterling, VA: Stylus, pp. 106–107. ***

2. Ibid., p. 8.

3. Ibid., p. 9.

4. John Ratey (2008). *Spark: The Revolutionary New Science of Exercise and the Brain*. New York: Little, Brown, pp. 245–6. **A great book, though quite technical in places.

5. Shari Bassuk, Timothy Church, and JoAnn Manson (2013). "Researchers Examine Why Exercise Works Magic." www.Scientific American.com./article/researchers-explain-why-exercise-works-magic. Preview retrieved September 17, 2014.

6. Daniel Goleman (2013). *Focus: The Hidden Driver of Excellence*. New York: HarperCollins, p. 16.

7. Ken Bain (2012). *What the Best College Students Do*. Cambridge, MA: Belknap Press, p. 259. *** This book tells the stories of successful adults and how they attained the kind of education they wanted and needed.

Chapter 2. The Four Approaches to Learning

1. Raymond S. Nickerson (1984). "Kinds of Thinking Taught in Current Programs." *Educational Leadership*. Alexandria, VA: ASCD, p. 25.

2. Daniel Pink (2009). *Drive: The Surprising Truth about What Motivates Us*. New York, NY: Riverhead Books. Pink summarizes the research and also quotes Harry H. Harlow from Harry Harlow, Margaret Kuenne, and Donald Meyer (1950), "Learning motivated by a manipulative drive," *Journal of Experimental Psychology*, 40, pp. 231–4.***

3. Edward Deci (1971). "Effects of externally mediated rewards on intrinsic motivation," *Journal of Personality and Social Psychology*, 18, p. 114. Quoted in Pink, pp. 5–8.

4. Edward Deci (1972). "Intrinsic motivation, extrinsic reinforcement, and inequity," *Journal of Personality and Social Psychology,* 22, pp. 119–20. Quoted in Pink, p. 8.

5. Ferrence Marton and Roger Säljö (1976). "On qualitative differences in learning. I. outcome and process." *British Journal of Educational Psychology,* 46, pp. 4–11.

6. Francisco Cano (2007). "Approaches to learning and study orchestration in high school students." *European Journal of Psychology of Education,* 22(2), pp. 131–51.

7. Maggi Savin-Baden and Claire Major (2004). *Foundations of Problem-Based Learning.* Berkshire, England: Society for Research into Higher Education and Open University Press, p. 197, as discussed by Karl Wirth and Dexter Perkins (2008), *Learning to Learn,* www.macalester.edu/academics/geology/wirth/learning.pdf. Retrieved August 29, 2014.

Chapter 3. The Five Characteristics of Meaningful Goals

1. John Barrell (1991). *Teaching for Thoughtfulness.* New York: Longman, pp. 72–3.

2. Edwin Locke and Gary Latham (1990). "Work Motivation and Satisfaction: Light at the End of the Tunnel." *Psychological Science,* 1, 240–6.

3. Linda Nilson (2013). *Creating Self-Regulated Learners: Strategies to Strengthen Students' Self-Awareness and Learning Skills.* Sterling, VA: Stylus, p. 3. This is an excellent book for teachers, mainly those teaching in colleges and universities, though some students might also find it interesting.

Chapter 4. Flexible Time Management

1. Laurie Hazard (1997). "The effect of locus of control and attitudes toward intelligence on study habits of college students." Unpublished Ph.D. dissertation, Boston University, discussed by Linda Nilson (2013), *Creating Self-Regulated Learners: Strategies to Strengthen Students' Self-Awareness and Learning Skills,* Sterling, VA: Stylus, p. 78.

2. Linda Nilson (2013). *Creating Self-Regulated Learners: Strategies to Strengthen Students' Self-Awareness and Learning Skills.* Sterling, VA: Stylus, p. 79.

3. Edwin Locke (1998). *Study Methods and Motivation: A Practical Guide to Effective Study.* New Milford, CT: Second Renaissance Press, p. 95. **

4. Daniel H. Pink (2009). *Drive: The Surprising Truth About What Motivates Us.* New York: Riverhead Books, pp. 90–1. Information based on studies by Edward Deci, Richard Ryan, and other researchers. (Bullets added.) ***

Chapter 5. Mindsets and Stereotype Threats and What You Can Do About Them

1. Carol Dweck (2006). *Mindset: The New Psychology of Success.* New York: Ballantine, p. 3.

2. Ken Bain (2012). *What the Best College Students Do.* Cambridge, MA: Harvard University Press, pp. 105–6.***

3. Alfred Binet (1913). *Modern Ideas about Children* [Les idées modernes sur les enfants]. Trans. Suzanne Heisler: Menlo Park, CA: S. Heisler.

4. Reuven Feuerstein (1980). *Instrumental Enrichment: An Intervention Program for Cognitive Modifiability*. Baltimore, MD: University Park Press.

5. Marian Diamond and Janet Hopson (1998). *Magic Trees of the Mind: How to Nurture Your Child's Intelligence, Creativity, and Healthy Emotions from Birth though Adolescence*. New York: Plume/Penguin.

6. Norman Doidge (2007). *The Brain that Changes Itself: Stories of Personal Triumph from the Frontiers of Brain Science*. New York: Penguin Books.**

7. Barbara Arrow-Smith Young (2012). *The Woman Who Changed Her Brain and Other Inspiring Stories of Pioneering Brain Transformation*. New York: Free Press.**

8. National Research Council (2000). *How People Learn: Brain, Mind, Experience, and School*. Washington, D.C.: National Academy Press. As discussed in Karl Wirth and Dexter Perkins (2009), *Learning to Learn*, www.macalester.edu/academics/geology/wirth/learning.pdf. Retrieved August 29, 2014.

9. Sian Beilock, Elizabeth Gunderson, Gerardo Ramirez, and Susan Levine (2010). "Female Teachers' Math Anxiety Affects Girls' Math Achievement." *Proceedings of the National Academy of Sciences,* 107 (5): 1860–3.

10. Kelly Danaher and Christian Crandall (2008). "Stereotype Threat in Applied Settings Re-examined." *Journal of Applied Psychology,* 38: 1639–55.

11. Claude Steele and Joshua Aronson (1995). "Stereotype Threat and the Intellectual Test Performance of African Americans." *Journal of Personality and Social Psychology,* 69: 799–811.

12. Jim Blascovich, Steven Spencer, Diane Quinn, and Claude Steele (2001). "African Americans and High Blood Pressure: The Role of Stereotype Threat." *Psychological Science,* 12: 225–9.

Chapter 6. Develop Willpower, Resilience and Concentration

1. Angela Duckworth and Martin Seligman (2005). "Self-discipline Outdoes IQ in Predicting Academic Achievement in Adolescents." *Psychological Science*, 6, No. 12: 939–44.

2. Roy Baumeister and John Tierney (2011). *Willpower: Rediscovering the Greatest Human Strength*. New York: Penguin Press, p. 10. Baumeister and Tierney discuss the research done by Walter Mischel in the 1960s, based on several summaries of the work.***

3. Ibid., pp 10–11.

4. Walter Mischel (2014). *The Marshmallow Test: Mastering Self-Control*. New York: Little, Brown and Co., p. 5. ***

5. Roger Crawford (1998). *How High Can You Bounce? Turn Your Setbacks Into Comebacks*. New York: Bantam, p. 2.

6. Ibid., p. 7.

7. Lydia Burak (2002). "Multitasking in the University Classroom." *International Journal for the Scholarship of Teaching and Learning,* 6(2), 1–12, p. 5.

8. Ibid., p. 7.

9. Daniel Goleman (2013*). Focus: The Hidden Driver of Excellence.* New York: HarperCollins, p. 16.

10. Daniel J. Siegel, Daniel J. (2013). *Brainstorm: The Power and Purpose of the Teenage Brain.* New York: Tarcher, pp. 288–9.**

11. Ibid., p. 289.

12. Baumeister and Tierney, pp. 133–6, discuss the work of Meg Oaten and Ken Cheng based on multiple studies, including their 2006 article "Improved Self-Control: The Benefits of a Regular Program of Academic Study," *Basic and Applied Social Psychology* 28, 1–16.***

Chapter 7. High School Skills Are Not Enough: A Brief Introduction to Part 2

1. Robert Carman and W. Royce Adams Jr. (1972). *Study Skills: A Student's Guide for Survival.* New York: John Wiley & Sons, p. 4.

2. Derek Bok (2006). *Underachieving Colleges: A Candid Look at How Much Students Learn and Why They Should be Learning More.* Princeton: Princeton University Press, p. 109.

3. Stephen Covey (2004). *The 7 Habits of Highly Effective People.* New York: Free Press.

Chapter 8. Rediscover the Excitement of Reading

1. John Dunlosky, Katherine Rawson, Elizabeth Marsh, Mitchell Nathan, and Daniel Willingham (2013). "Improving Students' Learning with Effective Learning Techniques: Promising Directions from Cognitive and Educational Psychology." *Psychological Science in the Public Interest* 14(1) 4–58.

2. Theodore H. Geballe, as quoted in an autobiography of Stephen Chu in Gösta Ekspong, ed., *Nobel Lectures: Physics 1996–2000.* Stockholm: University of Stockholm (2002), p. 120.

3. Donna M. Ogle. "K-W-L: A Teaching Model that Develops Active Reading of Expository Text." *Reading Teacher* 39, 564–90. As summarized in Nicole Strangman and Tracy Hall (2004). Background Knowledge. Wakefield, MA: National Center on Accessing the General Curriculum. Retrieved November 15, 2014, from www.aim.cast.org/learn/historyarchive/backgroundpapers/background_knowledge.

4. *The Harvard Report.* www.dartmouth.edu/~acskills/handouts.html#Reading. Retrieved August 30, 2014.

5. Sigmund Tobias. "Interest, Prior Knowledge, and Learning." *Review of Educational Research,* Spring 1994, 64(1): 37–54, from the abstract.

6. Terry Doyle and Todd Zakrajsek (2013). *The New Science of Learning: How to Learn in Harmony with Your Brain.* Sterling, VA: Stylus, p. 19.***

7. William Armstrong (1995). *Study Is Hard Work.* Boston: David R. Godine, pp. 38–9. *

Chapter 9. Take Notes You'll Want to Study

1. Ben Casnocha (July 2, 2013). *"If you aren't taking notes, you aren't learning."* Linkedin.com/today/post/article/if-you-aren-t-taking–notes-you-aren-t-learning. Retrieved January 4, 2014.

2. Gary S. Thomas (1978). "Use of students' notes and lecture summaries as study guides for recall." *Journal of Educational Research* 71, no. 6, 316–319: p. 316.

3. Linda Nilson (2013). *Creating Self-Regulated Learners: Strategies to Strengthen Students' Self-Awareness and Learning Skills.* Sterling, VA: Stylus, p. 37.

Chapter 10. College Level Research Can Be Exciting

1. Bill Coplin (2003). *10 Things Employers Want You to Learn in College: The Know-How You Need to Succeed.* Berkeley, CA: Ten Speed Press, p. 79.

2. Steven Bell. "What Employers Want from College Grads." *Library Journal*, October 30, 2013. http://lj.libraryjournal.com/2013/10/opinion/steven-bell/what-employers-want-from-college-grads-from-the-bell-tower/#. Retrieved July 29, 2014.

3. Donald Barker, Melissa Barker, and Katherine Pinard (2012). *Internet Research,* 6th ed. Boston: Cengage Learning, p. 111. This is an excellent book to read if you want to learn about doing research on the Internet **

4. *Resource Databases.* Prince George's Community College Library. http://pgccibguides.com/content.php?pid=291402&side=2405172-using-research-databases-research-guide-libguides.

5. *List of Academic Databases.* http://en.wikipedia.org/wiki/list-of-academic-databases-and-search-engines. Retrieved July 15, 2014.

6. *Database FAQs:* "Why use a research database?" Scituate (MA) Library. http://scituatetownlibrary.org/reference-db-faq.html. Retrieved August 2, 2014.

7. Harvard Business School Goal Story: "Study about goals at Harvard MBA program 1979." www.lifemastering.com/en/harvard_school.html. Retrieved August 30, 2014.

8. Sid Savara. "Writing Down Your Goals: The Harvard Written Goal Study. Fact or Fiction?" http://Sidsavara.com/personal-productivity/fact-or-fiction-the-truth-about-the-harvard- written-goal-study. Retrieved August 30, 2014.

9. Walter Pauk and Ross Owens (2011). *How to Study in College,* 10th ed. Boston: Cengage Learning, p. 379.

Chapter 11. Effective Writing Begins with a Purpose and a Plan

1. Richard Light (2001). *Making the Most of College: Students Speak Their Minds.* Cambridge, MA: Harvard University Press, p. 54.

2. Ibid., p. 10.

3. Ibid., p. 54.

4. William Strunk and E. B. White (1959). *Elements of Style.* New York: Macmillan. This classic book explains grammar, punctuation, and related topics so clearly and

briefly that it's a delight to read; most writers keep a copy on their bookshelves. Many writers refer to this book simply as "Strunk and White." ***

5. Vitaly Friedman (2009). "50 Free Resources that will improve your writing skills." www.smashingmagazine.com/2009/06/28/50-free-resources-that-will-improve-your-writing-skills/. *

6. Susan Rabiner and Alfred Fortunato (2002). *Thinking Like Your Editor: How to Write Great Serious Nonfiction and Get It Published.* New York: Norton. *** (mainly for those considering writing serious nonfiction).

Chapter 12. Develop Your Speaking Skills

1. To locate a Toastmasters group near you, either Google "Toastmasters" or go to www.Toastmasters.org. On the first page you can enter your zip code and find the group closest to you. If there are several, you can check the days and times you'd prefer and narrow the choices.

2. I learned to use a 3x3 chart (and a 4x4 chart) while working with a group called the Ecumenical Institute, or the ICA (Institute of Cultural Affairs). We taught workshops around the U.S. and later around the globe. We often used the same charts for our lectures but added our own examples or stories. Later, when making presentations at conferences or doing teacher training, I found it helpful to continue using these to organize information and help me remember what I wanted to say.

Chapter 13. The Never-Cram-Again- System of Test Preparation

1. Peter Brown, Henry Roediger, and Mark McDaniel (2014). *Make It Stick: The Science of Successful Learning.* Cambridge, MA: Belknap Press, p. 63.***

2. Terry Doyle and Todd Zakrajsek (2013). *The New Science of Learning: How to Learn in Harmony with Your Brain.* Sterling, VA: Stylus, p. 13.***

3. James Maas, Rebecca Robbins, and William Dement (2011). *Sleep for Success: Everything You Must Know about Sleep but Are Too Tired to Ask.* Bloomington, IN: Authorhouse. Quoted in Doyle and Zakrajsek, p. 17.

4. Doyle and Zakrajsek, p. 76

Chapter 14. Mental Processing Strategies: A Brief Introduction to Part 3

1. Arthur Costa, in the foreword to John Clark (1990). *Integrating Learning Skills in Content Teaching.* Boston: Allyn and Bacon, p. xii.

2. Terry Doyle and Todd Zakrajsek (2013). *The New Science of Learning: How to Learn in Harmony with Your Brain.* Sterling, VA: Stylus, p. 1.***

3. James Zull (2002). *The Art of Changing the Brain: Enriching the Practice of Teaching by Exploring the Biology of Learning.* Sterling, VA: Stylus, p. 178.***

4. Ibid., p. 185.

Chapter 15. Verbal Organization – Ten Strategies

1. David Hyerle (2009). *Visual Tools for Transforming Information into Knowledge*, 2nd ed. Thousand Oaks, CA: Corwin Press, pp. 75–6.

2. Matthew Lipman (1988). "Critical Thinking—What Can It Be?" *Educational Leadership* 38–43, p. 40.

3. Douglas Raybeck Herrman and Michael Grunebert (2002). *Improving Memory and Study Skills*. Seattle: Hogrefe and Huber Publications, p. 98.

Chapter 16. Visual Organization – Ten Strategies

1. Robert Marzano, in the Foreword to David Hyerle (2009). *Visual Tools for Transforming Information into Knowledge*, 2nd ed. Thousand Oaks, CA: Corwin Press, p. viii: a great book for elementary teachers.

2. Tony Buzan (1974, 1982, 1989). *Use Both Sides of Your Brain*. New York: Plume. This book begins with what was then the latest research on the brain and introduces many important learning strategies. Buzan's description of Mind Maps went on to be very popular. ***

3. David Hyerle (2004). "Thinking Maps as a Transformational Language for Learning" in *Student Success with Thinking Maps: School-Based Research, Results, and Models for Achievement Using Visual Tools*. Thousand Oaks, CA: Corwin Press, p. 7. This book was written for teachers.

4. David Hyerle (2009). *Visual Tools for Transforming Information into Knowledge*, 2nd ed. Thousand Oaks, CA: Corwin Press, pp. 18, 25.

5. Karl Wirth and Dexter Perkins (2008). *Learning to Learn*. This is a good summary of the research on learning, www.macalester.edu/academics/geology/wirth/learning.pdf. Retrieved August 29, 2014.

6. Dan Roam (2009). *Unfolding the Napkin: The Hands-On Method for Solving Complex Problems with Simple Pictures*. New York: Portfolio/Penguin, p. 50.

Chapter 17. Ways of Thinking – Ten Strategies

1. Keith Stanovich (2009). *What Intelligence Tests Miss: The Psychology of Rational Thought*. New Haven: Yale University Press, xi. ***

2. Ibid., pp. 71–107.

3. American Association of the Advancement of Science (1990). *Science for All Americans*. New York: Oxford University Press, p. 4.

4. The suggestions about kaleidoscopes come from one of my son's science fair projects, 1990. It was later revised, as a classroom activity called "The Human Kaleidoscope." He made a presentation on this at a conference of the National Science Teachers' Association.

5. Michael Michalko (2011). *Creative Thinkering: Putting Your Imagination to Work*. Novato, CA: New World Library, p. 1.

6. Thomas Vogel (2014). *Breakthrough Thinking: A Guide to Creative Thinking and Idea Generation*. Blue Ash, OH: HOW Books, p. 1.

7. Noreena Hertz (2013). *Eyes Wide Open: How to Make Smart Decisions in a Confusing World*. New York: HarperCollins, p. 1.

8. Edward Burger and Michael Starbird (2012). *The 5 Elements of Effective Thinking*. Princeton: Princeton University Press, pp. vii–viii. **

Chapter 18. Pathways to Memory – Ten Strategies

1. Judy Willis (2006). *Research-Based Strategies to Ignite Student Learning*. Alexandria, VA: ASCD, p. 3. This book is written for teachers and I'd recommend it for students planning to study education.

2. Tony Buzan (1991). *Use Both Sides of Your Brain, Third Edition*. New York: Plume. ***

3. Ibid., pp. 11–14.

4. Edward Hughes (2014). Personal email correspondence.

5. Edwin Locke (1998). *Study Methods and Motivation: A Practical Guide to Effective Study*. New Milford, CT: Second Renaissance Press, p. 59. **

6. Peter C. Brown, Henry L. Roediger, and Mark A. McDaniel (2014). *Make It Stick: The Science of Successful Learning*. Cambridge, MA: Belknap Press, p. 63. ***

7. Laura Papparo (2008). "Ultimate Study Tool: Testing." www.nytimes.com/2008/07/27/education/edlife/27test summarizing research by Professor Henry Roediger. Retrieved August 23, 2014.

8. P. C. Brown et al., p. 10.

9. Atsunori Ariga and Alejandro Lleras (2010). "Brief and Rare Mental Breaks Keep You Focused and Reactivation of Task Goals Preempt Decrements." *Cognition* 2011: DOI: 10.10161j.cognition 2010.12.007 as discussed on www.sciencedaily.com/releases/2011/02/11020813?529.htm. Retrieved August 30, 2014.

10. Willis, p. 4.

Chapter 19. What Employers Want Most: A Brief Introduction to Part 4

1. Derek Thompson (2014). "The Things Employers Look for When Hiring Recent Graduates." www.theatlantic.com/business/archive/2014/08/the-things-employers-look-for-when-hiring-recent-graduates/378693/. Retrieved September 3, 2014.

2. Hart Research Associates (2013). *It Takes More than a Major: Employers' Priorities for College Learning and Students Success: An Online Survey among Employers Conducted on Behalf of the Association of American Colleges and Universities*. www.aacu.org/leap/documents/2013-Employersurvey.pdf, pp. 13, 2. Retrieved August 14, 2014.

3. Ibid., p. 13.

4. Ibid., p. 6.

5. Ibid., p. 10.

6. Ibid., p. 8

7. Richard Arum and Josipa Roksa (2011). *Academically Adrift: Limited Learning on College Campuses*. Chicago: University of Chicago Press, p. 35.

8. Walter Isaacson (2014). *The Innovators: How a Group of Hackers, Geniuses, and Geeks Created the Digital Revolution*. New York: Simon & Schuster, p. 1.

9. Arum and Roksa, quoting Derek Bok, p. 1.

Chapter 20. Critical Thinking, Reading, Writing, and Listening

1. Stella Cottrell (2011). *Critical Thinking Skills: Developing Effective Analysis and Arguments*. New York: Palgrave, p. 8.

2. Stephen Brookfield (1987). *Developing Critical Thinkers: Challenging Adults to Explore Alternate Ways of Thinking and Acting*. San Francisco: Jossey-Bass, p. ix.

3. Ibid., p. x.

4. M. Neil Browne and Stuart Keeley (2007). *Asking the Right Questions: A Guide to Critical Thinking*. Upper Saddle River, NJ: Pearson/Prentice Hall, p. 125.

5. John Dunlosky, Katherine Rawson, Elizabeth Marsh, Mitchell Nathan, and Daniel Willingham (2013). "Improving Students' Learning with Effective Learning Techniques: Promising Directions from Cognitive and Educational Psychology." *Psychological Science in the Public Interest* 14(1) 4–58.

6. Cottrell, p. 147.

7. Dan Kurland (2000). www.critical reading.com/critical_reading.htm. Retrieved August 12, 2014.

8. Cottrell, p. 168.

9. Browne and Keeley, pp. 206, 207.

10. Cottrell, p. 6.

11. Brookfield, p. 171.

Chapter 21. Analytical Reasoning: Interpreting Numerical and Verbal Data

1. "Interpreting Data." InSites.org. 2007 www.insites.org/CLIP_v1_site/downloads/PDFs/TipsIntrprtData.5G.8-07.pdf. Retrieved August 21, 2014.

2. Gary M. Klass (2012). *Just Plain Data Analysis: Finding, Presenting, and Interpreting Social Science Data*, 2nd ed. New York: Rowman and Littlefield, p. xiii. ***

3. Catherine Pope, Sue Ziebland, and Nicholas Mays (2000). "Analyzing Qualitative Data." *BMJ*, 320:114. www.bmj.com/content/320/7227/114.short. Retrieved July 27, 2014.

4. Klass, p. 39.

5. Ibid, p. 39.

6. Gerald W. Bracey (2003). *Those Misleading SAT and NAEP Trends: Simpson's Paradox at Work*. www.educationnews.org/articles/these-misleading-sat-and-naep-trends-simpsons-paradox-at-work-htm. Retrieved August 26, 2014.

7. Edward R. Tufte (1983). *The Visual Display of Quantitative Information*. Cheshire, CT: Graphics Press, p. 13.

Chapter 22. Complex Problem Solving: The Five Levels of Complexity

1. "What Is an Analytical Approach?" www.thwink.org/sustain/articles/000_AnalyticalApproach/index.htm. Retrieved August 12, 2014. This is one of the most exciting sources of information I have found. The authors discuss problem-solving in the context of current global problems.

2. W. Schonwandt, K. Voermanek, J. Utz, J. Grunau, and C. Hemburger. (2013). *Solving Complex Problems: A Handbook*. Berlin: Jovis, p. 31.

3. Morgan Jones (1998). *The Thinker's Toolkit: 14 Powerful Techniques for Problem Solving*. New York: Three Rivers Press. This is the best book I know of about problem-solving. ***

4. Jonah Lehrer (2012). *Imagine: How Creativity Works*. Boston: Houghton Mifflin, p. 121.

5. www.Innocentive.com is a website that helps those with problems locate problem-solvers.

6. Joachim Funke, in A. Fisher, S. Greiff, and J. Funke (2012). "The Process of Solving Complex Problems." *Journal of Problem Solving* 4:1, p. 20.

Chapter 23. Big Answers for Big Questions

1. Terry Doyle and Todd Zakrajsek (2013). *The New Science of Learning: How to Learn in Harmony with Your Brain*. Sterling, VA: Stylus, p. 112. ***

2. Ibid., p. 12.

RECOMMENDED READING

All of these are excellent books. I cannot judge that some are better than others. The stars indicate my opinion of which books students are likely to find most helpful and interesting and are also most closely related to topics in this book.

*Good **Very Good ***Excellent

For ALL Students

***Ken Bain (2012). *What the Best College Students Do.* Cambridge, MA: Harvard University Press. This wonderful easy-to-read book tells the stories of successful adults and how they attained the kind of education they wanted and needed. If you read only one book on this list, this should be that book.

And here are three older books on study skills that I consider better than recent ones:

***Tony Buzan (1989). *Use Both Sides of Your Brain.* New York: Plume. This book, based on the latest research on the brain in the 1970s, introduces many important learning strategies. It made Mind Maps popular. Here you can read the full story of Edward Hughes.

**Edwin Locke (1998). *Study Methods and Motivation: A Practical Guide to Effective Study.* New Milford, CT: Second Renaissance Press. A small, older book with great information on learning.

*William Armstrong (1995). *Study Is Hard Work.* Boston: David R. Godine. A little old, but with good advice.

For Students Interested in Certain Topics

The brain and learning

***Terry Doyle and Todd Zakrajsek (2013). *The New Science of Learning: How to Learn in Harmony with Your Brain.* Sterling, VA: Stylus. A short, easy-to-read book with excellent information on brain research and learning.

*** James Zull (2002). *The Art of Changing the Brain: Enriching the Practice of Teaching by Exploring the Biology of Learning.* Sterling, VA: Stylus. While meant mainly for teachers, it was so exciting that I added it here.

***Peter Brown, Henry Roediger III, and Mark McDaniel (2014). *Make It Stick: The Science of Successful Learning.* Cambridge, MA: Belknap Press. Not easy but contains excellent information on research on learning

** Daniel J. Siegel, (2013). *Brainstorm: The Power and Purpose of the Teenage Brain.* New York: Tarcher. Some parts are fantastic. I skimmed through the rest.

Ways of changing the brain

**Norman Doidge (2007). *The Brain that Changes Itself: Stories of Personal Triumph from the Frontiers of Brain Science.* New York: Penguin Books. An excellent book for anyone interested in recent research on how the brain can be changed.

**Barbara Arrow-Smith Young (2012). *The Woman Who Changed Her Brain and Other Inspiring Stories of Pioneering Brain Transformation.* New York: Free Press. An inspiring story that is especially important if you are interested in learning disabilities.

Thinking

*** Keith Stanovich (2009). *What Intelligence Tests Miss: The Psychology of Rational Thought.* New Haven: Yale University Press. A fascinating book to read.

**Edward Burger and Michael Starbird (2012). *The 5 Elements of Effective Thinking.* Princeton: Princeton University Press. Easy-to-read book on thinking.

Creativity

Walter Isaacson (2014). *The Innovators: How a Group of Hackers, Geniuses, and Geeks Created the Digital Revolution.* New York: Simon & Schuster. (Not yet rated – new)

Willpower and motivation

***Walter Mischel (2014). *The Marshmallow Test: Mastering Self-Control.* New York: Little, Brown, and Co. This gives the latest information on research in the area and describes simple strategies for increasing willpower in children and adults.

***Roy Baumeister and John Tierney (2011). *Willpower: Rediscovering the Greatest Human Strength.* New York: Penguin Press. Excellent for those interested in willpower.

***Daniel H. Pink (2009). *Drive: The Surprising Truth About What Motivates Us.* New York: Riverhead Books. A great, easy-to-read book on motivation

The effect of exercise on learning and mental health
**John Ratey (2008). *Spark: The Revolutionary New Science of Exercise and the Brain.* New York: Little, Brown. An exciting book on exercise, though quite technical in places.

Internet research
**Donald Barker, Melissa Barker, and Katherine Pinard (2012). Internet Research, 6th ed. Boston: Cengage Learning. This is a good book about doing research on the Internet.

Problem solving
***Morgan Jones (1998). *The Thinker's Toolkit: 14 Powerful Techniques for Problem Solving.* New York: Three Rivers Press. The best book I know of about problem solving.

Analyzing data
***Gary M. Klass (2012). *Just Plain Data Analysis: Finding, Presenting, and Interpreting Social Science Data*, 2nd ed. New York: Rowman and Littlefield. After reading books on data analysis that were impossible to understand, I thought this book was wonderful.

Grammar
*** William Strunk and E. B. White (1959). *Elements of Style.* New York: Macmillan. This classic book explains grammar, punctuation, and related topics so clearly and briefly that it's a delight to read; most writers keep a copy on their bookshelves.

Recommended Reading for Teachers
*Richard Arum and Josipa Roksa (2011). *Academically Adrift: Limited Learning on College Campuses.* Chicago: University of Chicago Press. Describes problems but doesn't offer solutions.

*John Barrell (1991). *Teaching for Thoughtfulness.* New York: Longman.

***Derek Bok (2006). *Underachieving Colleges: A Candid Look at How Much Students Learn and Why They Should be Learning More.* Princeton: Princeton University Press. A classic in its description of how colleges and universities are failing to educate students.

***Peter Brown, Henry Roediger III, and Mark McDaniel (2014). *Make It Stick: The Science of Successful Learning.* Cambridge, MA: Belknap Press. One of the best books.

***Terry Doyle and Todd Zakrajsek (2013). *The New Science of Learning: How to Learn in Harmony with Your Brain.* Sterling, VA: Stylus. A short book with excellent information on brain research and learning. One of my favorites.

**Carol Dweck (2006). *Mindset: The New Psychology of Success.* New York: Ballantine. This is a classic book on mindsets.

** Linda Nilson (2013). *Creating Self-Regulated Learners: Strategies to Strengthen Students' Self-Awareness and Learning Skills.* Sterling, VA: Stylus. This is a great book for teachers, mainly those in colleges and universities. Some students might find it interesting.

*** Keith Stanovich (2009). *What Intelligence Tests Miss: The Psychology of Rational Thought.* New Haven: Yale University Press. It discusses why smart people do stupid things.

**Judy Willis (2006). *Research-Based Strategies to Ignite Student Learning.* Alexandria, VA: ASCD. Though this book is written for teachers, I'd recommend it for students planning to study education.

*** James Zull (2002). *The Art of Changing the Brain: Enriching the Practice of Teaching by Exploring the Biology of Learning.* Sterling, VA: Stylus. This book was so exciting that after looking at a library copy I hurried to get one of my own.

———•••———

Textbooks, although many were very helpful to me as I wrote this book, are not listed here.

Index